Becoming a Psychotherapist

A Clinical Primer

Becoming a Psychotherapist

Rosemary Marshall Balsam, M.B., M.R.C.P.E., M.R.C.Psych.
*Assistant Clinical Professor of Psychiatry, Yale University School of
Medicine; Staff Psychiatrist, Yale University Health Services, New Haven*

Alan Balsam, M.D.
*Late Assistant Clinical Professor of Psychiatry, Yale University School of
Medicine, New Haven*

Foreword by ROY SCHAFER, Ph.D.
*Clinical Professor of Psychology in the Department of Psychiatry, Yale University
School of Medicine; Staff Psychologist, Yale University Health Services; Training
and Supervising Psychoanalyst, Western New England Institute for Psychoanalysis,
New Haven*

Little, Brown and Company, Boston

Becoming a Psychotherapist: A Clinical Primer

First Edition

Library of Congress catalog card No. 74-125

ISBN 0-316-07980

Printed in the United States of America

To Catherine

Contributing Authors

IZA S. ERLICH, M.A., M.S.W.
Assistant Clinical Professor, Department of Psychiatry, Yale University School of Medicine; Psychiatric Social Worker, Yale University Health Services, New Haven

HENRY GRUNEBAUM, M.D.
Associate Clinical Professor of Psychiatry, Department of Psychiatry, Harvard Medical School, Boston

Foreword

Ideally, the psychotherapist at work should be thoroughly at ease.
By being at ease I mean securely open to what we call the inner and
outer worlds, ready to be responsive without being rigidly set in any
one direction, alert without being jumpy, curious without being intrusive, generous without being seductive, and definite without being domineering. But between the therapist and this ideal stands
the reality of the work itself. It is an activity that rarely leaves one
at ease for long. Almost unremittingly, psychotherapy stimulates
anxiety and indecision for the therapist: so much is unknown or
difficult to grasp; so often there is little ground for response with
conviction; and the therapist's aspirations reinforced by the patient's
demands can generate so much pressure to know, to grasp, to speak
out clearly, and act authoritatively! In this uneasy situation the
psychotherapist is often sorely tempted to play the part of un-
flappable master technician and purveyor of wisdom.

Although in this respect one may often succeed in fooling himself
(consciously), he rarely succeeds for long in fooling his patients.
However much patients may try to oversimplify themselves, their
problems, and their life situations, and however ready they may be
unconsciously to collude with the therapist in working out "magical"
cures, somehow they are also on to the ambiguities, intricacies, and
paradoxes of their existence, and on to relationships of these factors
to their present psychological distress as well. And given a chance,

they will let the self-deceiving therapist know it. They will do so either explicitly or, if necessary, by apathetic response, acute regressions, or sudden interruptions of the therapy.

To be at ease, the psychotherapist too must be on to these complexities and uncertainties. Moreover, to do beneficial work, he or she must be reasonably accepting of them. Here, acceptance means not being seriously threatened by them, not being hurried or demanding, and so not desperately trying to do something, anything, with the hope of "getting results," "making progress," or "effecting cures," whatever these phrases might mean in an as yet insufficiently understood human situation. For it to be reliable, this acceptance has to be based on a sufficient degree of that self-knowledge and self-acceptance that is given to some naturally and is gained, extended, or consolidated by others only through personal therapy or psychoanalysis. That acceptance also requires continuing experience in doing psychotherapy open-mindedly, that is, without rapidly and rigidly adopting bad habits and false postures. And finally, it requires good teaching, which may be had from some supervisors, some lectures and seminars, and some articles and books on the subject. Unfortunately, there is much inadequate and even bad teaching in the field.

In this book by the Balsams, we have a fine introduction to doing psychotherapy. It is fine precisely because it is itself at ease and because it sets forth the great variety of challenging therapeutic situations and options for intervention in a way that must help the thoughtful reader to feel at ease, too, at least as much as that condition is possible and appropriate for a student. Reading it is like listening to a favorite supervisor. Far from any exposition of rigid technique and any commanding and condescending tone of "this is how it's done, boys and girls," the student will find unfolding in these pages the benevolent curiosity, sensitivity, tact, thoughtfulness, enthusiasm, and humility that go into the making of all substantial human relationships, among which should be numbered that very special form of human interaction, the psychotherapy relationship. Additionally, as even a glance at the table of contents will show, the Balsams' exposition is wide-ranging and eminently practical. Many clinical illustrations are presented lucidly, concisely and instructively. Most important of all, the student working within its guidelines will be helped toward an excellent position from which to continue to learn from experience.

I must add that this book is deceptive in its accessibility. It seems to be merely a primer, when in fact, in its own graceful and modest way, it also advances many clinically sophisticated considerations and inventive suggestions. It provides, for example, a notable treatment of the interrelationships of the therapist's personal life and professional work, covering such topics as engagement and marriage, illness, and death in the family. And there is a valuable bonus for female psychotherapists in the forthright and helpful discussions of issues peculiar to their lives and work, such as being pregnant. Consequently, I believe this to be a work that will be read with interest and benefit also by experienced therapists and teachers of therapy.

In contributing so much and so admirably toward the completion of *Becoming a Psychotherapist: A Clinical Primer,* Rosemary Balsam has achieved not only an impressive remembrance of her late husband, Alan, but the position of being an outstanding teacher of psychotherapy as well.

ROY SCHAFER, Ph.D.

New Haven, Connecticut

Preface

This is a book about becoming a psychotherapist, a practical
guide to the art and technique of individual psychotherapy for the
beginner, whatever his previous experience. Competent therapists
have developed from many different backgrounds. We, the authors,
both came to practice psychotherapy by the medical route, but
this is only one possible way. We have attempted to draw together
here those aspects of our own experience that have proved most
useful. This means the book presents a point of view about psychotherapy, and, in light of that point of view, it discusses common
situations and problems that arise in learning to be an individual
psychotherapist. The book does not assess current trends in training or in the practice of psychotherapy. Nor does it review the
extensive professional literature on psychotherapy. Nor does it
describe the defense structure of different personalities or the
psychopathology in recognized neuroses. The psychotherapist in
training will have plenty of opportunities to delve into the literature and learn from his teachers on these topics. It is very important
for all therapists to read about established and current concepts
of normal and abnormal development.

However, the beginning psychotherapist may find that no matter
how much he knows of the theories, the myriad responses evoked
by the patient's describing and feeling episodes in his life experience
are mainly those that will elicit the therapist's nonverbal and verbal

reaction to him, temper the urge to say something, or hasten an action that seems appropriate. These are the communications that matter most to the patient, and within these is the potential to help the unfolding of the therapy process and the process of self-discovery for the patient. This is one reason why we have adopted the descriptive clinical approach, especially important for beginners.

I would like to say something of how this book came about. My husband, Alan, as a psychiatrist and teacher always wanted to write a practical book about psychotherapy. He felt that beginning therapists, in facing their first patients, were often expected to know too much at a stage when they had had little clinical experience. He also felt that the literature and sometimes the supervision were somewhat deficient on basic topics. Encouraged by the responsiveness of second-year residents to whom he gave a series of talks in 1970, he decided to gather the papers together in book form. In early 1971, he suffered a reactivation of lymphosarcoma that had been in abeyance for 14 years. He died in March 1972. At the time he was still working on the opening chapters of the book that was under contract to Little, Brown and Company. After his death, I decided to try to finish his book, not only because of the wish to create a memorial for him, but because I felt it was important work and in the spirit of our shared appreciation of the practice of psychotherapy and teaching.

The opening five chapters and most of the ideas on the handling of fees are, therefore, Alan's. The chapters on setting up an office, marriage, pregnancy, and illness reflect discussions we had about our reactions to our own joys and difficulties and how they could affect our work with patients. Alan's death was a painful and sorrowful event not only for me and our daughter, but for our friends, his professional colleagues, and his patients. He was a rich and complex person who had a great deal of love, interest, and respect for his fellowman. He knew how to care for others and convey his caring while allowing them their independence. Alan helped numerous people. He was a wise, kind, and good doctor, and he is greatly missed in our circle.

I know that Alan would join me in thanking primarily our patients. In studying and sharing the riches of their emotional experiences, we all, as therapists, can do our best always to learn from them better approaches to try to ease distress interwoven in the business of living.

But for the support of our friend Henry Grunebaum, Alan would have hesitated to present his work to a publisher at a time when it was less than completed. Thanks are due to him and his wife, Judy, for the subsequent encouragement they gave me. I would like to thank for their help and spiritual support all my friends and colleagues, particularly those on the staff of the Yale University Health Services — Robert Arnstein, M.D., Iza S. Erlich, M.S.W., Norton Garber, M.D., Rebecca Goz, Ph.D. (in particular for comments on the chapter about the pregnant therapist), Stanley Leavy, M.D., Jack Plunkett, M.D., Ernst Prelinger, Ph.D. (in particular for thoughts on the homicidal patient), Lorraine Siggins, M.D., Ann Oberkirch, M.D., and my supervisees. Judy Grunebaum, M.S.W., contributed ideas on the "recently returned" therapist. William McCormick, M.R.C.P., F.R.C.Psych., gave useful editorial suggestions on my thoughts about working with him in Belfast, N. Ireland. Anne Marie Foltz, M.P.H., and Gay Daly helped with some editing. Mary Jo Scrivani gave me invaluable assistance in looking after my daughter, Catherine, and in typing the manuscript. Albina Lipcius and my parents helped in very practical ways to allow me time to write, and I thank them.

I am particularly grateful to our beloved and admired senior colleague Roy Schafer, Ph.D. He is a magnificent teacher who radiates inspiration in his devotion, thinking, discipline, and integrity in his work with and care of patients. He kindly contributed the foreword and was always supportive and available to give constructive opinions on any part of the manuscript I presented to him.

I also appreciate the advice I have had from Little, Brown and Company, in particular the aid from the Medical Editor, Lin Richter, the Copyeditor, Diane Faissler, and the Copyediting Supervisor, Ferne Houser.

R. M. B.

New Haven, Connecticut

Contents

Becoming a Psychotherapist

1

A Way of Thinking about Psychotherapy

DEFINITION OF PSYCHOTHERAPY

Individual psychotherapy may be defined as an exploratory interviewing technique through which one person helps another to find relief from emotional pain. Its success depends on the therapist's ability to understand the patient and on the patient's use of the therapist's help to make decisions and changes that will reduce the pain in his life.

The psychotherapist's central task is learning to understand the patient. This understanding grows out of a reflective exploration for which the patient and the therapist share responsibility. It depends in part on the therapist's learning to be a skillful interviewer with facility in various kinds of inquiry and response and in unhurried listening and waiting. But it also depends on the therapist's understanding of people in general and of human psychology, on his intuition, and on his capacity for empathy. The focus of the exploration is on understanding the emotional experience of the patient.

The choice of an appropriate response to further the exploration may sometimes develop quite obviously from the story the patient tells, but often it requires careful preparation in the mind of the therapist. The richer the therapist's understanding of inner psychic life, of how feelings originate and grow, and of how personalities develop, the more flexible and resourceful he can be in the conduct of the interview. He needs to keep his mind open to the various possible meanings of what he hears and sees, and to the possibilities of discovering meanings that he had not previously considered.

The value of the therapist's understanding is in helping the patient to see his own situation more clearly — to get new light, for instance, on certain conflicts of values or wishes within his own feelings — or to gain objectivity about difficult relations that he has with other people. In this process the patient may learn things about himself that he did not know before or had forgotten. Feelings, assumptions, beliefs, and conflicts may be uncovered that have guided his life without his being aware of them. He may also get a clearer view of his own assets and capabilities. The ultimate test is whether his new understanding of himself enables him to make decisions or changes that lead to resolution of his major problems and relief of his pain.

Sometimes a person is able to achieve necessary or desired changes in his life with only a little bit of psychotherapeutic help. Occasionally a single interview or a brief series of interviews is sufficient. But commonly a longer period of joint effort is required, lasting several months, or even several years. Among the principal factors that influence the length of treatment are the severity of the patient's problems, his level of self-awareness, and his capacity for accepting responsibility for the solution of his own problems. Resistance to change is usually also important. Much as the patient may want help, it is not easy to change established patterns of adaptation, no matter how poorly they have been working. The patient's avoidance of change and his wish to maintain the status quo are constantly at work against his wish to get relief from symptoms or pain and his wish to be more self-reliant and self-respecting.

It often happens that neither the therapist's nor the patient's understanding of the problems is sufficient to enable the patient to bring about changes that he might feel he wants. Much of the work of psychotherapy is therefore spent in trying to understand what is keeping the patient from doing what he wants or what he knows will reduce his pain or make him happier. The inquiry can continue as far as is necessary to enable the patient to free himself from whatever inner forces are pushing him around.

Both patient and therapist usually recognize when therapy is going well, for both of them see the continued development and unfolding of their understanding of the patient and see him making changes in his life that are desirable. When therapy is not going well, therapist and patient together should consider whether it is because the initial goal has already been achieved and the work is finished; if it is not finished, they should try to identify the obstacles that are impeding progress.

THE IMPORTANCE OF THE EGO

The changes that occur in a successful psychotherapy may be thought of in terms of improvement in the functioning of the patient's ego. The term *the ego,* originally a psychoanalytic concept, now is widely used by mental health workers of many orientations. As used here it refers to the part of the personality or psychic structure that organizes and integrates everything that happens to a person, both inner and outer experience. It is the rational, thinking part of the psyche, and the defensive, protective part. It modulates and regulates inner drives, fantasies, and feelings; it weighs and responds to conscience and social pressures; it screens all perceptions, including those about oneself; it is the reality tester and the instrument of judgment, choice, planning, decisions, and orientation. The ego is the part of the mind that learns from formal education; it also learns from experience. It automatically processes experience in ways that it has learned, but it is also capable of reconsidering and changing its ways. The ego's defense mechanisms, such as repression, denial, displacement, and sublimation, defend and protect it against outer and inner stimuli that seem to be, or actually are, overwhelming.

The ego does not always function well. It can be overly strict, to the point of blocking nearly all experiences from one's awareness; or it can selectively block out certain kinds of inner experience or outer experience. If it is too strict, it leaves a sense of blankness, rigidity, or emptiness. On the other hand, it can be very loose or ineffectual in its screening and integration of urges or perceptions, causing a person to feel overwhelmed, inundated, out of control. The ego can also distort perception or understanding, causing difficulty in communication or in relations with others. The ultimate work of psychotherapy is usually helping the patient to correct or modify certain specific defects such as these in the functioning of his ego, which are responsible for his emotional pain.

When the ego is functioning reasonably well, it is flexible and enables one to modulate his perceptions and reactions, as one can control the volume on a radio. Under such circumstances one usually feels a sense of well-being and self-respect. When the ego is too harshly restrictive, too loose, or badly distorting, the sense of well-being and self-respect is low; the person feels that he is not master of his own life because strong outer or inner forces have taken over. The volume control is replaced by an off-on switch, offering all or nothing, without modulation or flexibility. A greater sense of well-being commonly is achieved as psychotherapy progresses.

Although almost all individuals have the same kinds of feelings, in varying degrees of intensity and at different times, and although there are many general principles of psychology that apply pretty well to everybody, each individual's experience and each individual's personality are unique. Things happen to people in different combinations and elicit different interpretations and reactions. General knowledge helps one to understand and often to anticipate correctly the experience of a specific individual. But it does not give the full picture. In the psychotherapeutic exploration the patient and therapist together try to understand the patient's unique experience in life, what he feels about the situations and relationships that have arisen, and how he wants to deal with them. They try to get as clear a view as possible of what it feels like to be that person, the patient.

2

People Becoming Psychotherapists

Everyone is doing psychotherapy! Psychoanalysts, psychiatrists, psychologists, social workers, nurses, nursing aides, clergymen, attorneys, teachers, group workers, communications specialists, and personnel workers. Adolescents and young adults in "crash pads," volunteers who talk to callers on hot lines and those who work in suicide control centers, recreation workers, volunteers in mental hospitals, vocational counselors, and those people who have a knack for helping their friends through talking their problems over with them all are practicing forms of psychotherapy. Medical practitioners often do psychotherapy. Parents do, too, and so do siblings and other relatives. Previously untrained "housewives" have learned to be good psychotherapists. All of these people do psychotherapy of varying degrees of depth and varying degrees of efficacy.

The words *psychotherapy* and *therapy* have become well established in our vocabulary and are often used to refer to a conversation that is helpful or clarifying or that relieves anxiety, or to some experience that leads to relief of tension. The general public is alert to the widespread need for relief of tension and reduction of pain. That is nothing new. But what is new in the second half of the twentieth century is the widespread awareness that there is professional training available that can teach an otherwise ordinary person how to help other people through talking with them. More and more people are seeking the help of trained psychotherapists, and more and more people from many different personal and professional backgrounds are seeking formal and informal training as psychotherapists. This book was written for the growing number of new psychotherapists.

THE PSYCHODYNAMIC MOVEMENT

Psychotherapy as it is practiced today grew out of observations made by Sigmund Freud at the beginning of this century. This is true of most varieties of current therapy, however different they may be from Freud's teaching and practice. It is particularly true of the approach to psychotherapy presented in this book. Freud's revolutionary contributions to human self-understanding involve his demonstration of the everyday importance of unconscious mental processes and of the absence of chance in mental processes. Thoughts and feelings develop in response to events or to other thoughts and feelings — they do not "just happen." And they exert their influence on the person even though he may not be aware of their existence. These facts, first clearly elucidated by Freud, provide a rationale for a practical technique of psychotherapy based on one person's trying to understand another's emotional experience. They tell us that a person's emotional experience is basically understandable and that understanding of one's own emotional experience can result in greater control of his life.

The first practitioners of this kind of systematic psychotherapy were Freud and his circle of colleagues and students, who were physicians. Freud had been trained as a neurologist. The others were psychiatrists and internists. Some psychologists, philosophers, and other "lay analysts" also learned the skills. By the 1930's many psychiatrists and some psychologists were learning the theories and skills not only of Freud but also of his students and colleagues and others whose theories had been influenced by Freud. These "schools" included those of Jung, Adler, Abraham,

Alexander, Reich, Rado, Fromm, Horney, Sullivan, Klein, and many others. They had different conceptual approaches to the understanding of human behavior, but their teachings about psychotherapy all emphasized the understanding of the individual person's emotional experience. They represent the early decades of the movement called *dynamic psychiatry,* which is devoted to the understanding of thoughts, feelings, behavior, and personality patterns of an individual as responses to earlier thoughts, feelings, and experiences, both conscious and unconscious. Their teachings had considerable impact on the development of modern psychiatry as well as on education, pediatric medicine, the social sciences, and pastoral theology. The fields of psychiatric social work and much of modern clinical psychology were dependent on the orientation of dynamic psychiatry for their development. The most widespread influence of so-called psychodynamic thinking on many professional fields and on popular thought has occurred in the nearly three decades since the end of World War II. What was begun by physicians and developed by psychoanalysts is now used by a wide range of professional and paraprofessional disciplines.

PSYCHODYNAMIC THINKING AND PHYSICIANS

Different backgrounds of education or experience produce psychotherapists with different skills and different orientations, and sometimes with certain handicaps. Until quite recently the majority of psychotherapists were psychiatrists, that is, physicians trained as specialists in psychological medicine. Many psychiatric training centers have offered high-quality training in psychotherapy, either as part of or as the center of the specialty training in psychiatry. The most intensive and most highly specialized training available is in a particular kind of psychotherapy called psychoanalysis. This training has been available mainly to physicians (in the United States). There is much debate about this approach and more doors are opening for trainees from other disciplines. The programs are run by psychoanalytic institutes which often are independent of psychiatric training centers. Many of the best teachers of psychotherapy have been and are psychoanalysts.

These circumstances suggest that there might be widespread affinity between psychiatry, psychotherapy, psychoanalysis, and medicine, but this is not generally the case in actual practice. In the first place, many psychiatrists trained in recent years are not dynamically oriented. Many are not particularly interested in and not at all skillful in psychotherapy. Training in psychiatry does not necessarily mean that one becomes a good psychotherapist. The orientation of many psychiatrists is much more biological, and the corresponding treatment orientation is to the organic therapies, including treatment with drugs that alter psychological processes, and to directive or didactic kinds of psychotherapy rather than to the form of psychotherapy based on self-discovery and self-direction, to which this book is devoted.

While psychodynamic thinking has had broad impact, and is now being taught in many medical schools as an important tool in the understanding of the human organism, it is not yet incorporated into the thinking of most physicians. Medical thinking is predominantly descriptive and organic. Physicians need to gather factual data in a systematic manner, fit them together into the most appropriate diagnostic pattern, and treat according to rational means, most often by "doing something" to the patient. The aspect of the physician's approach that attempts to support the natural healing processes of the human body is closest to the psychotherapeutic way of thinking that we are presenting. While the descriptive, organic, and directive approaches are very important in medicine and in psychiatry, psychodynamic thinking is still not a part of the basic armamentarium of most medically trained clinicians. It is, however, the stock-in-trade of those who are actively interested in the practice of psychotherapy.

It is often said that physicians who go on to get training in the medical specialty of psychiatry must unlearn much of what they learned in medical school. The physician who wants to be a psychotherapist must set aside the more rigid categories of what we are calling medical thinking. He has to learn to recognize different kinds of nuances and interacting forces, and learn to live with the uncertainty of not knowing just what is meant or how a situation will resolve itself. Within the medical profession, surgeons and those in surgical subspecialties, who rely more on quick decision and quick action, tend to rely more on "medical thinking," whereas the internist and the pediatrician, whose work makes them more dependent on the manipulation of complex interactions of physiological forces, tend to be more open to psychodynamic thinking. Pediatricians, who deal with the emotional as well as the physical development of their patients, are often more aware of and make more use of psychodynamic thinking than most general physicians. In all fields there are psychodynamic thinkers, however. We have portrayed here only general trends.

Is it necessary for a psychotherapist to be a physician or to have formal medical training? Not at all. The physician needs to shift in ways of thinking while learning to be a psychotherapist. However, there can be some advantages for the medically trained psychotherapist. The physician's training has taught him as much as is known about the physical organism that is the vehicle of the psyche. Very complex chemical processes occur with each thought or feeling; although they are still poorly understood, what is known of them is in the purview of the physician and is foreign to those who do not have the physician's training. Further, thoughts and feelings can profoundly influence any or all body functions, causing organic disturbances of all degrees of severity and complexity. One's emotional responses to the structure, appearance, and diverse functions of his body can also be intricate and far-reaching. This entire area of human experience is more accessible to the understanding of the physician-psychotherapist than of other psychotherapists.

Another unique part of the physician's experience is the fact of his having been responsible during his clinical training for the total welfare of very sick patients. On a 24-hour basis he has held the responsibility for life-or-death decisions about patients in his care. He has worked through many a night on lifesaving measures, both medical and surgical, on adults and children from many different life settings. In these situations he has learned a good deal about distinguishing between crucially important problems and less vital ones. He has seen his patients' reactions, as well as his own, to life-threatening illness, and he has learned to accept a special kind of responsibility for patient care. Nurses have similar experiences, but they do not carry the ultimate responsibility for the critical decisions (except in grossly understaffed hospitals), and they go home after their 8-hour shift rather than carrying 24-hour responsibility. Social workers and clinical psychologists are generally not at all familiar with this dramatic aspect of patient care. Hospital chaplains and clergy visiting hospitals may be closer to it, but in a different way. In many ways the training of the physician-psychotherapist has included broader and quantitatively greater "clinical experience" than that of any other mental health worker.

The physician who is learning to be a psychotherapist thus brings a certain kind of training and experience of patients to his new work. It may not make him a better psychotherapist. It merely makes him different. It may increase his understanding, but it may tend to make him overinvolved or oriented to "doing something" quickly. It may increase his awareness of interactions of psychological and organic processes, but if he clings to the traditional model, his understanding of these interactions may delude him into thinking that he already knows what is going to happen or that he can figure it out from basic principles. He may find it difficult to shift to the psychodynamic way of thinking that keeps an open mind and expects to be surprised. He has certain assets, but also certain liabilities. This is equally true of every discipline from which people come to learn to be psychotherapists.

The therapeutic community movement, defined in the early 1950's, brought all mental health professionals into more diversely responsible roles in the care of hospitalized patients. The observations about patients by all staff members were important to the overall understanding of the patient. And the conversations and interventions of all staff members with patients were important to the therapeutic process. The physician in charge of the ward was no longer seen as the single or central healing agent for whom all other personnel acted as assistants. All staff members therefore began to pay more attention to the meanings of their contacts with patients and to their clinical skills in talking with and working with patients. Initially there was a rapid expansion of training of all staff members in interviewing skills, and then in psychodynamics and in psychopathology. Before long it seemed reasonable to offer training in psychotherapy to mental health workers from many different backgrounds and many different levels of psychological sophistication.

A similar development followed in psychiatric outpatient services. Since about 1950 public outpatient clinics have appeared in more and more communities. When this development began, the roles of the staff members were defined along traditional lines. Therapy was done primarily by psychiatrists. Intakes or evaluations were done by social workers, and diagnostic evaluations, usually only on selected patients, were done by the clinical psychologist. If there were a nurse in the clinic, she most commonly dispensed medication or provided comfort to and physical surveillance of particularly distraught patients. Spouses and other family members were interviewed by social workers.

BROADENING THE SPECTRUM
OF PSYCHOTHERAPISTS

As skills were broadened and professional role boundaries were relaxed in the inpatient therapeutic community, staffs of outpatient clinics began to experiment with similar changes. Gradually everyone began to do psychotherapy, and everyone began to do intakes. The clinical psychologist retained his role as psychological tester and formal diagnostic evaluator, but he also expanded his horizons to include psychotherapy. Nurses were used increasingly to do intakes. More importance was placed on their other interviews with patients, and they began to make home visits, doing some psychotherapy in patients' homes. Not only psychiatric nurses but also public health nurses and visiting nurses undertook psychiatric intervention with patients in their homes.

There has been much debate about the appropriateness and the efficacy of nurses, in particular, but also of social workers, doing psychotherapy. As hospital chaplains and other clergy began to expand their pastoral counseling into psychotherapy, the same questions were raised. The debate goes on similarly over vocational counselors, school guidance counselors, and all of those agents of psychotherapy mentioned at the outset of this chapter.

Clinical Psychologists

Clinical psychologists with Ph.D. degrees are the largest group of doctors other than physicians who practice psychotherapy in America today. While there have been clinical psychologists practicing psychotherapy throughout this century, until about 1950 the principal work of clinical psychologists was in psychological testing and other diagnostic procedures. In the rapid expansion of training since the end of World War II, an increasing number of psychologists have been prepared to work as psychotherapists, both by academic training and by clinical assignments at predoctoral and postdoctoral levels.

The clinical psychologist generally has the broadest conceptual training of any of the mental health workers. He has learned many theoretical approaches to the understanding of the human psyche. He tends to be most conversant with the language of descriptive psychology, developmental psychology, and psychopathology. His formal training teaches him more about all psychic processes, including unconscious processes, than does that of any other mental health worker. His training in formal psychological testing enables him to elicit from patients responses to standardized inquiries, which responses he can then compare with those of other patients in such a way as to reach very useful descriptive and diagnostic conclusions. Some feel that this broad conceptual and diagnostic training equips the clinical psychologist particularly well to become a sensitive, skillful psychotherapist because he is so well trained to understand. Others feel that this background is too formal, too objective, and too rigid to be compatible with clinical skill in psychotherapy. In reality, both sides of that argument are often proved true, which suggests that other individual variations in training, interests and personal style may be as important as the general structure of the training.

Social Workers

Social workers are particularly trained in interviewing skills and in understanding the relationships of the patient with his family, his community, and the various community service agencies whose services he might use or need. Training in psychiatric social work has changed steadily through this century. It originated as training for social casework with psychiatric patients and their families but has gradually shifted to include a good deal of training in descriptive psychology, personality development, psychodynamics, and psychopathology. It is oriented more specifically to clinical service than is clinical psychology. Nearly all psychiatric social workers work directly with patients. With a typical training period of two years, the psychiatric social worker just out of school generally has less conceptual and less clinical training than the Ph.D. clinical psychologist, although the social worker's clinical experience may be more practical.

If one can generalize, the social worker often has a stronger orientation to being personally of service to others, while the clinical psychologist's orientation is more toward study and research about psychological processes. The psychiatric social worker, then, approaches his work with an orientation of psychodynamically aware clinical service. This prepares him for the traditional roles of doing intake evaluations, that is, selecting patients for psychotherapy, being responsible for decisions about other dispositions, and handling the dealings with patients' families and other community agencies. He has been the member of the clinical team best prepared to advise other clinicians on family interactions and on community and agency relationships. These are all very useful attributes to bring into training as a psychotherapist. Some say that the social worker's casework orientation suits him well for supportive psychotherapy in which he helps the patient to plan and rearrange his life without delving into the unconscious conflicts and motivations that would be considered in a deeper psychotherapy. Others find that the sense of personal involvement and eagerness to be of service give the social worker a particular empathy that makes it easier for him to seek and understand deeper meanings in psychotherapy than for some of his more theoretical colleagues. Social workers learning to be psychotherapists do commonly have to make a special effort to refrain from taking over the planning of the patient's life and from being too supportive, that is, to leave the initiative and responsibility in the patient's hands. Many social workers, like the many physicians and many clinical psychologists, have been able to utilize the particular assets of their training, and overcome the particular handicaps, to become excellent psychotherapists.

Psychiatric Nurses

The traditional experience of psychiatric nurses is farther afield from psychotherapy, but many of them nowadays are psychotherapists. Either advanced academic training or on-the-job training can provide further conceptual understanding of psychological processes and further understanding of the inner experience of the individual patient. Nurses have traditionally occupied themselves with more practical aspects of their patients' lives: medications, meals, beds, baths, occupation, and general mood or state of mind. Psychiatric nurses have seen as their role in the past meeting these immediate daily needs of their patients, reporting to physicians how things are going in these areas for individual patients, and reporting whatever else they learn from and about the patients in the course of their many daily contacts with them. They have also been involved in interpreting to patients the plans prescribed by doctors and in helping the patients to make sense or to make use of things doctors have told them.

The development of the therapeutic community has expanded the role of the psychiatric nurse — at first into the interpretive role, and then into a role of broader responsibility for participation in the overall therapeutic work, helping in the process of understanding the patient, and helping the patient to understand himself. This develops into direct participation in the psychotherapeutic work. Perhaps even more than for social workers, however, the traditional nursing role of practical helper, self-sacrificing servant, and friend of the patient makes it even harder for the experienced nurse to stand back, blend objectivity with compassion, and help the patient to take the initiative and responsibility in a joint endeavor to understand the patient's emotional life. The psychiatric nurse, being familiar with the daily life and experience of the patient in the hospital, brings a unique experience to the learning of psychotherapy. Her more limited conceptual education (except for certain nurses who have advanced training) and her practical here-and-now orientation may impose certain hurdles in learning to do psychotherapy. Again these need not limit her potential to become a good therapist.

Psychiatric Aides

Psychiatric aides are now often given responsibility for "following" a patient in psychotherapy, both during a period of hospitalization and after discharge. For some patients this amounts to a kind of counseling, reviewing the issues of daily life that the patient has to deal with, keeping the major emotional problems and stresses in focus, and reminding the patient what has been learned of a new approach to handling them. They may check on use of medication and report any major problems in the patient's mood or life experience to the clinical team or to one of its senior members. This practice is growing in acceptance in emergency treatment services, crisis intervention units, and short-term hospitalization services. It is also being used in public outpatient clinics, particularly among the growing number of walk-in clinics. Some psychiatric aides are learning to do a more exploratory form of psychotherapy.

There are widely divergent views on whether this use of psychiatric aides as primary clinicians working with very disturbed people is in anyone's best interests. One side of the argument holds that since they are often very bright people with much life experience, this is an effective way to utilize available skills and manpower, using the more highly trained personnel as supervisors. The other side holds that without more profound understanding of inner psychic processes than is possible in such limited training, no real change is made in the mental health of the disturbed patients who come for treatment, that only temporary first aid is given. Statistics have been amassed to support both views. This is not the place to attempt to resolve the issue. The point made in Chapter 1 is relevant: the richer the therapist's understanding of inner psychic life, of how feelings originate and grow, and of how personalities de-

velop, the more flexible and resourceful he can be in the conduct
of the psychotherapeutic interview.

It is not necessary to spell out the assets and liabilities of all of
the different kinds of people who are now doing or attempting to
do psychotherapy. The general point is clear. People bring different
skills and different problems to the experience of becoming a psychotherapist. They become different kinds of psychotherapists.
The work of psychotherapy is much less precise and standardized
than the work of the surgeon, for instance, who can name and define
the technique he will use in a certain operation right down to the
details of where he places sutures and what kinds of knots he ties.

PSYCHOTHERAPY MUST BE LEARNED

Psychotherapy does not come naturally. Regardless of the ac-
curacy of one's intuition or "gut reactions," not everything about
psychic processes is obvious. Conceptual learning means learning
ways of thinking about or ways of looking at things. Once a new
point of view is suggested, it may seem obvious. Before learning
the new point of view, however, the therapist may well have felt
that he understood all there was to understand about what the
patient was telling him. This is a very common experience for
therapists of all levels of sophistication. Probably the best, safest,
and most helpful therapists, however, are those who recognize when
they do not fully understand what they are observing and seek
further understanding through continuing their open-minded inquiry and exploration with the patient, through supervision, through
reading, and through formal courses.

CHOOSING PSYCHOTHERAPY AS A CAREER

Whether any individual becomes a psychotherapist is his own decision. Within the spectrum of disciplines there are people who are
interested in doing psychotherapy and people who are not. An individual may recognize that he has a temperament and a way of

thinking that will make the work easier or harder for him. Teachers or bosses often help to crystallize a trainee's choice of career path. Before making the choice, the prospective psychotherapist should learn something about what the work is like, the difficulties and the rewards, and then decide whether the work matches his interests and aptitudes. A few generalizations can be made. The person who likes finding quick answers or problem solutions, having information neatly categorized into pigeonholes, or being able to predict future developments with certainty will not be very happy doing the kind of psychotherapy described in this book. The person who likes open-ended exploration, who likes to watch the interaction of ever-changing forces, who likes to be more of a catalyst than a directly controlling agent in the process of change, and who enjoys working closely with another person is more likely to find satisfaction in this kind of work.

A psychotherapist, like anyone else, has his idiosyncrasies, his unresolved inner conflicts, and his extensive unconscious psychic life. One does not have to be a patient to have an unconscious. It is extremely helpful for every psychotherapist to become as well acquainted as he can with his own blind spots and inner conflicts. As long as he is unaware of them, they will control and guide him in his therapeutic work as well as in other aspects of his life. Blindness to his own feelings tends to make him blind to his patients' feelings in related areas. The limits of the therapist's self-understanding may become the limits of his understanding his patients' emotional experience. Personal experience as a patient in psychotherapy or in the more profound self-exploration of psychoanalysis is therefore extremely valuable to every psychotherapist. In addition to extending the therapist's self-awareness it provides him the invaluable experience of learning what it is like to be a patient. It may enhance his self-respect. It may help him to maintain or develop some humility.

3

Getting Started

A beginning therapist will feel some anxiety in starting this new phase of his professional career: it would be surprising if he did not. The most common anxiety stems from the prospect of confronting face-to-face an upset person in need of help. In need of what? How upset? How can one help anyway? This ambiguous demand sharply heightens the psychotherapist's awareness of his limited skills, lack of experience, and human frailties. At the same time he may feel that he ought to be a source of strength, knowledge, and superior wisdom. This paradox is even more apparent if one is called upon to cope with an emergency situation requiring a decisive course of action. For any beginner, then, concern about his performance is coupled with fears and lack of knowledge about what is expected of him (Judith Grunebaum, personal communication).

The beginner should try not to discount the validity of his own observations. The fact that a patient impresses one as funny or annoying or pleasing or confusing is in itself an important aspect of this person. As a clinician, one's principal help to the patient may be in noticing things about him that he does not know or does not understand about himself. One may try not to let his initial uncertainties about his new role and new surroundings, or his over-eagerness to be of help, keep him from observing how the patient dresses, looks, walks, shakes hands, sits, talks, etc.

Beginning psychotherapists are often very worried about making mistakes. If one is in immediate doubt, he may ask the patient to wait after the interview, and find a senior therapist to help. If one is in moderate doubt, he may ask the patient to return at least once more, and discuss the case with a supervisor in the interim. Even the most experienced therapists often take several sessions with a patient to complete an initial evaluation. The patient is also beginning something new and very important in his life. He is probably a good deal more anxious than the therapist as he comes to his first interview. Despite the appropriateness of the therapist's own anxiety, he may try to set it aside in order to focus attention on understanding the patient's experience in coming to see him.

SUPERVISION

Supervision by a senior colleague is extremely valuable. And it remains valuable through the many years it takes to become a good psychotherapist. The principal function of the supervisor is to supplement the perceptions of the therapist with another set of eyes, ears, thoughts, and levels of understanding. Any other therapist whom one tells about his work with a patient will immediately notice things that were not obvious during the session. It is not possible for the therapist, especially the beginning therapist, to observe and understand everything that is going on during a therapeutic interview with a patient. The greater the supervisor's experience, the more he will have to contribute to understanding the work with the patient.

It is a mistake for a beginning therapist to attempt to do psychotherapy without supervision. Whether the supervisor sits in the room with the patient and therapist (and later discusses the interview with the therapist), watches through a one-way mirror window, or learns about the interview from an audio or video tape or from the therapist's verbal report, it is crucially important that the beginning therapist have the experience of supervision. Supervision helps the therapist to expand his skills and to recognize his limitations. As one gains experience, the supervision process gradually shifts to more of a consultation. Even experienced, senior therapists find it helpful to talk over a difficult therapy problem with a colleague.

THE MIDDLE-AGED OR RECENTLY "RETURNED" BEGINNER

It is not an easy proposition to enter a new field when one has reached middle age or to re-enter the profession after a long absence. Beginning a profession is usually associated with being young. Indeed the majority of people starting careers are young, and they progress in direct, linear fashion from student to full-fledged practitioner. In psychotherapy, however, it is not particularly rare for a person to enter or re-enter the profession in middle age. A man or an unmarried woman may decide that his or her previous occupation was unsatisfactory and change fields. A married woman with growing children may either return to her profession after a long lapse or decide to begin training in psychotherapy. Consequently, a middle-aged beginner is still much more likely to be a woman. Many of the comments that follow are equally applicable to men, but for simplicity the pronouns "she" and "her" are used.

Learning to do psychotherapy presents a twofold difficulty. One is required to plunge into work and feel responsible for patients, while at the same time one has to become once again a dependent student working under the critical eye of a supervisor. For a mature woman whose home and children were her indisputable domain, this is not an easy step. At this stage of her life she may be facing simultaneously the waning of power over her growing children, her own aging, and a concomitant sense of diminishing sexual attractiveness. It is a time of increased need to bolster her feeling of self-worth. Returning to work may do precisely that for her. But it may also entail some threats to her changing self-image. She may come to the field with much more life experience, with many important decisions and steps already taken, a clearer recognition of her assets and limitations, a rich appreciation for the complexity of problems, and more compassion and wisdom. Yet with greater maturity may come increased rigidity and difficulty in seeing things in new ways and in grasping changing patterns of behavior (Iza S. Erlich, personal communication).

One may be more likely to imitate the style of a respected teacher without feeling free to experiment within limits; or one may so resent being taught that she pursues a certain path feeling inwardly "sure" that her style is preferable. All learning therapists should be encouraged to bring up areas of uncertainty and anxiety with supervisors — even if they are younger in age! Many anxieties and conflicts are necessary and natural aspects of becoming a psychotherapist. Time and experience ameliorate some of them — at least enough for the purposes of learning to do an adequate job (Judith Grunebaum, personal communication).

THE PATIENT IS STARTING TOO

Seeing a psychotherapist for the first time is an important event in any person's life. Some patients have vivid events preceding their visit and enter therapy in crisis. Other patients have been thinking about their problems for a long time, perhaps saving up money to afford therapy or awaiting the "right moment." Patients in the latter group thus enter therapy electively. Reaching the point of wanting to be in psychotherapy will involve more or less pain for each person. In addition to the internal conflicts, the social environment in which a patient lives may encourage or undermine his commitment. Thus a college student attending an institution where psychotherapy is easily available and where his peers may regard therapy as a valuable experience in increasing self-awareness may have less difficulty dealing with his external world on the issue. A patient from a community in which psychotherapy is regarded as a last resort for the "crazy" or deviant members may have great struggles in coming to terms with seeking psychiatric help, and may experience a great deal of initial resistance and need for secrecy at all levels in the therapy.

The patient must weigh the cost to himself of his decision. If the pain he suffers is interfering with his functioning, then the wish to have the pain relieved may transcend the cultural prohibition. Occasionally family members may pressure a person to seek treatment. The patient who is forced into the clinician's office will be a difficult person with whom to establish rapport and a working alliance. Indeed such an ideal therapist/patient relationship may never be established.

When a patient comes for psychotherapy, he and his family and friends and associates probably have already tried a variety of other approaches to helping him with his current life problems: advice, instruction, exhortation, explanation, encouragement, moral support, reward, or punishment. If other means had been successful, the patient would probably not be in the office. Any of these means may have their place in psychotherapy, but they are not central in exploratory psychotherapy. Although the patient wants help and wants to change, he may shrink from talking about himself because he feels it will be unbearable. He may be fearful of what he will find out about himself. These doubts and fears, which constitute resistance to all efforts at change, are attacked more head-on in the techniques just mentioned. Psychotherapy as presented here attempts to establish a more internal basis for change in the patient. It attempts to mobilize his ability to collaborate in identifying and questioning his doubts, fears, and blind spots.

A patient going into elective therapy may report that he has privately rehearsed describing his thoughts to himself. It takes practice to tell another person what is on one's mind, so it is too much to expect that a patient will enter the office and immediately do so without getting to know the therapist first. In fact, if an unknown patient spills out "everything" in a first interview, it may be a diagnostic indicator that he is generally feeling out of control.

A patient will have built up a set of fantasies concerning the therapist before he sees him in treatment. These may be enhanced by evaluation. His vision may be of a person who is all-loving and accepting, or cold and punitive, or wise and magical, or incompetent and useless. This wish for magic is more or less ubiquitous. Every therapist has had the experience at cocktail parties of people responding nervously, on being told one's profession, "Then you can

read my mind!" Another ubiquitous fantasy is, "You must be so
emotionally strong to stand hearing all those problems," as if the
therapist ought to have extra spiritual strength to emit to those in
trouble. Yet another fantasy represents the other side of the ambivalence; "Every shrink is mad himself." It is only in the course of
therapy that the therapist is, of necessity, knocked from his pedestal,
or elevated from the depths, as the case may be.

CHOICE OF A THERAPIST

Sometimes a patient will request to see a particular kind of person
in therapy. If a patient strongly wants a female therapist, an older
therapist, a black therapist, a distant or a warm therapist, having
such a request accommodated may make a great deal of difference.
This is particularly true in brief, less intensive psychotherapy, where
the transference factors are worked with in a more superficial way
and the reality of the therapist is primarily at the fore. It may also
make a difference in the initial engagement period of long-term
psychotherapy. After that span, for prolonged periods the patient
sees his therapist in the way he needs to see him based on earlier
experience with his parents.

In a clinic setting the practicalities of trying to mesh the ideal
therapist to the ideal patient are too complex. The organizational
needs have to be taken into account, although it may be possible
to compromise in many cases, especially when a strong request
comes from a patient. Black patients often want black therapists.
Unfortunately there are too few available, so the good black therapist
may have to protect himself from being overcommitted or having
only black patients in his caseload, especially when he is in training.
The black or foreign-born patient often complains that the white or
native therapist cannot fully understand his cultural position. This
may limit the effectiveness of these therapists in short-term therapy,
since many of the innuendos, such as the use of language, essential
to psychotherapy, may be missed. However, it may still be possible
to work under these circumstances.

Even in the absence of a wish for a certain kind of therapist,
anything obvious about the person of the therapist is of interest to

the patient and may bring specific topics to the fore. (One patient
who liked his foreign-born female therapist repeatedly reproached
her with her inability to understand him. Later he commented on
her accent, which much later aroused feelings about his mother's
speech defect. He had experienced anger, guilt, and a sense of loss
of contact with his mother. He had a hard time understanding his
mother, and conversely often assumed that she did not understand
him. His initial complaints had to do with isolating himself from
women, and it was an exciting insight for him to see that his present
isolation was connected to his old feelings about his mother and an
unquestioned assumption that no female could understand him.
The therapist's accent was thus an important facet of the work
[Iza S. Erlich, personal communication].)

Nowadays more patients, particularly women, are looking for
women therapists. It is sometimes felt that a woman can intuitively
understand more about women and their experience. This may be
true. Traditionally, men have cited the same position (at least toward women doctors of medicine): "Only a man can truly know
about me and be allowed to treat me." The "truth" may be less
important than the opportunity to have a choice. It is only relatively
recently, as the number of women professionals increases, that
women have a wider choice in the matter. "I am looking for a role
model" is frequently heard, expressing the wish to talk to a woman
who has both a professional life and a family life or the wish to talk
to a professional single woman. Talking with such a role model in
any capacity may prove a positive experience, but in exploratory
psychotherapy the female therapist will focus the sessions upon the
patient and her wishes and fantasies rather than emphasize a social
interchange about the therapist's life. The advisability of this approach is expanded later. So much depends on how the particular
woman patient views herself. The search for a role model may have
diverse implications. The patient may be looking for an idealized
mother she never had with whom to identify. She may want to re-
work some old unresolved conflicts with a mother figure. She may
wish for an ally against men because she has been ill-treated by
men. She may wish to recapture the closeness she had with her
sister. To discover the parameters and their value and hindrance
to the patient, one will embark upon the voyage of exploring.

In referral, one should always ask a patient whether he has a preference about the sex of the prospective therapist and try to accommodate him or her. There do not seem to be absolute indications that a male or a female therapist *must* be involved with a patient because he has a particular problem. The choice is often not predictable without exploring the preference with the patient. Adolescent patients often are more comfortable with a therapist of the same sex because of their conscious sensitivity to and growing awareness of their sexuality. It may also be part of their search for role models. In adolescence there tends to be an upsurge of conflicts from the earliest years, which may involve battling with the same-sex parent for the love of the opposite-sex parent. These conflicts are largely unconscious but could lead a particular adolescent to want to talk to an opposite-sex therapist. Female and male homosexuals often have strong preferences regarding the sex of the therapist. A person who actively dislikes either parent may wish to talk to a person of the opposite sex from the disliked parent, or if he mainly wants to re-experience and work on past conflicts, he may choose a therapist of the same sex as the disliked parent. A person whose father died early may want a male therapist to help. Or, since his mother was the major source of his emotional upbringing, he may wish to recapture some of that quality and look for a female therapist. As the involvement deepens in therapy, all may not proceed as initially planned by the patient, for example, a patient who feels that he or she needs mothering may react to any signs of mothering on the part of the therapist with discomfort and a great deal of hostility. Another patient may be very responsive to mothering-caring qualities in a therapist, either male or female, although she felt initially that what she needed was a "rational man's influence."

Equally as important as the sex of the therapist is his or her personality vis-à-vis the patient. There are strong, firm, aggressive women and soft, vulnerable, creative men in the profession. There are distant women and warm men. In other words, within the close interpersonal contact of therapy it may become clear to a patient that the therapist does not have the expected or stereotyped characteristics just because he is a male or a female. All one can do is be as aware as possible of the real attributes he can offer a patient, so that any interpretations about the patient's distortions will be more firmly based. A therapist can seek the middle ground in the discipline of conducting therapy without having to subordinate his entire personality to achieve it. This can be learned with the help of supervisors, colleagues, personal therapy, and patients themselves. To try to metamorphose oneself into an unmovable, unshockable, silent automaton would be too costly. Nor would it be desirable. Neither is it desirable to "let it all hang loose." One cannot underestimate the impact of one's words and behavior with any patient.

The "Right" Therapist

Patients considering starting therapy have a much wider choice, usually, if they can afford to go to a therapist in private practice. It is very intriguing to consider why one therapist should seem "right" and another "wrong" to a patient. Therapists of identical ideology may come across as entirely different to a patient. Aspects of each therapist's personality may coincide with or be at odds with a patient's need in a particular area. The patient should follow his "gut reaction," if he has one, in making his choice. Therapy has difficult passages for all patients, and times when the therapist is hated or is seen as uncaring and cold. Thus, to start therapy with an instant dislike, for whatever reasons, may put an unnecessary burden on the patient. Of course, a patient may start therapy with negative feelings and as these become resolved, grow to like the therapist and feel a consistent positive attachment and respect for him.

The "rightness" probably has to do with a meshing of the patient's preconscious wishes with what he observes in the therapist during initial contact. Deeper unconscious processes are also involved. One patient said that immediately on walking into a therapist's waiting room, although she had never set eyes on the man, she was instantly "turned off." The rug on the floor was crooked and stained. The curtains hung at different heights, with their linings sloppily bedraggled. The pictures were drab and hung at odd angles. While she waited, the preceding patient rushed into the waiting room looking upset, picked up her belongings, and rushed out. She immediately thought, "He doesn't care at all for his patients. Otherwise, he would protect their privacy and their physical comfort." Now, another patient waiting for the same therapist responded with, "Great! He clearly has no interest in his physical surroundings and will be more available to be absorbed with my internal life. He must be a great genius!" Another example. A patient in marital trouble wended her way nervously up a small staircase to the waiting area. Although tiny, it showed evidence of planning for the patient. It was partitioned off so that the incoming patient was shielded from the view of the outgoing patient, and the chair was very comfortable. She thought, "He must be a home-loving man who respects his children's needs. Perhaps he can help me with my marriage."

In other words, the initial and most pressing complaint of the patient will in part influence his feeling of the "rightness" of the therapist. One patient may be looking for comfort and search for signs of it in the place and person of the therapist. Another patient may wish for someone who will "not let me get away with anything" and look for signs of a sterner temperament in the person he is about to see.

WHERE THERAPY TAKES PLACE

The meeting place of therapist and patient may be anything from a small office in a hospital to a large suite in the therapist's house. Some therapists share offices, while others struggle to find a quiet corner in a hectic emergency room to interview their patients. One therapist had to conduct his weekly interview with one patient in a surgical ward sitting on the edge of the bathtub while the patient sat in her wheelchair. It is important to settle on a niche that one can call his own, if possible. If the therapist is attempting to do ongoing therapy while being buffeted from pillar to post, the quality of his work may suffer. Beginning therapists and those in transition often ask why a number of patients have fled from therapy, saying that it seems impossible to settle down to work with a single patient. On inquiry, it may become clear, particularly at the beginning of the academic year in a training setting, that no office has been established for the therapist and he is feeling left out, on the periphery of the "in-group" who have offices, inexperienced, and pushed around. All these factors, coupled with his feelings of uncertainty in his role, lead to a higher anxiety level than is ideal for his work. Often, once his specific location is settled, the patients, too, begin to settle down and come regularly.

Office Changes

Changes in office location will be noticed by patients at some level. If one temporarily changes his location with a patient, it will probably influence the content of that hour at least. It may raise all kinds of questions in the patient's mind. If Dr. Smith is using the office at a time when Mrs. Green would usually see Dr. Brown there, the patient may wonder what this means about Dr. Brown's status vis-à-vis Dr. Smith. Is he weak and unable to stand up for himself? Is he kind and making way for his pressured colleague? Is he being demoted, or promoted (according to the size of the office)? Does Dr. Brown feel that Mrs. Green is emotionally strong and able to stand the change? Does Dr. Brown think so little of Mrs. Green that he is pushing her around? One patient, turning her feelings against herself, said on such an occasion: "I feel like a beggar."

All kinds of questions about the worth of the therapist and the value of the patient may arise, and these will provide new themes or extensions of old themes on a different level. One patient's fantasy was that doctors had big offices and were therefore aggressive and sarcastic, while psychologists had small offices and were gentle and receptive. This patient had asked to see a particular psychologist who happened to have a big office. During an hour when the patient and psychologist had to use a smaller office, the patient chose to talk of how he had difficulty with his image of his therapist as gentle and the fact that his original office was large. He felt the therapist must be brooding, hiding falsely behind a gentle face, and waiting for a certain moment to explode. Later in the therapy it emerged that his mother was mainly passive but inexplicably explosive. He was working out whether or not he could trust this therapist to be predictable, and this hour in the changed office hastened the process into conscious awareness.

Changes in office location may be particularly upsetting for a borderline psychotic or psychotic patient. When his internal world is so chaotic, any discontinuity may heighten his anxiety to intolerable proportions. It is as if the therapist must be a new person if the location is changed. However, if such a patient is able to reflect on the effect of the change and if he has the experience of surviving it and examining how it was possible to change without anything terrible happening, the experience may be a solidifying one for him.

Décor

If one has an office, how should it be decorated? Some people feel that because they spend a great deal of time in the office it should be made as comfortable and pleasant as possible. Others feel that their immediate surroundings are of little consequence to the job at hand. Either approach inevitably reveals something of oneself. Patients will notice, too, and will weave it into the therapy to reveal something about themselves. It is a delicate and uncomfortable issue how much of oneself he should display for scrutiny. Of course the therapist is the only person who can decide this.

Personal photographs are one of the trickiest issues. If pictures of wife, husband, or children are in the office, why are they there? There are all kinds of reasons. On a gloomy day when nothing goes right with patients, they may provide comfort. They may be there to show a patient that one is married, which may increase the feeling of safety on both sides. They may demonstrate that one knows about children, too, and therefore can empathize with a patient's problem. From the patient's standpoint they often become a focus for fantasy. The patient may long to have such a beautiful wife, or despise the therapist for having an ugly spouse, or admire him or her for seeing past the fleeting external value of physical beauty or handsomeness. He may envy the children, or wish or fear to be treated as he fantasizes the therapist's children are treated. The permutations and combinations are endless. The only rule of thumb is that if photographs are displayed in the office, the therapist ought to be prepared to listen to what patients say about them. One may expect any kind of reaction, and it will tell one something about the patient.

The same thing goes for wall hangings, ornaments, and books. One patient described an office as "the usual psychiatrist's office, you know — bad taste and pseudo-intellectual, expensive paintings." This may be a valid stereotype, but this patient was annoyed with the particular therapist. The patient chose to expand the comment at this level and tried to find out more of why he was angry. Abstract works of art may be frightening to more disturbed patients. For this reason one may have to reconsider their placement or whether one's office décor is adding to human pain. One might question whether the décor is so distracting it leaves almost no room for the patient's concerns. One therapist kept a piano in his small office. Introducing such a major piece of equipment was perhaps going too far, even if the therapist felt it was necessary for revitalization of his soul between patients.

The choice of chairs for the office is a fascinating business. This is not such an issue if one works in an institution, because the furniture is provided. Some very democratic institutions seriously take into account the therapist's opinions about furniture for their use. This is ideal. Should the chairs be equal in size for therapist and patient? Equally soft? Equally hard? High or low? Should the therapist spend more money on *his* chair, since he sits in it much longer than any patient sits in his? Should a chair rock, or swivel, or will an agitated patient drive a therapist to distraction by unwittingly using every angle of the chair that is mechanically possible? Will an anxious therapist do the same to a patient? Should there be a couch in an office that is used only for psychotherapy, or will the mere sight of it cause too much regression? There are, of course, no "shoulds," except that the therapist and patient be comfortable and not be disturbed by chairs that are falling apart.

Different chairs will evoke interesting reactions in different patients. One office that a female therapist used had two very different chairs. The "therapist's chair" was leather and capacious. The "patient's chair" was soft, with a linen slip cover and a flounce around the bottom. On first entering, a young male patient immediately took the "therapist's chair" leaving the more "feminine" one for his female therapist. He turned out to have particular problems with his father. For this one hour a week he could in part assume the strong father role, "displacing" the therapist. At the same time he showed his masculine caring side in showing her to the softer chair. He talked about it in this way later. When the same patient felt crushed by his father's disdain and expected criticism from the therapist, he sat in a side chair across the room, and when he felt childlike or seductive he sat on the couch. Thus one may be able to use such peripheral pieces of information to assess the forthcoming climate of a particular hour. A patient with hallucinations, being interviewed for the first time, sat on a couch at the greatest distance from the therapist and proceeded to shout information at him from across the room. Since the patient assumed he was speaking in a normal voice, it seemed that his perceptual senses were altered, which led the therapist to consider organic investigations. A phobic patient bitterly complained that the side wings on a wing chair were making her feel smothered. In such cases it is good to have an alternative chair available, if one is causing too much discomfort. The same patient began to use her tolerance of this chair as an indicator to her whether her symptoms were flourishing or decreasing.

Whether diplomas should be hung on the wall is a moot question. Some therapists regard it as too exhibitionistic and flaunting. Others consider it necessary information that should be available to a patient. Patients may be irritated if there are no diplomas, since they may use them as an index of competence: "No *proper* doctor could look so young," etc. One therapist, a young Aryan, might have saved himself and his patient some phone calls had he displayed his diplomas. A Jewish family was questioning his competence to treat their daughter. To the therapist's face they were very obsequious: "Anything you say, doctor." He found out a week later that on various pretexts they had called many of his colleagues to "get a second opinion" on his credentials. It was obvious that they were annoyed, suspicious, and frightened of the therapist. Even if his diplomas had covered the wall, suspicion would still have been an issue, but their presence would have saved this family the trouble of reality testing. One may cite examples to illustrate heightened suffering on the part of an envious patient due to the presence of diplomas, but these issues occur anyway in the therapy. It is a matter of what the therapist deems comfortable for him.

The only furniture a therapist really needs is two chairs, possibly a desk and chair, a phone, a locked filing cabinet, a clock, and an ashtray. Other items contribute to comfort but are not essential. Adequate soundproofing is vital. Landlords often do not appreciate this necessity. The beginning private therapist may need to arrange for soundproof panels and double doors. A separate exit and entrance are ideal but may be too hard to arrange.

The more private the waiting area, the better. All patients are concerned with privacy, and it is within the sphere of the therapist to respect these feelings of the patient as far as possible. A minimal outside noise level is helpful. The tone of the room should be professional, comfortable, and not visually distracting. A seductive bedroom atmosphere, with very muted lights and flouncy trimmings, is best avoided. Bright lights should not glare in the patient's eyes. Care should be taken with the placing of chairs. As long as they are placed so both people can talk easily but can also look away from each other, the arrangement will be fine. A distinctly marked clock may be placed where both parties can see it without having to do gymnastics. Ashtrays should be easily available.

One can debate about the best telephone arrangement. It should not be interrupting. A low tone or a flashing light discreetly placed may be used. The therapist may want to see these to know when to call his answering service. Some therapists turn the phone off and call the answering service at regular intervals.

4

Evaluating the Patient

Regardless of who has seen the patient previously, who has referred him, or what is known about him from any source, the current clinician will want to make his own assessment. The first order of business is to try to come to an understanding with him about several specific points: What major problems does he want help with? What success or failure he has had in grappling with these and other major problems in the past? What immediate dangers or problems is he facing? What does he expect of the therapist? What help can be offered? What will be required of him as a patient in psychotherapy? Do the therapist and patient want to work together? One does not have to cover all of this in one hour, but these issues should be kept alive until there is some understanding of them. The decision to work together in psychotherapy depends on discussion of the earlier points.

APPROACHING THE PATIENT

In response to a question by a beginning therapist on how to approach a new patient, this was one experienced therapist's account of his own behavior.

I begin by identifying the patient in the waiting room, introducing myself to him by name, and asking him to come with me into my office. If it is a public or shared waiting room, I greet him as discreetly as possible, trying to avoid calling his name out loud for others to hear. If the office is not beside the waiting room, I tell him where it is, as we start to walk together, so that he won't have to wonder where I'm leading him. I walk with him, not ahead of him or behind him, unless he clearly makes an effort to walk separately.

Once in the office, I close the door. If there is a chair that I want him to sit in, I tell him which it is; otherwise I invite him to sit down and watch to see how he goes about it. Then I sit down, look at him, and pause for a moment, long enough for us both to collect ourselves. If he begins to talk, I listen. If not, I say something.

If I know anything at all about him I usually make a very brief statement of my understanding of how he happens to be here, such as, "When we spoke on the phone the other day, you said that you're hearing voices and you're afraid that you're going to lose your mind." Or, "I know very little about you except that your wife has been worried about you, and I believe you've been worried about yourself." If a simple statement like that isn't enough to enable him to begin to expand and clarify, I might add, "Can you tell me some more about it?" If I know nothing at all about the patient, I usually begin by asking, "How can I help you?" In either case, with just a few words, I try to get the patient telling me in his own way what the problems are, what he expects of me, what it means to him to come to see me. If I have comments to make in response to his, I keep them short.

Sometime early in the first interview I like to let the patient know how much time I have set aside for this interview, and to make explicit the purpose or goal of this interview. For example, after there has been time for him to tell me something of what problem brings him to see me, I might say something like, "I would like to use our time together today to get as clear a picture as I can of how these problems developed, and of what has made it hard for you to find your own solutions to them, and then to talk with you about what would be the most helpful way for us to work on them. We have until 3:20 today, and if that isn't enough time we can schedule another meeting. In other words, we're not going to decide on any program of treatment for you until we both have a pretty clear idea of what we might be trying to treat."

The patient may have some response to your comments, such as, "Oh, I thought that this was the treatment now, just talking with you," or, "Aren't you going to hypnotize me?" or, "You don't have a couch. I thought I'd lie on a couch," or, "I don't know if I'll be able to come back, it's so hard to get time off work," or, "You mean I have to convince you that I need help?" or, "Oh, that's fine. I expect to be coming to see you for a long time." Whatever the response, it should be taken seriously and expanded upon.

The patient's expectations about seeing you are just as important at that moment as the problem in his own life that made him decide to come. If you ignore his responses relating to your work together, and merely press on to an understanding of "his problems," you will be working with him in a vacuum.

This applies to the first interview as well as to any longer course of psycho-therapy. That is the reason I advise letting the patient know early in the first interview what you have in mind for that interview and listening for his reactions. Some of that work, of course, may have been done over the telephone at the time the appointment was made, or in some other way at the time the patient was referred. But it is important to be quite clear about it.

OUTPATIENTS

Some outpatients will have been hospitalized, but the majority will not have been. Some may *want* to be hospitalized; most will prefer not to, even if they find the idea tempting. Mostly they want help *while continuing the struggle* rather than during a period of hospitalized moratorium. The therapist will not have the benefit of 24-hour observation by a hospital staff. For many patients there will be no information from other members of the family. Usually the therapist will not see, hear, or get any new information about the patient except during the single hour or two hours a week that are spent with him. One must rely primarily on the increasing skill of his interviews and perceptions during the scheduled hours, and on the help he gets from supervisors, colleagues, and readings, for his understanding of patients.

TRANSFER OF A PATIENT

Therapy may be begun after someone else has seen the patient for evaluation. An old patient may come to a new therapist with the previous clinician's recommendation that he undertake psycho-therapy with, say, "a doctor coming to the clinic in July." The patient may come with some sense of contract. He certainly will come with some thoughts about the new clinician, as well as hopes, fears, or resentments.

The therapist may know some facts about what is troubling the patient from a summary by the evaluating or previous clinician. A good summary will give an impression of what kind of relationship and interaction the patient and the previous clinician had together; it will tell how the other clinician understands the patient's situation, to what extent he and the patient seem to agree about what are the patient's major problems, and to what extent he and the patient agree about the expectations of and reasons for continuing treatment.

Here are some examples of the kind of brief comments one might use, during long pauses, to evaluate a patient referred from intake or from another therapist.

I understand that you saw Dr. Jones for a couple of interviews in May.

Dr. Jones said that you were having troubles with your teen-age son. He said that you wanted some help in sorting out why it is so hard for the two of you to get along together.

You've decided to undertake a period of psychotherapy? How did you come to that decision?

I understand that you've been in treatment with Dr. Jones for the past seven or eight months?

You felt that you wanted to continue with therapy even though he was leaving the clinic?

How did you decide that you would continue at this time?

He has told me some things about your work together, but it would help me if you would tell me about it in your own way. [This applies whether the previous clinician was the patient's therapist for many months or only did the intake interview. In either case, he was important to the patient. It will be helpful to you to hear the patient's version of his own problems, and his responses about the previous clinician.]

In assessing what it means to the patient to be coming to see the present therapist, one will usually ask every patient who has already seen another clinician questions such as these:

What is it like for you to stop seeing Dr. Jones? [This may elicit important data, the implications of which are described in Chapter 10.]

What do you think it would be like to work with me?

What did you think I might be like? [This may be a useful question. People have very diverse expectations of psychiatric help. The answer to this question may help in understanding the position from which the patient approaches his work with the new therapist.]

One's views about the patient may be very different from what the previous clinician's comments had led him to expect. If so, he should not assume that either is wrong. Instead, he should try to understand what might account for the disparate impressions. Some of the more common explanations include the following:

1. The patient may present different sides of himself to different people or to the same person at different times. Sometimes this is done intentionally, sometimes unwittingly. Different clinicians, with different clinical skills, elicit different responses from people and thus have different interactions with them. Both therapists may have perceived accurately.

2. The patient may have changed. He may have had considerable relief from anxiety or other symptoms as a direct result of the previous contact, no matter how brief it was. Or he may feel calmer and reassured just to know that treatment with the new therapist is in the offing. On the other hand, the patient's symptoms may have worsened in the interval. His anticipation of revealing his private thoughts may have activated fears of reprimand or reprisal from the therapist or from other important individuals in his life. Sometimes relatives make dire threats to keep a patient away from psychotherapy. Disparate impressions about the patient may be no more than manifestations of his own inner conflict about entering treatment.

3. There may have been other changes, for better or worse, in the patient's life circumstances that now cause him to seem quite different than he did to the previous clinician.

4. The previous clinician may have made a mistake. He may have made an inappropriate referral. He may not have known how to get rid of the patient any other way than by referring him for further treatment. He may have misunderstood the patient's situation or feelings. He may not have recognized the patient's feelings about termination and therefore left an important part of his work undone. Often, however, there just is not time enough to work out termination issues, and further treatment may be indicated specifically for the purpose of continuing that work.

The new therapist will have many impressions about the virtues and vices of a previous clinician working with a patient who comes to him. One who has turned over any of his own patients to the care of another clinician may recall the feelings he had about it. The *other* clinician is usually the villain in the therapist's eyes, whether he precedes or follows. One cannot assume that the patient feels the same way about the therapist in question, however.

MUTUAL EVALUATION

The first interview opens, then, with interwoven development of the patient's presenting problem and assessment of his attitudes to the evaluating therapist. This is very much a mutual evaluation. Since the patient's anxiety is probably greater, since he may be embarrassed about exposing his private affairs to the scrutiny of another person who up to now was a total stranger, and since he has the disadvantage of needing the help of the therapist, the patient may be shy and secretive about the fact that he too is assessing the therapist. It is part of the therapist's skill to recognize these concerns of the patient and to help make them explicit if that is indicated. Frequently the uncertainties and misconceptions of a new patient, if they are not brought out into open discussion, lead the patient to decide against continuing. Another way of putting it is that the anxiety about coming for help is usually very nearly as great as the anxiety about the problem that leads him to come, and unless both anxieties are dealt with simultaneously, it is hard for the patient to feel free and open enough to discuss the things he came to talk about.

FEELINGS ABOUT ASKING FOR HELP

Many of the problems that bring people to seek help in psychotherapy have to do with anxiety about what "other people think." The fear or expectation that "other people won't like me," that "I will be left alone," or that "I won't be able to get along with the other people who are important to me," is usually woven into the matrix of the problems that bring a person into therapy. "Who cares about me?" seems to be a universal underlying concern. This concern does not suddenly go away upon seeking professional help for current discomforts. On the contrary, the therapist is immediately drawn into the web of the patient's concerns about himself. Open discussion of these issues, as they occur in everyday life and as they occur in relation to the therapist, may convey to the patient that the therapist is not dismayed by them but is as much available to hear about this important aspect of the patient's problems as any other. It sometimes happens that the patient's concerns about seeking professional help are so great that several interviews may be taken up in dealing with this issue before the patient feels ready to go on to discuss the pre-existing problems that prompted him to come.

The problem of how far to go in pursuing the patient's reaction to the therapist and the setting, while discussing "his problem," represents a special case of the need to follow the patient's affect. If the patient's strongest affect at the moment is invested in the meeting with the therapist, then that must take precedence in the discussion. If the other problems that the patient brought with him are more pressing, then they should be discussed without delay. No rules of interviewing technique should be followed blindly to the exclusion of the source of the strongest affect of the moment.

WHY DOES HE WANT HELP?

Attention to the patient's feelings about talking with the therapist should not, however, obscure the importance of learning why he wants help. Sometimes that can be learned quickly, sometimes not. Some people will be able to describe very succinctly what the problem is, how it developed, and how they seem to be stymied by it. They may only want help in sorting out the things about it that they have not understood, or in getting over specific hurdles. An example of such a situation might be the 30-year-old man whose wife has just left him, taking the children with her to her parents' home. He is able to describe carefully how they met and got ac- quainted. He describes the good and bad aspects of their relation- ship, putting it into a reasonable context of what he had learned about marriage from observing his parents and his older brothers and sisters. He considers how this relationship is different from those he had had with several other girls he'd been seriously interested in before marrying this one six years ago. He can see it all very clearly, but he claims he cannot understand what finally happened this time to make her decide to leave. He is depressed and discouraged, and very angry at his wife. He finds it too confusing to think about by himself, and thinks "It would be very helpful if I could come in and talk with you every week for a while." The presenting problem and its history and context are pretty clear.

At the other end of the spectrum is the patient who is unable to make any clear statement of what is bothering him. "I don't know what it is. I just feel upset all the time. Sometimes I can't even seem to think straight. I don't know if I'm losing my mind or what. Other people used to ask me if I'm feeling all right, but they've stopped that. I have the feeling that people are avoiding me. My family seems to steer clear of me too. I thought I was run down and went to the doctor to get some pep pills or vitamins or something, but he just told me to come and see you. What do you think is the matter?" The therapist must then undertake a slow process of trying to find out what the patient thinks is the matter, and if that is of no avail, he must inquire into the areas in the patient's life that he knows are emotionally important for most people, until some clarification begins to emerge as to what the patient is so upset about.

OTHER INFORMATION

Whether the initiative is taken by the patient or the therapist, there are a number of areas that the therapist wants information about. Again, he chooses among them by following the lead of the patient's affect. At the head of the list are relations with other people. It is important to know who are the important people in his life. If it is not immediately evident from the patient's age or from the conversation, one can assume that spouse, children, parents, siblings, employer, friends, and neighbors might be significant. If the therapist needs to ask, open-ended questions will yield more information than factual cataloguing questions. "Tell me about your wife," or, "How are things between you and your wife," is better than, "Do you get along all right with your wife?" If the answer is monosyllabic, such as "Fine," the open-ended question should precede more specific questioning. "Can you tell me a little more about it?" for instance, should precede such specific questions as, "Are you able to talk things over together?" or, "How is your sexual relationship?" Elucidation of the picture of the patient's important relationships with others will give you a pretty clear picture of his emotional life. If the picture is of few relationships with others, or none, that too is important. Relationships with others revolve around the central question in everyone's life, "Who cares about me?" which is very closely connected with each person's sense of self-respect.

Work is another important area. How does the individual feel about what he is contributing to his own welfare, to the welfare of his family or of his society? Successes and failures in work, whether the patient says, "I'm only a housewife," or "You mean you've never heard my famous name before?" profoundly influence his sense of emotional well-being.

Play is also important. What does he do for fun? What pleasure does he get out of life? For some people there is no clear distinction between play and being with other people that they care about. For others work is the major source of fun. But many persons have more formally organized play time, with hobbies or sports or family recreation, for instance.

As the information accumulates, the evaluating therapist can begin to put together tentative partial pictures of the patient's experience in his own life. He will begin to develop a picture of what emotional pain is bothering the patient, and will begin to formulate some idea of why the patient is suffering in this way. The therapist may try to keep his own thoughts a few jumps ahead of what the patient is saying, attempting to formulate tentative hypotheses or psychodynamic formulations that would explain the development of the problems in the particular way they developed. As new information is contributed by the patient, the formulations are either confirmed, revised, or abandoned, and new ones are formulated *in the therapist's head* to lead his thinking and understanding as the patient continues to unfold his story.

ASSESSMENT OF DANGER

In the course of assessment, one must ascertain whether there is serious danger that the patient will harm himself or another person or property, and whether his inner emotional life or outer life experience is so intolerable as to require more active intervention. This requires active inquiry and active listening. Occasionally a patient's distress does require more active intervention, that is, hospitalization. This is discussed in later chapters. Having decided that active intervention is unnecessary, one may limit his activity to trying to understand.

RECOMMENDATION FOR THERAPY

Sometimes, toward the latter part of the first or second interview, a brief summary statement is made to the patient, of the therapist's view of his major problem. It might be something like this:

From all that we have talked about so far, it seems that you've had tendencies toward nervousness for some time, and that it sometimes gets so bad that you feel miserable much of the time. You can't sleep, and you can't seem to help yourself. Now it's so bad that your friends and family seem to be avoiding you, and your boss is threatening to fire you. We don't yet understand all that goes into causing that, but I do think that it is a kind of problem for which psychotherapy could be very helpful. I can't *promise* how much it will help, but it seems to me the chances are very good that it can, if you are willing to put into it the time, energy, and money that it requires.

The content of such a summary is just the sort of issue the beginning therapist might want to discuss with a supervisor, after a first interview before communicating it to the patient in the next hour. If one is thinking seriously of changing the proposed contract with the patient, that is, if the patient or the therapist has serious doubts about the advisability of proceeding with psychotherapy, the therapist might find it helpful to suggest to the patient that they both think it over and meet again at a specified time to discuss it further. In the meantime, the therapist can discuss it with a supervisor.

Summarizing the patient's problem, letting him know what the treatment possibilities are, and making a recommendation to him, are standard practice in any professional work. They are equally appropriate in psychiatric assessment.

EDUCATING THE PATIENT ABOUT PSYCHOTHERAPY

Either in the process of deciding whether or not the patient wants therapy, or after that agreement has been reached, it may be helpful to educate the patient a little bit about psychotherapy. Some therapists wait till later, and "educate" the patient during the process as it evolves. One experienced therapist uses comments like these from the beginning.

In psychotherapy you and I would meet regularly to try to figure out what has happened in your life to get you into this kind of difficulty that you've been unable to get yourself out of. It is not yet clear what has caused it. You may have forgotten, or pushed out of your mind, some unpleasant experiences or thoughts or feelings that are contributing to the problem or causing it; our work in psychotherapy would be to try to find out what they are. If I am to be able to help you, I'll have to know a great deal about you, about your present life and past life, your thoughts and feelings, the things that go well in your life as well as the problems. That means that you'll have to tell me all you can about yourself. We also try to examine what goes on between us, since this is my most direct experience of you, and we may learn something useful here that applies to outside relationships. Much of the time I'll listen. I will make comments. We can talk about how or whether they apply. Mostly it will be up to you to tell me about yourself. It seems to work best if you just tell me things as they come to you. Sometimes that may be hard to do, or may seem foolish or embarrassing. But we're looking for things that aren't obvious, so we really have to look at everything that comes along. We work at it together. You do a lot of the work; I try to help you in some of the hard places. It's hard work, and you have to think about whether the problems in your life are bad enough to make it seem worthwhile for you to go through the effort, expense, and aggravation it will take to try to make some changes.

SETTING UP THE CONTRACT

It is important to discuss the mechanics of the therapy at the beginning of the work together. Fees are expanded upon in a later chapter.

Very often the therapist respects the frequency suggested by the neurotic patient. It may be a practical issue of money, or it may be an internal sense of how intense a relationship he can tolerate. His wishes will be balanced by the therapist's available time, and together they may decide on one, two, or three meetings a week. Since any therapist is unsure how treatment will develop, he may suggest starting with one meeting a week with an option to increase if it seems advisable to both. A stabilized psychotic or borderline psychotic patient may know intuitively that he could not tolerate the regression of being seen three times a week and may wisely opt for once a week treatment.

There are exceptions to trusting the patient's judgment. A very turbulent patient may suggest coming once a month. The therapist may be worried about unpredictability and variability of impulse control, and he may need to tell this to the patient as a reason for seeing him much more frequently. The negotiation may be more complex and prolonged. For example, the patient may insist on infrequent visits but make telephone calls in the interim. These mixed messages may need to be taken up in therapy before the patient will agree to regular treatment. He may need to test the therapist to see if he is available before trusting him enough to make a commitment.

If any very difficult patient (judged by his behavior outside of therapy) refuses to come often enough, leading the therapist to feel he cannot be responsible for treatment, then this issue should be discussed. Discussion about hospitalization may be considered. If this is not appropriate, the therapist has the option to refuse to treat the patient, or else to settle for less, when the patient and possibly a relative are aware of the limitations the patient is placing on the therapist.

An exception in the other direction, toward recommending fewer appointments than requested, might be the following. A very paranoid, perhaps previously hospitalized patient, who is functioning well in his environment, may ask to be seen three times a week "to finally get to the root of my problems." The therapist may be wise to begin warily on a once a week basis, to assess over time how rapidly he may be drawn into the paranoid system or how the close interpersonal contact may reactivate the problems. Later one may change his opinion and increase the frequency.

SPELLING OUT THE CONTRACT

Let us listen again to the therapist quoted at the beginning of the chapter, talking to beginners. Parts of it may be relevant for particular patients.

I tell the patient that we will meet for fifty minutes each time, and I explain that when he comes he should let the receptionist know he is here, and that I'll come out to the waiting room to get him. I stress the importance of regularity of our meetings, stating that I see it as a two-way contract in which we both agree to make every effort to keep all appointments and to start and end the hour on time. I also explain that I have different kinds of responsibilities in the building that may occasionally delay me, but that if I am late I will make up the full fifty minutes. (This is not a question of full dollars' worth but of conveying my sense of the importance of each of our interviews together.) Of course, my subsequent behavior will tell him more than my initial speeches, but until he has time to see how I behave, it seems to simplify matters to take some time at the outset for explanations. I always tell the patient that there will be times when he will feel like not coming, often for seemingly very valid reasons; these often work out, I add, to be the times that it is most important to come. I tell him my rules about paying for missed appointments.

As for how long we'll work together: I suggest that we try it for a specified period from one to three months to see how it goes. I personally like to let the patient know whatever I may know about how long I might be available to continue, if we decide we want to.

The first interview ideally should be started and stopped on time. The patient watches the therapist's nonverbal behavior as well as verbal expressions. Probably everything will not have been covered in one session, so one may make it clear that this kind of preliminary discussion can be continued next time.

5

Tuning In to the Patient in Early Psychotherapy

TRANSITION FROM EVALUATION

After the relative activity of the evaluation sessions, the therapist begins to settle into a less active role, particularly if he feels that the patient is going to come for at least several months. It may be a good idea to tell the patient the reason for this, since then, at least, he knows there is a purpose. One might say, for example, "When you came, we needed to have an active discussion about what was going on, and what you wanted. Now we'll settle in to work on the problems. At this point it is better for me to question and interrupt less because you need time to go into things in detail." This may be followed up by a question on how he feels about the change, later in the hour, or in the following hour if he is running aground or obliquely referring to it.

Patients will react to this change. They may be annoyed and find it difficult because the therapist is less "giving." They may be relieved and have a sense that therapy is really under way, giving them a chance to expand in depth upon the first version. Some may feel tricked, others may have fantasies that the therapist has suddenly become angry or withdrawn in reaction to his story. Lack of reaction may indicate something too. If one has acknowledged the reason for the change from the style during evaluation, then one may store the information, wondering how it fits with the person's expectations and dynamics.

If one is starting treatment with a patient evaluated in the same clinic by another clinician, there may have been a detailed face-to-face discussion between therapists on the patient's problems and motivation for treatment. He may then choose to abbreviate his own evaluation if after meeting the patient it seems compatible with the other therapist's views. No matter how treatment begins, there will be a point at which the therapist becomes more silent with a less disturbed patient. Longing to be in treatment with the lost "giving" person may be at the fore, or perhaps there is relief in escaping from the "organizing" person.

Some needy patients may have to be "weaned" over a period in terms of responses from the therapist. The most needy — psychotic and borderline psychotic patients — usually call for more activity on the therapist's part throughout therapy.

PATIENTS ON A WAITING LIST

Patients who come from a waiting list and finally see a therapist after a long wait will have a lot of feelings about it. A new assessment may have to be formulated. Such patients are often angry at the wait, and feel pushed around and neglected. If the therapist cannot hear their feelings, they may leave and vow not to return. Empathy with the patient's feelings about the delay on the therapist's part is often all that is needed. Circumstances may have changed, and in the interim he may have reasonably decided against therapy. This has to be assessed too.

THE THERAPIST'S STANCE

In exploratory psychotherapy, the therapist tries to remain fairly uniform to his patients in order to maintain clarity about the patient's concerns. This may be a source of frustration to patients as they struggle to define the relationship for themselves. As a human life experience, the psychotherapeutic relationship *is* a peculiar situation. It is one-sided by design. "A friend in need" is one view (Dr. Roy Schafer), with the words carefully chosen so "the friend" keeps his own narcissism under control in order to be able to concentrate on the troubles of the other. Everyone has experienced friends who scarcely allow one to begin to complain before they are saying "Gee, that just happened to me, too," and follow it by exhaustive reports on the ideal way they handled the event. Mutual sharing is part of true friendship, and in that sense the therapist can never be the same as a social friend. "Friendship that you pay for" was one patient's definition of therapy.

The longings for mutuality are present in most patients, but difficult though it may be at times, the longings may be accepted as such and gratified only in controlled ways. "Caring" for the patient can be demonstrated by being reliable, being on time, listening attentively, remembering, being interested, and being emotionally available. More will be said about this in various ways throughout the book.

An example comes to mind about a female patient who was full of questions about the therapist's life. The therapist, full of doubts about the efficacy of the stance outlined, unsure how it could possibly be helpful, especially when the patient asked for much more, decided to experiment with a mutual back-and-forth to see where it would lead. He was also annoyed with the patient's demands to prove his intelligence. They shared an interest in films. She came to a session enthusiastically, saying, "Have you seen Jean Luc Goddard's *Weekend*? What did you think of it?" The therapist responded, "Yes. It seemed disjointed, and divorced from reality, but artistically significant [etc.]." They discussed the directing, the photography, and so on. It was a short-term therapy, and the rest of the hours were equally pleasant conversations. At the end of therapy he said she seemed annoyed that he would not meet her for a date.

This therapy was not harmful. It was not frightening, and at worst, not particularly helpful. The patient soon entered therapy again with someone else. In a discussion with the next therapist, the first therapist was shocked to hear that during the course of their meetings the patient's sister had been killed in a bloody automobile accident on a holiday weekend. He remembered that that was just about the time they had been chatting about the film, with its multiple automobile accidents. Now one wonders why she could not tell him about it. The reasons may have had to do mostly with the patient, but since the therapist did not give her a chance, there is no way to know if it was a problem in which the patient needed help elaborating her feelings. Had he maintained his initial, more listening, less involved stance, and confirmed that he had seen the film but accompanied this with a patient-centered query as to what was important to her about it, she might have been able to use the approach to her advantage. Had she not been able to use it, then one might wonder constructively about her fear, denial, or unreadiness at that time, and there would have been a greater possibility of understanding for both patient and therapist, even if it was discussed in retrospect.

PSYCHOTHERAPY IS FULL OF SURPRISES

At the start of any new therapy, both therapist and patient will have fantasies and expectations about the work that lies before them, including reactions to each other, information that will be uncovered, difficulties along the way, and the ultimate outcome. But neither knows just how things will develop, or how helpful the joint effort will be. At some time in the work together, the therapist's understanding will be far ahead of the patient's, and he may often correctly anticipate what will be told. At other times, things will be quite clear to the patient but make little or no sense to the therapist. This may be because of illogical leaps in thinking, false assumptions he makes, or feelings he cannot describe adequately. Sometimes it is because the therapist's previous experience does not enable him to understand what is being uncovered. On the other hand one cannot jump too quickly to the conclusion that he understands by assuming that the experience is a shared one. The patient has to tell the therapist what he means or feels. If the work together goes reasonably well, many surprises will be encountered.

WHAT PATIENTS WANT FROM THERAPY

It is usually hard to predict in advance how far the patient wants, or needs, to extend his self-understanding to achieve the freedom he believes he seeks. It may evolve that he wants informed advice on a certain issue so that he can go off and try it out. Having assessed the whole situation with him over a few sessions, it may be appropriate for the therapist to give an opinion on what would be the best course of action and not persuade the patient into prolonged therapy. The door can always be kept open for such a patient. The chances are that if there is more to the story than first met the eye, he will return if he had a satisfactory trial experience.

The patient may want an advocate in resolving some issue. It may or may not be appropriate to take a position of advocacy. In general this position is better avoided, but at times the external situation is very clear, and all the patient wants is support from a sensible, responsible person. A 20-year-old girl came to therapy for three sessions. She wanted to rent an apartment away from home. Her parents opposed this, but the girl had been offered a potentially satisfactory job and felt the need to run her own household and be away from her parents. She wanted to talk over the issue, to see if it sounded reasonable to an uninvolved person. There was also discussion of the pulls against independence, both from her parents and herself, since she had her temptations to remain dependent. She had thought the issue through but needed a little extra encouragement to act on it. She did not want longer therapy, thus she got what she wanted and did not return.

IDENTIFICATION OF A PROBLEM

With certain patients, coming to recognize an area of avoidance is enough to enable them to change. The following example of the helpfulness of this kind of superficial intervention in a brief therapy may seem overly dramatic, but it is not uncommon:

A bright college dropout, age 21, applied to a public clinic, asking for psychotherapy because he found himself chronically unable to make a career choice. He thought it was due to hangups with his domineering father and thought he needed help in dealing with his father. In a few introductory interviews he described complex and painful relationships with his father and elder brother, and a more pleasant relationship with his sister. He consistently failed to mention his mother, and brushed aside every inquiry made about her.

In the fourth interview, the clinician pointed out that he seemed to be avoiding any thoughts of his mother. This angered the patient. He accused him of treating him according to some old Freudian textbook. But he came into the next interview announcing that the clinician had really hit the nail on the head. He then poured out a long account of his mother's "silent disapproval" of everything he ever did, and added that he thought the "hangup with my mother" might be what was really keeping him from making any choices in his life. Feeling considerably relieved, he thought he did not need to continue in treatment. He terminated therapy and later reported good progress.

Identifying his avoidance of thoughts about his mother was nearly all that was needed in this situation. In the same interviews, the patient's description gave the therapist the impression that the mother sounded chronically depressed. He told this to the patient, to whom it seemed a new idea but one which he was then able to use in privately re-evaluating the thoughts about his mother that he had been avoiding. He did most of the re-evaluating on his own, after the therapy had formally ended.

VARYING DEPTHS OF INTERVENTION

Consistent avoidance of important experiences or feelings may cause a person to live with emotional blind spots that limit his adaptability to the changing circumstances of life. New problems and symptoms may then develop as a result of unsatisfactory efforts to evade earlier painful situations. Before a particular patient can meet at least a few life situations more confidently, a further phase of therapy may be needed, in which the patient comes to recognize that the blind spots are serving self-protective, pain-avoiding functions. The following is an example.

A 16-year-old high school girl was in psychotherapy for treatment of acute anxiety attacks, hyperventilation, and fainting. In her therapy interviews she brought up one anxiety-laden topic after another but avoided any serious discussion of any of them. She brushed aside discussion of nearly all unpleasant feelings. She discussed many unpleasant events in her family but denied or explained away the associated feelings. As the therapist more forcefully drew attention to her avoidance of feelings, she insisted that she did not want to talk about these feelings. When the therapist continued to inquire, her anxiety and hyperventilation increased, both at home and in the therapist's office. Slow, repetitive work was needed to develop a sense of collaboration with her before she could allow herself to see the recurrent relationship between discussion of certain topics and onset of symptoms. She then began to tolerate discussion of the forbidden feelings that had been terrifying her, and to recognize that she had been eluding them with fainting episodes or pleas for medical attention. Gradually the symptoms began to diminish. Identification of the blind spots was not enough. It was also necessary to help her see the protective function that the symptoms were serving before she dared to try to give them up.

A third phase of therapy may develop spontaneously from the second and may require substantial further therapeutic work. It leads to the patient's recognition of his present feelings as derivatives of old experiences. Once they are uncovered, the patient may become able to assess the appropriateness of the hidden feelings in light of his adult capabilities for coping with problems. For example:

A 33-year-old floor sander was admitted to a psychiatric hospital in a near-psychotic panic. He had lost more and more time from work due to anxiety attacks, and the tranquilizers given him by his family doctor had lost their efficiency. The anxiety was quickly brought under control in the hospital, but severe anxiety recurred with each visit from his wife and with each effort at discharge planning. Psychotherapy in the hospital covered many troubled areas of his life that he "had never thought of before" but failed to avert new anxiety attacks. While taking the Thematic Apperception Test, the patient bolted from the room in panic at the card showing one person in bed and another in a doorway; later that day he told his therapist of the unpleasant scene. In response to a comment from the therapist, he then blurted out the memory of his father walking into his bedroom while he was masturbating under the covers, at age 13. The patient had felt extremely guilty and extremely angry, and had consciously suppressed the memory as too painful. Over the year before his hospitalization, his wife had often left their double bed in anger and slept in the living room. The patient had sometimes masturbated, which stirred up the old familiar guilt and the anxiety. The recovery of the memory from adolescence led to a great sense of relief and a sense of embarrassment at being so "foolish" as to still be frightened by that old memory. It also led the patient to initiate and carry out a plan for discharge and return to work and to his family. Much therapeutic work was still to be done, but this important hour, with its concomitant relief and increase of self-trust, gave impetus to a forward progression, at least sufficient for him to leave the hospital.

THE PACE CANNOT BE FORCED

It is prudent to allow the patient to reveal himself slowly. It is generally useless, if not harmful, to attempt to rush toward insights or explanations before the patient is ready for them. When the therapist's understanding of the patient is far ahead of his own, it is generally not helpful for him to share with him new ideas about him as soon as he sees them. Here is a clinical example that illustrates the unpredictable development of a therapy.

A young woman entered therapy profoundly depressed following a significant professional success. She was not satisfied with her accomplishments, and her social life was almost nil. Early in treatment she mentioned in passing that as a child she had considered herself a failure because she could not equal her older brother's athletic accomplishments and was not as pretty and flirtatious as her little sister. Almost in so many words she declared that she had considered herself a failure as a boy and a failure as a girl, but she was unable to see any connection between that early conviction in her mind and her current difficulties. Many months later in therapy, after she had come to recognize her massive efforts to avoid painful thoughts, she was able to come back to rediscover the same childhood conviction that had unconsciously plagued her for so many years, and to see that it played an important part in her current depressions. The therapist's early recognition of this connection was not useful in bringing immediate relief to the patient, but it was quite useful in alerting him to important material that unfolded along the way so that he could ultimately help the patient to make the necessary connections.

Understanding can advance no faster than the gradually growing sense of trust in the therapist and in the patient's own capabilities. His defenses and resistances, his forgetting, his avoidances, all exist for psychologically important reasons. They will be automatically supported and strengthened if one attempts to undo them too quickly, before the patient feels sufficiently in control to acknowledge them and give them up or change them in his own way.

At every point it is well for the therapist to try to respect the unsteady balance between the patient's wish to proceed further with the therapeutic work and his wish to slow down or stop. A patient may wish to stop because the treatment is becoming too painful and the therapist is not adequately helping him to defend against or cope with the pain, or he may wish to stop because he got what he came for and is feeling better.

The therapist cannot accept at face value everything the patient says. The patient may think he understands himself, but he may be unaware of large areas of his feelings. He must be encouraged to talk, to tell the therapist about himself at length, about his present life, his thoughts and feelings, his strengths and weaknesses, the pleasant experiences he has and the unpleasant ones, the memories of his earlier life, and his reactions and feelings in the relationship that he and the therapist share and can both observe.

THE OVERLY CONTROLLED PATIENT

The unfolding and clarification of the patient's outer and inner life experience develop more smoothly if the therapist keeps his attention on what the patient is feeling at the moment. A patient who shows no affect and talks very concretely might be feeling nothing at all, or he might be feeling a need to keep everything under rigid control and avoid any emotion. After listening at some length to what such a patient has to say, the therapist would be well advised to inquire directly as to the patient's feelings about what he is saying. If that is unproductive, the therapist might comment on the patient's apparent lack of feeling in what he says. He might acknowledge the patient's apparent interest in avoiding emotions or keeping them under control. These are ways in which the therapist attempts to clarify his own awareness of what the patient is experiencing and helps to make the patient aware of his own experience. At the beginning of treatment and until it is evident that the patient dares look a little further, it is well to limit the inquiry and comment to the most obvious surface feelings that the patient is already aware of, or partly or nearly aware of. One hopes this will lead in time to the patient being at least comfortable enough to tell the therapist of whatever tightness, rigidity, constriction, or fear he recognizes in himself and in his relationships with other people.

THE POORLY CONTROLLED PATIENT

Patients whose emotions flood their minds and flood everyone they talk with need help in regulating and modulating the flow of their feelings. The technique with these patients is somewhat different from the technique with overly controlled patients. With some of these patients the therapist may observe that such regulation will be accomplished by the patient himself if the therapist does not rush in too fast. For example, some patients are flooded with feelings and words in response to anxiety aroused by the new, uncertain relationship with the new therapist. A patient therapist may give the patient enough sense of comfort that his anxiety will decrease and the pressure of thoughts, feelings, and language will abate.

Sooner or later, the therapist and patient will discuss the experience of the patient that led to the observable nervousness. One hopes they will come to a shared understanding of the inner experience that the patient can use to manage the flood of feelings and words in subsequent similar situations. The therapist can assume that the patient's flooding will become understandable, and possibly controllable, when they know what the patient is experiencing and how he is reacting to what is going on around him.

If waiting and inquiry do not lead to some calming of the patient, the therapist may begin to comment on the evident turbulence of the patient's words. He might inquire if the words represent a lot of mixed feelings that the patient is having trouble sorting out. He might inquire if the flood of feelings has something to do with the patient's uncertainty about the new therapist or what the new experience in therapy will be like. If the patient is not able to respond coherently to such a discussion, the therapist might comment on what he senses to be the underlying feeling, possibly fear or anger, from the effects he feels the patient is creating in him. Another approach is to direct the conversation intentionally to some structuring aspects in the patient's life. In such cases it is often useful to review the patient's daily activities in careful detail, including practical discussion of what the patient eats, how he manages his money, his laundry, transportation, the details of his sleep patterns, his job, family, or children, and whatever matters are pertinent to his getting to and from the therapeutic interviews. Such an approach may serve the dual purpose of reducing the patient's anxiety and confusion so that the interview can continue more productively and so that the patient can carry on essential activities more satisfactorily by himself.

REQUESTS FOR THE THERAPIST TO INTERCEDE

The patient may try to get the therapist to do more: to explain himself or his philosophy, or to intervene in his life problems, such as with his draft board or his job or his parents or his legal problems. The therapist may not know how to respond because he does not fully understand what the request means to the patient, or because he is unsure of his own feelings about the matter. This might be a point for discussion with a supervisor. In the meantime, the patient can be told that the therapist wants time to think over his request, and that the main purpose is to try to understand his problem and what caused it, inviting him to tell more of what is on his mind about it. It is helpful to try to get the patient to consider consciously why he needs intervention. One may suggest figuring it out together, to see what keeps him from working it out for himself — not that help is being refused but that one needs to understand more before he can really be helpful.

FOLLOW THE AFFECT

One may listen first for the affect. Where is the affect, and where is it going? As long as it is developing, unfolding, clarifying, even if very slowly, this is an appropriate stance. One may wait through silences for him to continue. If necessary, in a long silence, one may interject, "Go on," or "What made you stop just there? You were talking about . . . ," and then listen some more. As a general rule, one tries to avoid frequent inquiries about factual matters. Sometimes the factual detail will be needed for clarity, but often not; and often it will ride in on the waves of the affect. One attempts to avoid filling every pause with a leading question. If the patient keeps stopping, it is helpful to point that out to him. It might lead to comment or discussion about what inhibits him, or what he wants or expects of the therapist. If his affect is involved in baiting or teasing, or getting the therapist to do all the work, or getting him to try to dig out information, then *that* experience might well become the object of the therapist's attention. If, at the moment, his affect is invested primarily in some aspect of his relationship with the therapist, it may be fruitful for the therapist to give his attention, and perhaps a comment or inquiry, to that rather than to set it aside as an interruption to getting details of what he is talking about. His affect may at some times be invested in what he is feeling and at other times in how he is telling or not telling the therapist. These are important observations to make about the patient, in the therapist's mind at first.

Another way to think about deciding which thread in the pattern to pursue is: what is most striking about all that one hears or sees of the patient? It may be his dress, the tone of his voice, or the topics he is talking about; or, it might be the details of what he is saying. If he were bleeding visibly from cuts on his wrists, one would not ignore that while pursuing the content of his comments about, say, his anger at his girlfriend. Similarly, if something about his appearance or style is more striking than what he is saying, it should not be ignored.

Then, when something clicks in the therapist's mind, or he is thoroughly confused, he may decide to *give* a little back to the patient, such as:

It's hard for me to follow all of the things you've been talking about. I don't understand yet how they are connected.

Of all of the things you have been talking about, I find it hard to tell which are more important to you.

You've made several comments about illnesses today, is there some illness on your mind that you might not have mentioned yet?

You seem to be amused at the things you are saying, is that true? What is it that's making you smile like that?

You looked and sounded particularly irritated when you mentioned your mother, but it wasn't clear from what you said what it was about her that annoyed you.

And then one listens some more. If the comment leads further toward what the patient is feeling, then one is probably on the right track. If the patient talks a lot about strong feeling but seems bland or unconvincing, after a while one may mention to him that although he's talking about something that caused strong feeling in the past, or might be expected to stir up some feeling, he doesn't look or sound as though he's feeling very much. He may relax the inhibitions on his feelings, he may go on and talk about how hard it is for him to feel anything, or he may get angry at the supposed accusation that he is insincere. Any response, of course, is a bit of evidence that may eventually help the therapist and the patient to understand what he is experiencing.

It is very hard for the therapist to know where the patient's affect will lead. One cannot assume that it will follow the chain of association of his own thoughts or feelings, even though those responses can be suggestive guides or clues. Patient waiting, simple inquiry, brief comments about one's most superficial observations, and avoidance of deeper interpretations will allow the patient to unwind at his own pace. One may inquire along the way as to what the patient observes of himself or tell him a little of what he sees. Instead of questions that can be answered with yes or no, inquiries may be framed in a way that invites unfolding and clarification: instead of, "Did you go to college?" or "Do you get along well with your father?" one may try, "Tell me about your schooling" or "How did you and your father get along together?" Understanding of the patient will grow faster with this kind of approach than with cross-examination or tug-of-war.

THE TIDES OF PSYCHOTHERAPY

The patient sitting and watching that is required in doing psychotherapy is in some ways like watching the tide come in or go out on a beach of sand and rocks. The sea fills or empties pools, overcoming resistant barriers if they are soft enough or small enough, moving on inexorably. There is nothing one can do to speed up the tide or change the direction of its flow, yet a well-placed touch of a finger or toe will speed the filling or emptying of a pool; moving a rock or a log, or smoothing out a hillock of sand, will allow the successive waves to advance or retreat more smoothly. Sometimes the obstacles are huge boulders, cliffs, or man-made seawalls; they, too, can be moved or fortified, but at the cost of far greater effort. The sea has no consciousness or awareness, and in that sense it is unlike the patient in psychotherapy. Watching one's patient in psychotherapy is like watching the tremendous power of the sea moving at its own pace: one can observe and describe it but one has no ultimate control over it. The intensity and direction of the patient's feelings gradually become apparent, as do conflicts between separate feelings and resistances to self-awareness. The therapist's intervention, if well placed, helps the patient to observe the forces at work in himself and to recognize the psychological sandbars, rocks, logs, and seawalls that inhibit the flow of his energies, so that he can move them if he chooses, or leave them alone if he likes their effect. Unlike the sea, the patient can join in the observation; he can make decisions about the use of energies he comes to recognize in himself and can decide whether or not to move obstacles that are identified. The therapist can point out the choices, but he cannot make the ultimate decisions any more than he can speed up the tide or change its direction.

6

Working with the Therapeutic Relationship

Much of this chapter will revolve around the uses and problems of the therapeutic relationship. Some aspects of working with transference, resistance, and dynamic content are described. These are essential aspects of working in therapy and are an integral part of the process. The middle phase of therapy is too variable an experience for which to lay down rules. A few components of frequent and important situations are mentioned here, since it is not possible to attempt to cover every area that might arise with a particular patient.

THERAPY AS A LIVE EXPERIENCE

By the time the patient is engaged in therapy, the therapist will be full of working hypotheses to test. He may have a general idea of the dynamic framework, but he can have no fixed notions about how the hours will develop. Each hour is a live experience, particularly when taken in conjunction with the preceding hour. Rather than trying to remember every single detail of what the patient says, one can remember groups of ideas in order of presentation, with

63

emphasis on transition points. Transference, affect, and content themes develop together, the small perspective of the hour imposed on the larger perspective of an aspect of the patient's life experience. It can be difficult to keep track of each patient if one sees twenty patients in once a week therapy. In many ways it is easier to follow interlocking themes if one sees each patient two or three times per week.

If a literary analogy may be used, it is as if the experience moves from a story told in the third person to one told in the first person. It becomes further animated as the therapist is increasingly involved by the patient in the action. The patient sets the stage and stimulates anticipation of events. He proceeds, now in mime, now verbally. The therapist is both a participant-observer and a catalyst. By feeling for himself and reflecting upon the events, the patient becomes better acquainted with himself. He learns about his areas of constriction and his areas of freedom. Within this framework the psychotherapist tries to be sensitive to any particular patient's need for an abbreviated therapy that suits his life-style at the moment.

TRANSFERENCE

Patients develop all kinds of feelings about their therapists. These feelings play a central role in therapy. Attention to and exploration of the relationship will provide opportunity for the identification of pleasures and difficulties the patient is having in his other human relationships. The therapeutic environment sets up a situation in which the patient's fantasies and wishes or fears about the therapist may flourish. He will recreate and strive to repeat familiar patterns of behavior, which may be helpful or harmful in his everyday life. Often it becomes clear that the activation of feelings about the therapist comes from the patient's private repertoire and has little to do with the present reality. When this occurs in the therapeutic relationship it is called *transference.*

Transference refers to those internal images, feelings, and modes of coping which arose in earlier situations with important persons from the patient's past. They may now be imposed upon the

therapist with built-in assumptions appropriate to the early experience. There is a purpose in one's interest in helping bring to
the surface these complicated, disguised, often buried assumptions
and feelings. They may be connected with the symptoms for which
the patient seeks help. Some of them will also be conected to adaptive aspects of his personality with which he becomes familiar con-
currently. One's developmental years are at least in part complex,
confusing, painful, and hard to understand. In the relationship to the
therapist, the old sufferings and misconceptions are gradually brought
to light, where they can be reconsidered. Ideally, the patient is able
to work through the old feelings and has less need to recreate painful situations. He can then make conscious choices about whether
he wishes to continue his life playing out the old relationships or
to develop new ways of relating that are more appropriate to his
current life situation.

CLINICAL VIEW OF REACTIONS TO THE THERAPIST

Clinically it may be useful to consider a patient's reactions toward the therapist as a series of layers, from those of which he is
consciously aware to the most buried (unconscious) ones. Some
feelings expressed are based on reality; some are based on fantasy.
Some have a partial base in reality but become elaborated in an individual way for that particular patient. Any comment by the
patient about the therapist or therapeutic situation may therefore
have *potential* transference aspects. Some facets may develop more
than others. Whether one chooses to take up any of the aspects of
transference will depend on how they arise, how troublesome they
seem, and how available they are to awareness. Making transference interpretations will depend on one's concept of their use to the patient at
that moment. Thus choices are constantly being made by the therapist.
The open-ended, exploratory approach to such communications
is a good principle because certain realities perceived by the patient
about the therapist and fantasies on the patient's part about the
therapist may be intermingled. One does not know in advance which
layer will develop. Isolated innuendos or comments about the

therapist will usually have fewer implications. Reality-based feelings may call for minimal or no comment. Both patient and therapist are aware and await the developments, if any. If the patient seems to be expressing clearly what he feels, there may be no technical problem about it. Affectionate feelings expressed toward the therapist usually should be left alone unless there is some problem — for example, if the personal element becomes abstract or intellectual. They provide the motive force for the therapeutic work. They help the patient to feel that it is all right to talk to the therapist about highly personal matters. They may give him courage to discuss difficult material when in a phase of disliking the therapist. Annoyance and irritation with the therapist for mistakes and misunderstandings may be reality-based and can be discussed and validated. If they are part of an extended reaction, this may need to be separated from the reality of the mistake. One reason for attending carefully to current observations about the therapist is to set the tone of therapy as a live interpersonal experience. It encourages freedom in the working alliance. Keeping track of groups of feelings as they wax and wane will alert the therapist to the buildup of connected deeper feelings of which the patient is less aware.

The upsurge of feelings that have little to do with the reality of the therapy situation will often be observed in the hesitancy or blocking with which the patient is burdened while approaching them. The therapist will almost always be aware of them sooner than the patient. The patient might preface a comment with, "I know it's stupid, but I feel this or that about you." He may just slow down, his thoughts seeming to halt; or he may seem covered in shame or fear or anger to an intensity out of proportion to the stimulus at the time. Other times he may flood the hour with apparently disconnected accounts, if he is warding off some difficult issue. Forgetting an event or arrangement with the therapist may indicate resistive feelings. In everyday life one may not go on to sort out the mechanism behind such seemingly involuntary behavior. In therapy the therapist will be interested in it. He will want to help the patient see that it is not just stupid or weak but has a purpose that may be important in the persistence of maladaptive patterns. The resistance to the flow of feeling rather than the feeling itself may be the most important aspect he can address himself to. Pointing it out and making a joint effort to understand its function may help to relieve the tension engendered and elucidate the conflict behind it.

During the course of psychotherapy, things do not usually unfold in a well-ordered, stepwise fashion. Current feelings about the therapist may be told in the midst of childhood memories and related adult feelings. Events associated by similar feelings will often be mentioned in juxtaposition. The emotional experiences will come up in their own order. By observing the repeated situations with the therapist the patient and therapist gradually build the concept of exaggerated responses linked to problem aspects of the transference Many fragments of information and reactions will never fit together in psychotherapy, however one can usually see at least part of the pattern of what would develop into the "transference neurosis" observed in psychoanalysis.

RESISTANCE

Resistance is a concept that is illustrated in many of the clinical examples in this chapter. It is resistance on the patient's part to feeling and knowing more about himself and his reactions to the therapist. Sometimes one hears the term used pejoratively, as if it were a fault of the patient. Multiple resistances are in fact a necessary part of the patient's psyche. They are neither bad nor good. They are simply his characteristic ways of defending himself against early powerful feelings. Resistances demonstrated in therapy may show something of the way he forms his intimate relationships. The transference feelings themselves are a form of resistance, a natural resistance against early situations and powerful associated feelings.

The therapist's task is to work *with* the resistances. Identifying them with the patient is itself a complicated business. It is a mixture of observation, an intuitive knowledge of what lies beyond and how much the patient can tolerate at any time. Thus, for example, the therapist may have an idea how the ambivalence is balanced and what affects lie beyond, but he chooses to work in such a way that the patient himself can take the initiative to explore. Thus the patient's autonomy is respected, while at the same time enough intrigue is preserved to give him courage in the exploration. In psychotherapy the patient will necessarily maintain many resistances. The therapist does not wish to precipitate acute regressions in which powerful feelings from early childhood states may be experienced, perhaps for prolonged periods. These can occur if the patient's defenses are attacked unwisely, unremittingly, and too vigorously. Due attention must be paid to how much emotional turmoil the patient can stand at this moment in his life. Active promotion of regression is not the purpose of face-to-face psychotherapy, particularly where the patient only sees the therapist once or twice per week. Some regressive elements will show themselves in the transference feelings, activated by the patient himself. It is these which the psychotherapist can help the patient understand, learn from, and tolerate while preserving other areas of defense. With patients whose hold on reality is weak, for example psychotic patients, the task is rather to help bolster their resistances and defenses to try to help these patients regain their integration. Some of these techniques are described in Chapter 14.

FEELINGS BASED ON THE REALITY OF THE THERAPIST

If a patient says to her female therapist "You are a woman," this is an obvious instance of a reality-based comment. "I'm glad that you're a woman" is more complicated. The "gladness" may turn out to be reality-based for the patient, depending on the therapist's style. For example, the woman may want and like a therapist who allows her to finish sentences without interruption. This may be something the therapist knows she generally does; hence, if the patient comments on this, it can be considered reality-based. On the other hand, the gladness may involve all kinds of internal wishes and expectations that the therapist does not want to fulfill because she views it as unhelpful. With one patient the gladness was an expectation that the therapist would automatically help her with her homework because "women should be helpful"; her aunt always wrote her papers and she liked it. The therapist did not comply when asked to write a paper for her. In her reaction to the refusal, it became clear that the patient's initial "gladness" had to do with the experience with her aunt and was not reality-based in the relationship with the therapist.

The therapist may be aware of his own tendency to be gruff, harsh, or even cruel under certain circumstances. If a patient labels the therapist's silence as cruelty or his frank discussion of delicate issues as rudeness, the therapist, aware of the tendency, may consider whether it is indeed true. The beginning therapist, in particular, may have some uneasy moments when patients reveal observations about him that either are new to him or touch on things about himself which he dislikes or fears. The idealistic young therapist, for example, may see himself as all kindness and may be quite unprepared to accept a patient's observation that he is cold or unreasonable. He might find it hard to differentiate between accurate observations and projections by the patient if he does not have some acquaintance with his own hostility and the circumstances that can arouse it. While it is indicated for him to inquire into the basis of the patient's observations, it is not appropriate to assume that the patient is always wrong or always distorting. The therapist's task in this regard is continually to try to differentiate between the reality about himself and the distortion.

Realistic compliments from the patient may be disquieting and may throw the therapist off base. They may create a situation in which the therapist thinks, "He's so *nice*! How can I pin him down to talk about the unpaid bill? Am I being too mean to him?" While it may be true that the therapist deserves the compliment and that the patient is a nice fellow, there should be a balance in the consideration. One also asks himself, "Is there an added reason for his special niceness today?" "What is he doing with me that he may also be doing with others?" The therapist may accept the warm intention while pondering on development of other meanings within the hour. He may decide to inquire further at present or decide to wait for further evidence or repetitions.

POTENTIAL TRANSFERENCE COMMENTS

How can one be alert to the levels of communication, and how can one make choices about when to intervene and when not? All verbal and nonverbal behavior are relevant in trying to decide on the timing of comments.

A patient may begin the hour by looking cheerful and saying, "Isn't it a nice day? It's so cozy and bright in here." This, if followed by an easy flow, will mean "I'm pleased to see you. I like you." Nothing needs to be said about this, except perhaps a pleasant nod or "Yes, it is." With another patient the therapist may notice that on days when he is more open, the patient takes off his coat, and on days when he is defensive, he huddles with his coat on, regardless of the weather. If he is struggling and hesitating on a theme of openness, it might be useful to draw his attention at some point to his behavior with his coat in order to learn more about his varying levels of vulnerability and what situations with the therapist increase or decrease them.

Displaced references to the therapist are commonly heard in stories about people who sit a lot, who are quiet, who are "good listeners," who are passive, or who give little. These may be negatively or positively loaded. While hearing the content, the therapist is also registering the temperature of the current therapeutic relationship. Suppose the transference is building negatively. The patient is becoming hesitant. However, the next hour there occurs an active discussion about something he faces the next day. Meanwhile, the therapist stores the potential transference information, both positive and negative, to see how the climate develops. In the next few hours the patient freely reveals more detail about his life. Since the affect is pleasant (seen by his greeting and cooperative attitude), at a deeper level the therapist wonders if it is in gratitude for his "giving" in the preceding, necessarily active discussion. Remembering the patient's previous growing sense of annoyance, the therapist speculates that it may reappear. The next hour the patient is fifteen minutes late. He apologizes and says he was unavoidably detained. As the hour develops, he looks anxious, fidgets, and has a hard time saying anything. He relates a fight that he had with his girlfriend. He says, "What do you think of that?" The therapist asks the importance of the patient's knowing his reaction. He replies, "I was just wondering. It's too hard for me just to go on as if I were talking into mid-air." The therapist stays silent. The patient demands, "Tell me something, can't you? I'm getting angry with you. You never say anything, you just sit there."

The therapist knows this is not true, and indeed he has demonstrated that he participates in active reality discussions when it is indicated; the patient has "forgotten" this. It is being revealed that in the larger perspective he is very sensitive, for some reason yet to be discovered, to the lack of equal interchange. The therapist attempts to clarify the connection:

Therapist: I wonder if your growing annoyance about my not talking to you all the time may be connected to your lateness today?

Patient: It could be. I remember feeling a bit annoyed a while back about it. You know that's the very problem with my girlfriend. She's too silent — I never know what to expect — I think she's criticizing me all the time when she doesn't react. I have to have feedback.

Therapist: You feel I too am critical of you when I don't react immediately.

Patient: Yes.

A discussion might ensue about the patient's good feelings the day the therapist did talk a lot and more about his difficult feelings concerning the therapist's silence.

This is an example of how such storing of information for use at the appropriate time may occur. The different parameters of the patient's assuming criticism where it does not necessarily exist and his resultant defensive annoyance will be interwoven themes in this therapy. One might suspect that mother or father had often behaved like this at an earlier time when he was particularly vulnerable; for example, when little, he may have felt that his parents could see through to his angry thoughts. The patient will not get to this unconscious level for a long time. It may take many discussions of naturally arising instances of assumed criticism in the transference before he is able to feel adequately protected and not "seen through," hence less likely to react to assumed criticism. The basic level may never be reached in psychotherapy. However, in living through some upward derivations in which it becomes clear that the therapist cannot "see through" him, the patient may begin to feel stronger in this regard.

To test the temperature of the relationship, while listening to content, past and present, the therapist may ask himself:

What mood is being created with me?

Is he pleasing, flirting with, or palliating me?

Is he fearful, despising, or resentful of me?

Is it some repetition of the past?

Is it feeding into his present problems?

One has to choose when to use a self-related comment or question based on the thought, "For what purpose am I saying this?" The planned purpose may be to help the patient pin down a feeling, to release an affect or a resistive barrier, to clarify something puzzling, or to connect the present and the old experience.

The following is an example of a therapy summary, with emphasis on the use of transference.

A young adult male patient came to therapy because he was chronically bored. It turned out that he was depressed three years after the death of his father, a difficult man. Over the first year and a half of treatment it became apparent that his boring, evasive style with the therapist was a replay of years of ambivalent interaction with the irascible father. He seemed to be waiting silently for his father's loving or angry response, or provoking it. A big step in the clarification of this process occurred following an auto accident in which he was involved. The patient volunteered, "My father would never have let me go on driving the car if something like that happened." That led to a new phase of open discussion about missing the old man, which the patient had not consciously experienced before that. It led on to extreme guilt and anxiety over a memory of sex-play with a younger sister. "If my father had been home he never would have let that happen . . . but I would never have been able to talk with him about it." The discussion went on to the patient's view of therapy as seeking and anticipating reactions from the therapist with no real expectation of talking things over with him. The emphasis, unconsciously determined by the patient's earlier partially gratifying, unsettling experience with his father, was on seeking signs of interest or caring through eliciting some negative response rather than talking things over, with which the patient had had minimal earlier experience.

Interwoven in the therapy with the father and sister issues were the patient's repeated efforts to embroil his mother in contacts and conflicts with the therapist. The focus in the therapy would go from one of these important early relationships to the other, dealing now with each of them separately, and now with the complex interactions that went on within the family, as the varying old feelings and conflicts were displaced onto the therapist and played out in the relationship with him. The maladaptive aspects in the here-and-now were constantly explored at the same time and reappraised.

In any single case the consideration of transference comments can be very complex. The suggestions given above are only a few simple schemata that can be used as initial points of reference.

INTEREST IN THE THERAPIST'S PERSONAL LIFE

A beginning therapist often feels uncomfortable when a patient asks something directly about himself. If in doubt about the implication of a question (as is appropriate), one may say something like, "I would be glad to say more about this or that. But maybe first you could tell me why it would be important to you?" Or, "I wonder why it should seem important to you just now?" Or, "I wonder why you bring up that question?" He might reply briefly and then ask what it means to the patient. After exploration it often becomes clear to the patient why he wanted more information. It may become unnecessary or seem an irrelevant intrusion to give information after both the therapist and the patient understand the nature of the question. Information gained during exploration may also guide one's answer.

A question about one's personal life in general is an expression of a patient's wish. Attempts may be made to understand it in the same way as any other piece of behavior. It may be a wish to put the therapist on guard or a wish to complain in a disguised way. It may be a wish to be closer or a wish to assault. At deeper levels it may be a wish to incorporate knowledge of the therapist, as if it were a piece of his person, to fill an inner void. Some patients are afraid of knowing anything about the therapist, in spite of constant questions, lest it mean too close a relationship.

Here is an example of elaboration on many levels that were not obvious at the moment the patient asked the question. An 18-year-old male patient in ongoing once a week treatment enters the office and says sharply to his female therapist, "How pretty you look! That dress has a shell pattern. Does that mean you like the sea?" What can this mean in the context of what is happening in therapy? His manner is coy, but at the same time he is embarrassed and looks anxious. He takes the chair farthest from the therapist and inclines his head, waiting for the next comment. It seems that he would like to say something kindly, or seductive, but his manner and affect betray his mixed feelings. If the therapist says, "Yes, I love the sea. How are you today?" the discussion is closed quickly. It may relieve her own feelings of anxiety about hearing this patient making sexualized comments to her. After all, there is an air of personal interest and flattery about the statement. The therapist is not immune to needing gratification, especially if she has just finished an hour with an angry, "ungrateful" patient.

The contrast between the content of the patient's statement and the affect revealed provides a much wider area of inquiry. How come he wants to be nice? Is it niceness or is it hostility? What occurred in the preceding hour that might lead to either response? What does "pretty" actually mean to him? Why should he choose to see shells in the circular pattern of whirls? And why "the sea"? Does the therapist look so distant, dreaming of beaches and vacation, or is *he* thinking of the sea? These are a few of the questions that might run through one's mind. For purposes of this example, let us assume that the therapist is not feeling unloved and has not dressed up specially with a view to eliciting a gratifying comment from this patient. Neither has she been yearning for a vacation. Nor is she angry with the patient, provoking a need for palliation by the timid young man. After one has scanned his own associations, there will be less need to be anxious or defensive or to collude with the patient; an atmosphere of open inquiry is more easily established.

In this example there is actually no need to respond verbally. The comment may be regarded as an opening gambit, the significance of which will become apparent if one waits. For one therapist that may seem too cold, unresponsive, and out of character. For another it may come easily to wait but nonverbally encourage further elaboration by facial expression. To say, "Thank you," smile in a pleasant way to the compliment, pause, and say, "How come you ask that?" may come more easily to another therapist. There is of course no correct response to be learned. The only ultimate test of what is said will be revealed in the close observation of the effect on the patient.

In this vignette the patient was silent for a few minutes of reflection and then began a replay of what he felt about complimenting the therapist for the first time. He had expected her to be annoyed and tell him not to be so personal. The ultimate fantasy was that she would stop seeing him. He elaborated on some of the difficulties of expressing more tender feelings to girls. Every time he was beginning to be attached to a woman, he felt paralyzed about telling her that she was attractive. If he did say something, either the woman would overreact and expect too much of him, or else she would ignore him gradually because he seemed too pushy. The reference to the sea turned out to be a projection, since he himself was planning a vacation and he had a fantasy of the therapist coming along. In part the compliment was an amelioration for the therapist's assumed anger at his leaving temporarily. Another factor was his anger at the therapist for not coming along. At last, as he was about to depart he felt safe enough to make a tentative overture. In part he was telling the therapist that he liked her and wanted to continue in spite of the break.

Interested neutrality in all this was therefore of maximal importance. Later he said that had she answered directly, he would have been scared — perhaps she could see that he felt too pushy! Perhaps his ambivalent fantasy would come true and she would want to go with him to the sea — what then? The attitude of inquiry thus created an ambience of real safety for the patient. Together they learned something of his timidity with women and his ambivalent attachment to the therapist. He experienced a first inkling of the meaning of separation from the therapist. Each area in itself was worthy of exploration. The issues became clearer over several hours. This patient was able to do most of the work himself. Here it was relatively easy to promote exploration, partly because the therapist was not enmeshed in the content and affect.

A patient may want or need to discuss his thoughts about

whether the therapist is a Christian or a Jew or a Catholic or an atheist. He may want to know whether the therapist's political views are "as radical as most psychiatrists" or "as reactionary as most other doctors." The question in the therapist's mind should always be the same: what observation, what interest, what concern is behind the patient's thoughts?

While the therapist is building his own new skills and self-image, he may find it hard to restrain his concerns about himself in order to give his full attention to the patient's feelings. Experience will yield the information that the beginning therapist urgently wants about how the patient sees him, how effective he is as a therapist, and what the patient's distortions are likely to be. All therapists learn, all the time, what they are really or objectively like as therapists to their patients. If the therapist is experimenting with a more open sharing of his own personal experience with the patient, perhaps in order to be a real person to the patient and to make the therapeutic relationship "a real relationship," he may freely confirm a patient's statement about him. Such a response may be unhelpful. It may shift the focus of attention away from the patient. The outside experience of the therapist is primarily his own private affair or for conversations with his friends. The patient may welcome such intrusions and may find more equal personal interchange with the therapist more comfortable than the continuous attention to his own feelings. Giving information about oneself may also be tantalizing to a patient, since one is bound to offer more at one time than another. The patient's curiosity and anxiety may be heightened by an uneven approach to the issue. A beginner may be cautious, but at the same time he has to discover for himself how it can be unhelpful, or what modifications are helpful with a particular patient.

HOW MUCH TO REVEAL?

It is not always a mistake to reveal more of oneself. Sometimes sharing knowledge about oneself will support the side of the patient that wishes to explore further. This might help decrease the patient's resistance. It depends on both therapist and patient and the timing. Some therapists use personal anecdotes in a didactic way to illustrate some point of universal human experience. For example, a therapist was with a patient who was very confused and bogged down during termination hours. He described his recurrent anger at people whom he liked generally. The therapist said, "As you know, I'm leaving town, too. I, too, find that annoying things which haven't been so important about my friends are suddenly growing in importance and make me aggravated. People often get angry with those they're close to before leaving. We all have our own reasons. . . ." The patient was able to use this to continue his self-examination. It was a time for giving and supporting the patient, but attention was brought back to his concerns.

Some people can show their humor with patients in the same way. A girl full of fears reported that her last therapist often had laughed and said, "I don't think the roof will fall in if you try such and such that you suggest." The patient said it was helpful because it pointed out an aspect of absurdity in the larger perspective. It helped support a side of her that wished to be less fearful. It never made her reticent to tell the therapist her feelings, and she felt treated with respect. One should, however, be cautious that humor is not used for evasions or sadistic purposes and that the patient does not feel ridiculed, since these aspects could oppose the exploration.

Whether or not one chooses to reveal something of himself, he may at the same time be alert to the patient's reactions to the comment, answer, or explanation. Often one's responses have more than face value to the patient and may be viewed in a more complicated way than he intended.

PACE

Doing long-term work is one of the best ways to learn to do short-term work. It is a good idea for trainees to see at least a few suitable patients for over a year. By comparing different durations of therapy one gets a sense of pace and how much can reasonably be accomplished.

In all therapies there are times of speed and times of lag. This is hard for the beginning therapist to appreciate. He may become discouraged in periods of lull. If it is reasonably clear that counter-transference is not interfering, then it is just that the patient goes at his own pace. The therapist may be excited for his patient in some new development and follow with annoyance that the patient cannot keep up the speed. The therapist also moves at his own pace.

The patient's internal experience of pace and the therapist's experience of pace may not mesh. The therapist may feel there is "nothing happening," while the patient is in the process of solidifying a development and feels a faster pace. The patient may complain that there is "nothing happening," while the therapist senses a heady pace and is tuned in, for example, to the patient's growing anger or love, of which he is as yet unaware. In therapy there is rarely "nothing happening." One cannot jump too quickly to the conclusion that the process is stalemated or that the patient is "unsuitable." Discussion with colleagues can often shed light on the value of continuing on course or suggest a change in strategy to revitalize the hours. If the work is truly halted, whether because it is approaching material the patient prefers to leave untouched or for whatever reason, it is better for patient and therapist to decide together that the patient does not want therapy at this time than for him to be passively pushed out because the therapist believes him to be "unmotivated."

Boredom may cast a pall and make the pace seem slower for the therapist. Often this involves an undertone of powerful feelings which the patient is keeping in check. The therapist may be tuned in to the undercurrent preconsciously, resulting in a kind of over-stimulation. He may have a paralyzed, restless sensation of being unable to work with the feelings because the patient is too distant at that point. Sexual and aggressive feelings often lie behind the boredom. In this dilemma the therapist may bide his time, be aware of what is going on, and work on the patient's experience of the hours, gathering hints as to why the patient needs to keep such a tight control on himself. This patient waiting may build trust so that the patient feels safer and more ready to loosen up. Particularly with an obsessional patient, a lot of seemingly repetitive work has to be done on his style and what it feels like for him to reveal more, before one can come closer to the feeling tone. As alterations and shifts occur, it may seem like one step forward, two backward. The pace depends on the state of the transference, the resistance, and the constant mixed feelings within the dynamics.

What follows is a bare outline of a two-year, twice a week therapy, summarized and annotated with respect to pace. It is structured via the attachment to the therapist. Each new paragraph shows a change in pace roughly representing speed of talking and eagerness or lack of it in introducing new ideas.

Beginning
Jane is 14 years old. She comes to a female therapist.

[The pace is medium fast.]

She complains of not loving her sister.

It is very important to her father that she love her sister.

Two Months
Jane remembers that her father's sister was tragically killed in infancy. She likes her therapist because she resembles mother, who can be trusted. Guilt, fear, jealousy, and envy of sister pour out. Father beats her for fighting.

Six Months
[The pace slows.]

Suspicions arise about the therapist. Lack of effusive response is too much like father.

Jane is afraid that the therapist's rage is gathering. This is tested and verbalized, and proves to be her own fantasy, connected with telling the therapist her angry feelings about sister.

[The pace speeds.]

Maybe the therapist is like both mother and father? More detailed complaints follow about sister and similar friends.

Eight Months
[The pace slows.]

Jane is angry with the therapist for suggesting that she contributed to a fight with sister.

At home she walks away in fury or is beaten by father. Neither happens with the therapist. Instead she talks of her urges and feelings.

[The pace evens.]

A new closeness develops between Jane and her therapist. She decides that the therapist implicated both Jane and her sister. She says it is good not to be singled out for blame.

[The pace slows.]

How can she be the therapist's favorite patient if she is not singled out? She struggles with mixed feelings and decides that perhaps each patient is different and is treated in a different way.

Twelve Months
[The pace slows further.]

In a labored way she "confesses" painfully that she so loves father that she wants him to single her out for attention, even by being beaten. That way they have something special.

[The pace varies erratically for about four months.]

Jane's feelings are unstable. There are more rows with sister, mostly when Jane sees her sister having more from father. Simultaneously she derides her love for mother and is angry that mother does not protect her. Further anger with the therapist because she won't call in father to talk to him (and thereby insure first place for Jane).

Sixteen Months
[The pace steadies.]

After all this turmoil she wonders that the therapist is still with her. Mother and father seem to be steady too, in spite of Jane's anger. Sister is as usual.

[The pace is faster.]

Jane sees herself as like father in some respects. She talks to him more. He too was the oldest. They compare experiences as children. She finds out more about the circumstances of his sister's death. He says that having a sister seems extra-precious to him, and Jane points out that he did not actually have to grow up with his sister.

Eighteen Months
[The pace is slow and steady.]

Toleration of her sister increases. Now when she feels like fighting, she can control it. Jane evaluates all her own good points. No one now pleads with her to "love your sister." She also becomes very interested in mother's early life, and talks about her own femininity. She is full of questions about the therapist's life.

[The pace is even.]

Therapy becomes more "chatty." She talks about her future. Arguments with sister largely cease. Jane offers to help her with school work. Sister openly admires Jane's cooking and tennis ability. The therapist becomes more peripheral.

Twenty-two Months
   Stopping therapy is discussed.

   [The pace slows.]

   There is anger about the therapist pushing her out to make room for the next patient. She sees connection with the old pattern.

Twenty-four Months
   [The pace evens.]

   Pleasure at independence is experienced. Therapist and patient say good-bye.

This therapy dealt in a broad way with some of the oedipal up-surges of Jane's adolescence and old sibling rivalry. By no means did it cover all aspects in depth. Enough work was achieved to suggest that she could proceed to the next developmental step of becoming interested in boys, establishing beginning independence, and thinking of her future.

Slowing of pace during the therapy occurred at transition points of leaving the area of positive feelings about the therapist to become more involved in the negative feelings. Through most of the first year of therapy this happened when constellations of feelings from aspects of anger with the father became focused on the therapist, for example, Jane's complaints about not enough encouragement, blaming her for fights, not being first favorite. At about one year the protective function of the negative feelings — saving her anticipated pain because of her extremely positive feelings for father — became more apparent. The pace varied erratically as she made attempts, now too close, now too distant, to modify the quality of love for him. In the process she manifested more directly loving and hating feelings to both parents and therapist. Her wish to be punished for her "special" love for her father probably was somewhat relieved by the parents and her therapist remaining constant while she became more aware of her own need to be rejected. After this there was a faster pace, as she allowed herself to become attached to father in a more grown-up way. Then for about the last six months, there was a slow, steady period of general internal integration, exploration of her own femininity, and external experimentation. Termination involved a slowing, related to an upsurge of turmoil in further working through of ambivalent feelings about rejection. This was followed by a steady pace as the therapy closed with a mixture of loss and pleasure at freedom.

PSYCHOLOGICALLY INFORMED COMMENTS

Many of the comments offered in psychotherapy are psychologically informed comments which incorporate transference and dynamic overtones. They are mixtures chiefly of *clarification, confrontation, ego support,* and *dynamic interpretation.* Most therapies involve more of the first two and perhaps the third kind of comment. Here there will be more of an emphasis on how they can be used clinically rather than the intellectual ambiguities of the separate situations. After a comment one can choose whether to pursue the patient's reaction to it or to pursue the dynamic aspect, according to how it is received. An example follows.

A depressed 30-year-old housewife in her second year of once a week therapy tells her therapist that she will go to Mexico in two weeks. Her maternal uncle is paying for the trip. He will accompany her and her family. He is old and infirm. It may be his last opportunity to travel. The patient is depressed at the prospect.

The matrix of the patient's depressive problems involves undue ambivalent dependency on her mother, with repetitive conflicts between wanting to be adult and decisive, and wanting to slip into a familiar, controlled, childish position.

At the end of the hour the therapist says, "Do you really need to go? Why can't you say no?" She seems baffled and perplexed. She mumbles something about cruelty. It is the end of the session and she wants to leave quickly. The patient cancels the next session, and the following two hourly sessions she is in Mexico.

Why did she cancel her appointment? It must be presumed that it was in large part in reaction to her therapist's suggestion. The therapist had forcefully addressed the forbidden side of her ambivalence (a confrontation) while she was also reacting to leaving him for vacation. Seeing him the week before she left would have further increased her ambivalence. She wanted to please both her uncle and the therapist. In a sense she became super-independent by staying away. She was too guilty to please herself in a self-serving way. In therapy she denied herself the session, and in everyday life she denied herself the thought of compromises with her uncle.

The next session she arrived suntanned and sullen.

"Well, I went, and it was awful." She wept. Her children had constantly disobeyed her, and she was angry for the whole trip.

Therapist: How come you missed the last hour?

Patient: I felt too upset. I *had* to go with my uncle and you didn't seem to understand.

Therapist: You mean by suggesting you had the power to say no? *[A clarification]*

Patient [Angrily]: Yes. Don't you understand how awful I feel? You were so cruel and unfeeling. The family might have said I'd killed the old man with disappointment.

Therapist: You were very angry with me. *[Another clarification, with a transference overtone]*

Patient: Yes, you were just like my young brother. He always goes off and leaves me to bear the burden.

Therapist: Was I leaving you to bear the burden?

Patient: It felt like it at the time. I mean, you couldn't come with me. I felt no one was being helpful. I guess I could have tried coming in to talk about it. In a way, I felt pleased to let you down. I was saying, "Screw you! I can get along on my own." Besides, I thought you sounded angry.

At this point, the hour was running on at least three levels: (1) reaction to leaving the therapist; (2) reaction to him as her young brother; (3) reaction to his comment suggesting she could have independence. All were interrelated. Illustrated below is the follow-up to his confrontation at the end of the hour before her absence.

Therapist: Given the way you felt, I think that you could have had other options. *[An ego-supportive comment]*

Patient: Well, I clearly had blown up the whole bit about your anger. I couldn't take the suggestion of depriving my uncle, but I think I could have explained why, and who knows, maybe I. . . . Another way just occurred to me. I could have gone with him myself for a couple of days and settled him, and I could have asked my young brother to bring him back. He was in a different part of Mexico. [Etc.]

This comment worked differently, since the therapist had heard the affective reaction to and transference implications of the first comment. This kind of work on a comment directed to the center of the patient's neurotic conflict, offered at an important time, can be part of the work of the middle phase of therapy. The constellation may appear in different disguises over and over again before the patient begins to make freer decisions for herself.

EGO-SUPPORTIVE COMMENTS

Another kind of comment has to do with ego support. This in a way is "giving" something to the patient in a thought-out manner. It may help with a needy patient, particularly in the first few months, or at times of stress in therapy when there will not be an opportunity to meet till the following week. Suppose an acute life stress is about to be approached by a patient who frequently panics. The therapist may want to try to help the patient think in advance, envision problems that might arise, and then try to work out a course of action to try to avoid disorganizing panic. The encouragement even to allow himself a prior fantasy may be helpful in mitigating the anxiety. It calls up the patient's ego resources in preparation. It communicates an expectation of less helplessness. Simultaneously one may hear what the patient feels about the therapist doing this, which is helpful — one wants to leave all doors open, so that if he panics again, he can return to examine the situation without an added burden of shame at having "failed." This burden may be present anyway, so one wants to avoid injunctions to "succeed."

Encouragement after a patient has overcome a barrier or persevered with something difficult may be very appropriate. Such a comment may be framed around the patient and his needs, for example, "You seem to have handled that very well" (or with increased comfort, etc.). Or in the process of ending therapy, when a patient has struggled with the difficult affects involved in such an experience, one might say, "You made use of our time together very well." One may search for something that he believes to be true rather than be tempted to give a sweeping, ill-founded reassurance such as, "I'm sure you'll have no trouble again."

At the end of a painful hour one might choose to say to a timid patient something like, "It must have taken courage to discuss that fantasy with me." As with all other comments in therapy one should try to be alert to reactions to them and in general try to say nothing to provide closure or cut off further feelings. Ego support can be reassuring to patients by helping them to experience, for example, "My way of feeling is acceptable to others," or "Perhaps I *do* have the ability to act differently." Acknowledgment of a patient's valued achievements is important for the patient's self-respect, and also for the therapist's fuller view of him. The side of himself that the patient presents in therapy may be very different from other sides of him that meet the outside world. These sides the therapist will never encompass, and it is valuable to try to appreciate that there are many facets of the patient so one does not maintain a reductionistic view of him and his problems.

DYNAMIC INTERPRETATIONS

At one end of the scale is the trial interpretive comment offered experimentally to test the climate. The patient may or may not be ready to use it. It may be attempted if there is enough of a working alliance; if the patient has curiosity to explore on his own; and if one suspects that the idea is not too far from consciousness. These are more appropriate with resourceful patients in brief therapy. They may be worth trying in acute crises. An example follows.

A female sophomore transferred from a major college in her home town to another major college away from home. She found herself in constant anxiety, clinging to roommates and teachers for comfort. She was sleepless and lost her appetite. After three weeks of school she came to a therapist. She indicated that she liked him because he had responded to her promptly. She decided to postpone her decision to drop out for a few weeks.

In the first three hours she talked mostly of her symptoms. As an aside she mentioned that her father had wanted her to attend this prestigious school. She too had an emotional investment. The first school was her mother's choice, since it was near home. Her parents were divorced when she was 4 years old.

The fourth hour started, as usual, with high anxiety and description of multiple physical aches. She said, "I can't stand it any longer. I'm going." After a pause the therapist offered a trial interpretation: "I've been thinking about what you said about your parents. It occurs to me that this may be the exact situation you were in when your mother and father split up. You must have felt torn apart in your loyalties." She stopped. She thought. She replied, "I never thought of it like that before," and proceeded to describe what it was like for her with divorced parents. She decided not to leave school and stayed in therapy.

The interpretation could easily have proved useless. The patient could have retorted, "You shrinks are all the same. That can't have anything to do with it." And if she had needed to go home to her mother, she would have gone.

If a dynamic interpretation is wrong, the patient can usually tell the therapist why it does not make sense. If he is very defensive, or overly enthusiastic about the interpretation, one may want to explore his reaction rather than become invested in its veracity. There is a delicate problem in offering interpretations to patients who have a very low opinion of themselves. They tend to hear everything as an accusation, which only serves to prove internally that they are just as bad as they "know" they are. Thus one often has to shift back to the affective or transference level and view the process partly as the long haul of building an atmosphere of trust.

In a long-term process with a neurotic, content interpretations may be offered when detail is known about the patient's life, usually when the transference is neither too loving nor too hating, and when the patient is actively involved in reflecting upon his reasons for this or that way of being. One is usually on the right track if the patient shows intrigue. A flurry of denial or enthusiasm does not necessarily mean that it is wrong or that it is right. The reaction may warrant a lot of attention before it can be assessed.

Dynamic interpretation is a very large subject, which has been only briefly touched on here.

TIMING OF COMMENTS

Good timing is a question of knowing when to wait and when to say something about the process evolving. It is not so much a matter of making mistakes as a matter of trying to maximize the use of the material for the patient. Comments that are made when patients are running into difficulties in the hours often turn out to be important. The problem is when to intervene. Would it be best to intervene quickly, or to let the patient struggle for awhile, or to let him weather a passage of hesitancy and unrest entirely on his own? There are times to address oneself to something about to happen. There are times to address the situation of the moment. There are times to wait till the experience is over. In any given hour one may be almost entirely silent or may use all three methods. Consideration of alternative responses in consultation with supervisors is the best way to continue learning. The therapist may also experiment and learn from the effects brought about.

A comment or suggestion can be made about *an anticipated event*. For example: A patient is in treatment for six months. His main complaint is unreliability. It unfolds that he is particularly sensitive to separation, because he moved a lot as a child. There were missed appointments and problems in building rapport because he felt that the therapist would leave him at any moment. It is now a month before the ending of therapy. The therapist could choose to focus on these themes and tell him that over the last month he may feel tempted to miss hours but that coming regularly will be helpful to him in trying to understand his feelings. There is no suggestion of an ultimatum. If it is internally essential for him to avoid the pain, he will miss sessions. But the explanation described may help bring his conflicts to a higher level of awareness for self-assessment.

Suicidal patients may at times benefit by this approach: "As you've described it before, you may begin to feel like harming yourself during this weekend with your parents. If you begin to feel this way, please call me, and we can at least talk about it. We can arrange to meet if it is necessary."

If a patient is recovering from a deep depression and has had periods of unstable affects, poor impulse control, and self-destructive fantasies, the therapist may choose to say something to the effect that it would not be unusual in this phase of therapy for him to begin to feel more actively suicidal, and that, ironically, it may be because of his improvement. These alerts are often most useful either in brief therapy or in the management of and attempts to abort crises in disturbed patients.

The following is an example of a few of the intracacies involved in deciding how, or whether, to address *a present event*.

A beginning therapist was doing a good job helping a patient elaborate conflicts underlying his symptom of intermittent stomach pain. Earlier material had suggested an association with being angry. He was in heavy competition with his successful twin brother. The working hypothesis was that the stomach pain was connected with guilt about angry feelings, in particular toward his twin.

The hour started with the stomach symptoms. He moved to musing on his brother's reactions, and his parents' reactions. Then he talked of going to church as a child and his feeling of freedom when he gave it up during adolescence. "Maybe I should go back to church — [laugh] — maybe my stomach pain is my judgment?" The therapist opted to stay silent at this point, but he complained to his supervisor later that he was sure he had made a tactical error: "After all he was just avoiding the issue. I should have cut through that and got him back to talking about his twin." This approach would have been less helpful. The patient was merely disclosing a lower level of guilt and wish for absolution. He was obliquely confirming that relief of his guilt might help his stomach. He was also talking of the price he paid for independence from his parents and how hard it was to bear his strong feelings alone without "forgiveness." He may also have been complaining that the therapist was doing nothing magic to help him. It was very wise for the therapist to remain silent at that point.

Further in the hour the patient spoke of his parents' mistrust of psychiatry. He ground to a halt. The therapist took this cue to help.

Therapist: That makes you fall silent.

Patient: I don't know why. Maybe I don't trust you either. I don't see how you can help. . . . *[Silence]*

Therapist: It is very hard indeed to talk about strong feelings.

Patient [Speeding up]: It is. I never talked to anyone like this. [Etc.]

The therapist's comment, empathizing with his difficulty, was all that was needed at that point. His words touched in a nonspecific way on the patient's struggle with anger, guilt, fear, magical thinking, and most of all on his fear and ambivalence about revealing himself. The patient was supported in the right way at this point. It was respectful of the complexities yet to be revealed, which they could tease out later.

A rule of thumb in choosing levels to work on is to try to work with the most revealed and pressing levels first, even though the deeper levels are implied. Sometimes in once a week therapy, if the patient is well known by the therapist, one might ask which level the patient feels is right to explore, spelling out the options, for example: "You tell me about this new problem with Jack. We could take it at the level of why you want me to know at this time, or your thoughts about my possible reactions, or further exploration on something you want to change about it." The patient may then indicate his preference, knowing that something is to be understood at all levels but realizing the limit of time.

Other options available at a point like this may be to take up the patient's difficulty in choosing, if that is upper-most. This may at the same time provide clues as to the appropriate level to pursue.

An equally reasonable response would be to state the dilemma without asking that the patient choose. In this way, one may learn more about why it should be difficult to decide. For example, one may hear the patient complain about feeling too rushed in the time available, or about some more manifest urge to "put it all in place" before the next meeting.

Sometimes a situation is best brought to the patient's attention *after the event.* The therapist may feel he has nothing to say for an hour or a number of hours. If this is the case, it will be because a patient is continuing on his own and the therapist is gathering information. A patient who fills the hours may be afraid of what the therapist might say and may need to be in control. One may want to observe variation in this over a few hours before interrupting to comment on the patient's need to keep talking. Another patient may present a number of equally weighted issues simultaneously, and the therapist may want to say at the end of such an hour, "I am not quite sure where we are going at this point. We'll just let it unfold, and see where it takes us." Or the therapist may say nothing, advisedly. Although silence is a contribution, "saying nothing" is not necessarily exquisite technique. It could be withholding. Psychotherapy is a much more reality-oriented situation than psychoanalysis, and few hours pass without some spoken contribution from the therapist.

Again, the decisions may be very complex and ambiguous, and the beginning therapist will have much discussion and practice in interrelating levels of awareness to timing during his training.

WORDS USED IN PSYCHOTHERAPY

Words become vital and highly loaded in psychotherapy. They are a major tool of the therapist's trade. Every innuendo is expressed in words or lack of them.

The closer the therapist can come to expressing the live experience, the better. Rather than say to a patient "the therapy" or "the session,' it is preferable to say "when we meet," or "your hour," "our time together." One tries to deemphasize theoretical terms, such as *ambivalence, conflict, separation, termination.* It is preferable to say "mixed feelings," "torn between wanting to and not wanting to," or "when we stop meeting," or "when you stop seeing me." It is closer to the patient's experience to speak of "your mood," "your feeling," or "my feeling," rather than "the affect created." Different intensities of feelings may be expressed, with "annoyed," "irritated," and "aggravated" as variations from "angry" or "mad." "Fury" and "raging" are very strong and are best used only if they truly reflect the patient's feeling tone. If a patient uses "pissed," "shitty," "fuck," or "balled," it is not necessary for the therapist to step out of character to try to reassure him by a sense of camaraderie and acceptance by using the patient's own vocabulary. If it is in character for the therapist, it does not seem so foreign to the patient. "Low," "down," or "burdened" can be variations on "depressed" or "sad." There is obviously plenty of room for experimentation.

Occasionally a therapist may want to help a distant, restricted patient toward more feeling words. This may be appropriate so long as one does not use shock tactics. For example, if a patient says, "I intimated to the secretary that she best investigate if your last client had departed," it is out of key to blurt, "You're mad I kept you waiting again." It would be better to start by suggesting that he *had* feelings about it and help him elaborate if they were available. He might settle on "a trifle annoyed," which might be progress indeed, even if he looks thunderous.

The middle phases of therapy therefore concern everything to do with the tending of the therapeutic relationship and the exercise of technique so that the process can unfold. The therapist learns more all the time, as does the patient while he experiences the situations and conflicts. All the while he is building up to termination, when everything he has practiced will be put to the test.

7

The Therapist's Feelings about the Patient

Henry Grunebaum
Rosemary M. Balsam

The relationship between therapist and patient can be understood
as containing elements of two different kinds of relationships — the
professional relationship of expert and client, and a unique human
relationship involving two interacting individuals, both of whom
have strong feelings. Part of the information the therapist has about
the interaction is his own feelings. His continuous monitoring of
these, while keeping himself separate, so that he can gain clues as
to what the patient is feeling at any given moment, is one of his central
tasks. The use of the therapist's own feelings is a delicate matter,
since he is involved both as a professional and as a human being at
the same time. Insofar as the relationship is a professional one, the
therapist does not permit himself certain kinds of gratifications, and
he endeavors to be guided by what he considers to be in the best
interests of the client. He attempts to remain objective so he can
offer maximum help. Insofar as the therapeutic relationship is a
human interaction it will involve a dynamic interplay of the ideas,
fantasies, and feelings the therapist has about the patient. This
chapter offers some guidelines for thinking about these feelings of
the therapist and their possible use.

WHAT IS REQUIRED OF THE THERAPIST

Part of the therapist's contribution to the work of therapy therefore is trying to sort out his own feelings about the patient. Like the patient, these range from the most available levels of awareness to the most buried. The therapist, too, often experiences an uneven mixture of available and less available feelings while with the patient. The unconscious responses are most correctly called *countertransference.* Here our primary interest is in briefly describing multiple feelings on all levels, possible situations in which they may occur, and how they may affect therapy.

Many therapists doing exploratory psychotherapy have a special interest in trying to be sensitive to current affect in themselves. Some have a further interest in exploring and recognizing the roots of these feelings. This helps in tuning in to various levels of patients' communications and may help in deciding which feelings are nearer the surface for potential use in therapy.

Awareness of the current affective situation between therapist and patient may be a major source of data for understanding the patient. Familiarity with the therapist's own range of feelings may help in hearing and tolerating these in other people. The therapist may have less need to cut the patient off in his own anxiety, and he may communicate a sense of tolerance that in turn can help the patient to bear to articulate his own feelings. Picking up affective highlights in his own free-floating fantasies stimulated by a patient's account of an event may be useful in tuning in to the preconscious parameters of the presented material. Some knowledge of his own particular psychological responses can help the therapist to be aware of those situations in which the major portion of the interaction is due to himself and the lesser portion contributed by the patient.

A kind of emotional agility or flexibility is useful, and therapists develop this in their own way. Learning the discipline of a fairly neutral therapeutic stance for some therapists seems like learning classical ballet. Very strong feelings are present and felt, but the emphasis is on defining, describing, and following themes, and connecting vignettes, rather than entering into an unplanned rough-and-tumble. All therapists practice recognizing when to be still, when and where and how to move. Other therapists learn to have more confidence in loosening up to be available for a wider range of expression.

A simple example may be useful at this point. The therapist in the outpatient department of a community health center is listening to his patient and finds himself growing increasingly annoyed. How can he understand his feelings? Are they the result of the overcrowded intake clinic that morning, making it unlikely that he will have time for lunch? Is he perhaps experiencing an empathic bond with his patient as she relates how her employment is being jeopardized due to a cutback in government funds? Do his feelings arise mainly from the argument he had with his wife at breakfast? Are they related to the fact that the patient is an older woman complaining about her husband, reminding him of his mother and her complaints about his father? The feelings of therapists toward their patients are a standard topic of conversation among supervisors, therapists, and patients. Fairly frank discussion of these feelings can occur when a small group of colleagues shares clinical experiences in regular meetings over a long period of time. Even there, the feelings of therapists about their patients are difficult to discuss, because of their intimacy and one's sense of not wanting to be exposed. Individual supervision and consultation are also useful places to learn about one's own feelings as they affect psychotherapy.

The topic will be approached here by considering the external factors which influence the therapist's feelings about patients in general or a particular patient, and progressing to internal factors arising from the therapist.

THE THERAPIST'S EMOTIONAL FIELD

Sometimes therapy is described as if the therapist and patient met alone in an office surrounded by empty space. Particularly in clinics, the meetings are influenced by many forces arising from the emotional field in which therapy occurs.

When the therapist is newly arrived, he has time on his hands. He anticipates seeing supervisors, to whom he must soon present cases. In this situation few patients may seem too disturbed or too unmotivated to be of interest. It is different when, later in the same year, the therapist is busy, sometimes too busy, and has hardly enough time to discuss his problem cases with his supervisor!

The beginning therapist is often more eager than the patient to see diagnostic assessment lead to therapy. Therapy may be "sold" to the patient only to be terminated by him later with little gain. On the other hand, the overburdened therapist is unlikely to be keenly interested in exploring the patient's ambivalent desire for help. He may decide that anything less than a clear, explicit commitment to psychotherapy is "inadequate motivation." Sometimes it is said of these reluctant patients that if they really wanted psychotherapy, they would be willing to come in the evening or get a babysitter, or leave work early, or ask their parents for funds to support therapy. The situation is often more complicated than that. The patient has problems and wants help but is unclear as to the help required. The busy therapist may be too tired and ambivalent to clarify for the patient the kinds of therapy available for his difficulty and assist him in determining the most appropriate mode and therapist. The patient may leave perplexed and decide against psychotherapy even though it is objectively appropriate.

Institutions have their own unique dynamics determined in part by history but also by present events. If the director of the institution is about to resign and a new, unknown replacement is coming, this will impinge on the feelings of all the therapists. It may make everyone anxious about who will be in charge. Similarly, the death or divorce of a devoted teacher will have its impact on the staff of his institution. The occurrence of these dynamics on a particular day on which the therapist and patient first meet is likely to have a considerable impact on the feelings of the therapist about the patient and on his ability to listen.

INFLUENCE OF REFERRAL SOURCE

Referral is sometimes from a senior colleague and sometimes from a friend or another patient. The referral may be one that the beginning therapist, especially, cannot gracefully refuse. For instance, if the colleague is the administrator in charge or a senior, respected teacher, one may accept the patient even if he is reluctant. A request for help with a very difficult patient by a colleague or friend who needs to be "bailed out" may readily lead to agreement to see a patient.

The presenting problem may be one that particularly interests the therapist, in which case he might find "yet another hour"; or the problem may be one with which he has had previous difficulty and on which he would like a second chance. While the emotional field in which the evaluation occurs may lead to a general inclination leading either toward an interest in psychotherapy or toward a reluctance to engage in psychotherapy on the part of the therapist, it may also have more specific consequences.

An individual patient may arrive in the therapist's office with "a reputation." Sometimes his reputation is of short duration, since the clinic secretary or the therapist's own receptionist handed him the patient's chart with only a few words. This introduction may lead to antagonistic feelings, as when the patient arrives in the clinic accompanied by a large chart containing the previous therapist's notes. The patient may be a young adult or late adolescent whose parents made contact with the therapist. They may have been officious, manipulative, and controlling in their approach, resulting in negative feelings toward them and the patient. Or they have been diplomatic towards the therapist, and thus eased his anxiety about seeing their child. A young female colleague of the therapist may hesitatingly ask if he has time to see a troubled friend of hers, a shy girl who is earnestly pursuing her studies with modest resources. The therapist may feel sorry for her even before he sees her and feel committed to helping her. The therapist may be particularly interested in a certain group of patients, or on the other hand may have a general dislike of them. He may be treating too many women or too many men. He may be asked by his supervisors to treat a certain patient to increase his experience. His financial situation may also be related to his attitudes about starting therapy with a patient. Thus, the patient who arrives in the office enters a situation that is already partly structured.

The above illustrations are provided to suggest that one of the first things to be done is to clarify the emotional field in which the therapy is occurring. This may help the therapist to set stronger feelings aside, at least temporarily, in order to decide on his willingness to make a commitment to treat a patient and to assess more clearly the patient's presenting problem and need for treatment. Any therapist, as he becomes experienced and works more often in his own office by himself, is more likely to be familiar with his own emotional field and to be practiced in self-preservation. A delicate balance must be struck between allowing oneself involvement with a patient, caring about him, and wishing to be helpful, and excessive feelings of professional obligation that might lead one to become overcommitted and thus have less emotional resources available for his work, which might be damaging both to himself and the therapy with any particular patient.

WHAT THE THERAPIST'S FEELINGS INDICATE ABOUT THE RELATIONSHIP

The therapist's feelings can be looked at in different ways. First, they can be classified into various types, such as anger, anxiety, or sadness. Second, the therapist can attempt to apprehend the nature of the relationship between the patient and his therapist at that moment. Examples will help clarify these ways of looking at the issue. A therapist may recognize a feeling of sadness because his patient is sad at that moment. Or he may feel like teasing his patient because she is acting exceedingly coy at that moment. In the former instance he is experiencing some form of the same feelings as the patient. In the latter case the patient creates a situation in which the therapist experiences the natural counterpart to the patient's way of relating.

In a simple way it may be said that the therapist can relate to his patient in three different modes: (1) an empathic mode, in which he experiences something of the same feelings as the patient, (2) as a significant other to the patient, frequently in the role of a parent or sibling, and (3) in the position of the patient, who may act the role of his own parents, casting the therapist as the "child-patient." This brief introduction to this part of the chapter is not intended to clarify all the issues raised by this scheme but rather to place it before the reader so that he will understand the general framework of the rest of the chapter.

EMPATHY

In a general way, a major response that therapists have about many of their patients is empathy.

Many beginning therapists are concerned lest they find their patients unattractive, unpleasant people, with whom it is uncomfortable to sit. Curiously enough, this rarely happens. It is a rare patient who, even though he may be unprepossessing, gauche, or even boorish at the beginning of therapy, does not gradually arouse more interest or for whom one does not feel more empathy as his story unfolds. However, if a therapist thoroughly and continuously dislikes a patient, for whatever reason, it may be better to consider giving the patient an opportunity to work with someone else. People have differing views about this, some asserting that it is the therapist's job to begin to help the patient understand his distasteful presentation of himself. If it occurs with the therapist, there is a good chance that it is one of the patient's life problems. An example of a "mismatch" of patient and therapist follows. Soon after World War II, a young Jewish psychiatric resident was assigned to work in therapy with a former German storm trooper. His negative feelings were so strong that he felt unable to work with the man. His associates and supervisors were unable to agree about what was the best course to follow. Some people felt that, theoretically, he ought to be able to work with the person. Others felt, on "humanitarian" grounds, that it was impossible. Clearly this kind of predicament is a difficult one to resolve.

Empathy is having some sense of what a feeling is like for the other person. A patient may talk of being sad. The therapist does not necessarily feel sad at that moment, but enough of the quality and intensity is transmitted so that the therapist recognizes its components from some part of his own inner affective repertoire. He may retain his own affect of the moment, feeling separately his deeper level of recognition. One therapist said that when a very depressed patient began to talk of "nothingness" or of "the future being black," she felt a certain "gunk" in the pit of her stomach that she used diagnostically as an indicator of suicidal despair in the patient. Another therapist said that when a chattery, elated manic patient began to tell him how wonderful the world was, his "blood ran cold"; this was in recognition of difficulties yet to be experienced by the patient. Sometimes, depending on the mood of the therapist and how ready he is to be cheered up, or saddened, or sexually titillated, he may find less clear the distinction between his own and his patient's infectious affect.

Continuously matched feelings in therapist and patient may indicate evidence of some less consciously available feelings in the therapist. For example, a therapist with a consistently cheerful patient might say, "I really like Jack. He cheers me up every time I see him." The therapist may be relying on Jack to relieve his tiredness at the end of the day or there may be more complicated reasons. If he considers the interplay of feelings no further, he may be subtly influencing his patient away from troublesome concerns.

Another type of response related to empathy is "intuitive feelings." These, again, may be far from the therapist's prevailing affect of the moment but are part of his own psychological makeup derived from past experiences and are not necessarily consciously available to him at the time he connects with some feeling cues coming from the patient. To take two simple examples: a patient's face is radiant as she talks concretely about an achievement. The therapist says, "That must have made you happy." She agrees. Another patient crosses and uncrosses his legs, and lowers his head or blushes while talking of telling a lie. The therapist says, "You sound ashamed," and has it confirmed.

When the therapist experiences these feelings connected with the patient's feelings, of whatever origin, how can he use the information? He may say nothing, and wait to see how matters evolve. He may restate the feeling, helping to identify it, as in the examples in the preceding paragraph. Sometimes the therapist will experience feelings because of an incident which the patient relates but about which the patient himself does not experience direct feelings. Any verbalization the therapist offers may then be likely to draw a blank or a denial, and he may decide to store the information about the feeling to work with after the resistance has been considered. Or he may point out the absence of an expectable feeling.

Some empathic feelings call for direct expression. Certain tragedies demand a compassionate response; certain dangers require that the therapist be concerned, for instance about a young mother's sick child; some situations require outrage, others a laugh. These are spontaneous human responses to meaningful events. However, based on a patient's previous painful account of a struggle, one may have reason to believe that the patient might have a strong negative reaction to a direct expression. Or he may seem to be trying too hard to share one's response. These might be areas to take up with him. For example, a therapist had seen a student who took many years to pass his final examinations. At last, after all the travail, panic, depression, and fear, he came in and announced that he had "done it." The therapist said sincerely and with relief and pleasure for his success, "Congratulations!" The patient then, expectedly, thoroughly scolded the therapist. This was not to say that the therapist should not have given a normal response. But the meaning of the patient's inability to accept the standard human response was an issue for work in the therapy.

COMMUNICATED ANXIETY

Some patients, because of very intense and continuous feelings under pressure in themselves, can communicate them almost en bloc to the therapist. The psychotically anxious patient, for example, may arouse much anxiety in the therapist, a major clue that one is hearing about psychotic experiences. One teacher of residents has described this as a feeling that "the hair on one's neck is raised." The patient's panic may arouse thoughts that one does not know what to say or what to do. Following themes may be next to impossible, especially if there is a great deal of abstraction. At a basic level the anxiety may touch the therapist's own anxiety about his reality testing and the frailty of his own humanness. He may be over-burdened in a particularly uncomfortable way. Searles has written movingly of his inner experience in working intimately over long periods of time with borderline and schizophrenic patients.[*]

SEXUAL FEELINGS

Another set of feelings that seem particularly difficult to cope with are sexual feelings that the therapist may have about his pa-tient. Anger is often more openly discussed with patients or with supervisors than sexual feelings. These may concern only the ther-apist, or they may be coming from interactions with a flirtatious patient. Therapists, as well as patients, can be aroused by physical beauty or handsomeness, and they too are concerned with their own attractiveness. Therapists, as well as patients, enjoy erotic flattery. There are probably wide variations among therapists in the ease with which they are sexually aroused. The waxing and waning of life gratifications may also lead to greater or lesser receptivity and stimula-tion due to a patient's attractiveness, whether or not he or she is also flirtatious. A therapist, feeling aroused, may become anxious or annoyed with the lack of outlet and the constraints on the rela-tionship. Thus, one might hear a young male therapist adopt an ac-cusatory tone while deciding unilaterally that his young female pa-tient needs a woman therapist because she is "too seductive with men" (it is quite a different matter if the patient herself says it). The accusatory way this adjective may be used suggests how threat-ened a therapist may become in this situation.

At the lower end of a scale of sexual arousability, one male and one female therapist stated that they never really had experienced sexual feelings due to involvement in a patient relationship. The necessary established lack of mutuality seemed to be enough to pre-vent any constant or growing stimulation with the patient per se.

---

[*]Searles, H. *Collected Papers on Schizophrenia and Related Subjects.* New York: International Universities Press, 1965.

Both therapists felt that they could admire or appreciate a physically attractive patient of either sex as they might aesthetically view a lovely painting. This was a pleasant feeling which would easily give way to whatever affect was presented by the patient in the hour. These same therapists felt it might be sexually stimulating to hear a patient's account of an erotic event, but this had a voyeuristic, secondhand quality, like watching a sexy movie, rather than direct involvement with the patient.

Midway on the scale are feelings reported often with particular patients because they have a specific significance to the therapist. Thus, a female therapist talked of being sexually aroused in her first meetings with a male patient who resembled an old boyfriend. She wondered if this would interfere with the work together, but she said as she continued and got to know him as a very different person, the patient became more separated from the image of her boyfriend, and his physical attractiveness to her markedly decreased.

Some therapists at the upper end of the scale have said that they are easily aroused, by a patient's manner of speaking, deportment, handsomeness, or beauty, even if the patient is not being flirtatious. Again, they say that as they get more involved in the therapy process, their sexual feelings often diminish or at least seem manageable.

Beginning therapists, in particular, sometimes talk as if a patient's sexual overtures were directed solely at them. They are, at one level, in the hour. Yet more broadly speaking, one may view the overt aspect of the sexuality as having past and future components in fantasy, as well as the present obvious aspect. All of these are parts of the therapy. The process of beginning to think about the sexual feelings and their wider complexities, for either the therapist and his or her own needs, or the patient for his or her needs, may diffuse their intensity for the therapist. They may therefore be less dominant and less likely to affect the therapist's stance. The therapist may be less likely to stimulate the patient further or to push him away as being too demanding.

Sometimes the therapist's sexual arousal can be an indicator that the patient is similarly sexually aroused. A patient fully aware of her attractiveness may be telling a therapist, and he may be getting the message, "You see, I *do* have areas of expertise, so please don't

think I have no talents." Another may be saying, "All my relationships are sour. Maybe I can get you involved in a fuller way with me."
A patient who relates to peers, or to older men and women, mostly
in this way, may start treatment seductively, this being a familiar
stance, since he or she is fearful of what this strange relationship
demands of him or her. Another patient may only become seductive
or flattering when mainly angry or confused or afraid or grateful, or
when he or she wants to keep the therapist at arm's length.

Occasionally the sexual arousal felt by the therapist is really not
on the same plane as that felt by the patient. The behavior of one
young girl patient who used to pull up her stockings or lift her skirt
to fix her garters was misinterpreted as conscious seductive behavior
because it was arousing to the therapist. This patient was only dimly
aware, if at all, of its effect on anyone else because it was a cover
for a regressed schizophrenic position. Taken in conjunction with
her other problems and childlike relationships, it was very seductive
in the little-girlish sense. As the meaning of this patient's behavior
became clearer, the therapist became more comfortable and the work
proceeded.

With a flirtatious patient, therefore, the question for the therapist
may become, why is he feeling aroused, and what else is the patient
feeling or doing? The sexual feelings and behavior may be very
complicated. Over time, the therapist can communicate either nonverbally or verbally that mutual sexual activity is not part of the
therapy and that this, like other behavior and feelings, is open for
discussion. By further consideration of them, the aroused therapist
can often prevent his feelings from clouding his vision of the patient's
problems, and the anxious therapist usually becomes less threatened.

It is very common for therapists to feel fondness and affection
for patients, and, like the patients' positive feelings, they help in the
therapeutic alliance. Sexual feelings or affection, like pity, anger,
and any other feelings aroused, can be observed, thought about, and
clarified for the patient at points in therapy where they may be useful, and when they are related to other situations in his life.

How one learns to trust one's own feelings is a complex problem.
Too much rumination may be as little help as too little thought. In
many instances the patient himself is naming his feelings, and the

therapist gets practice in recognizing what is happening inside himself as the patient talks. At other points the therapist may hypothesize either from his personal past experience or his experience with other patients, what the patient is likely to be feeling. He may identify the feeling for the patient, and the feedback gained from patients' responses provides valuable practice. The patient may deny the feeling as labeled by the therapist, but follow with a theme in which he uses the same affective language; the therapist can then trust more firmly his initial prediction.

This is a simplification of a very interesting topic, further discussion of which is beyond the scope of this chapter.

THE THERAPIST IN THE ROLE OF SIGNIFICANT OTHERS

It is quite natural that the therapist should find himself in the role of the patient's significant others. The defenses and character of the patient was formed with these people, and the patient often recreates the original situation. If the patient feels sad and the therapist is aware of it, he may naturally wish to ameliorate it. He may desire to nurture or comfort his patient. For instance, an experienced therapist was seeing a young woman who found her situation as a teacher in a school increasingly difficult. She seemed bewildered by the social field in which she was operating, and he found himself drawn into offering what amounted to advice rather than psychotherapy. He viewed his course of conduct in terms of helping the patient to deal with her anxieties about the situation, which at times seemed overwhelming. It finally became clear to both participants that what was necessary was an exploration of her anxieties rather than consultation on how to face her current situation.

In desiring to nurture the patient, the therapist assumes the stance of the patient's significant others, often his parents. The lonely, sad patient and the comforting therapist are, therefore, a complementary pair. In the example just given, the therapist found himself taking the role of the patient's mother, who had given the patient advice in detail and at length on how to conduct herself in all the various and possible situations in which she had found herself during her school days. The patient had learned to gain some gratification, if unsatisfactory, from having social problems. Other examples are the worried, hypochondriacal patient and the reassuring, symptom-oriented psychiatrist; or the meek, masochistic patient and the therapist who finds himself unwittingly the inquisitor, whose questions seem invariably to provoke pain rather than clarify issues.

The therapist may find himself afraid of a patient. If not sensed directly, this may become noticeable to the therapist in the form of his subtle compliance with patient's requests and avoidance of direct confrontation of certain issues. These observations often constitute suggestive evidence that the patient is paranoid and that the therapist is concerned lest he incur the patient's wrath. This may be an important feeling that is shared by others in the patient's environment. For example, if a family in bringing a member to the clinic has told him a fictitious story about where he is being brought and why, it is often because they are afraid. It can also be seen that the patient has ample reason to distrust his relatives, since they don't tell him the truth, and that he and his family are in a vicious circle.

One way a therapist can recognize his unwitting collusion with a patient's neurotic needs is that he may over time begin to feel that he is detoured or is meeting constant resistance to forward movement. If the therapist finds himself at such a point with a patient, once he realizes what is or may be happening to him he may be able to understand how the pattern arose with the patient and what can happen as a result. It may be part of the live experience of the patient for the therapist.

In the work together, the therapist is a target for all of the patient's usual and neurotic ways of engaging other people. He sometimes finds himself going along, to a point where both he and the patient find they are in a familiar cul-de-sac. He may then discover for himself, and if necessary help the patient to discover, why this mode is unrewarding. For the patient, it was a set of responses chosen early in life for want of a better one, when the alternatives seemed even less rewarding. Now, as an adult, the patient can perhaps reconsider it and try out new ways of relating, experimenting first with the therapist.

THE THERAPIST FEELING AS THE PATIENT USED TO FEEL

Another stance that patients take with their therapists arises out of their own identifications. They have come to resemble their parents in crucial ways, often unconscious and sometimes much repudiated. Everyone has noticed that much as young parents resolve not to treat their children as they were treated, in certain ways they cannot help doing so. Examples arise frequently with young therapists treating older patients, as in the following:

A young female therapist was constantly scolded by an older female patient for wearing pantsuits and no makeup, and having long hair. The patient's daughter of similar age was also the object of such criticism, which to the mother symbolized unreliability and lack of caring. The feelings were connected to fear and suspicion that the therapist was incompetent. There were many other aspects, but one that began to emerge was that the patient's own mother had been fearful of the patient's independence and sexuality, and mostly she was fearful of being left alone and sick in her old age. The patient had had a very turbulent and defiant adolescence, and had suffered greatly from guilt for cutting herself off entirely from her mother at 15 years of age. It seemed that in the unresolved separation, she had taken on the angry, controlling, clinging qualities which she had repudiated in her mother but which she was repeating with the daughter and her therapist. She was putting the younger women in the same position she had been in as a teenager.

Another example of the therapist finding himself in the position of the patient while the patient seems to have taken on an aspect of his parents occurs when the therapist of a psychotic patient feels lost in a maze. His task seems to be to find a way out of the maze, and only as he does so can his patient follow him. Some of these feelings seem to arise because the patient is recreating for his therapist the puzzles his parents presented to him, with resulting mixed messages and confused emotions.

An example of the patient's reaction to a parent role imposed on the therapist is the obsequious patient who claims he will do anything the therapist suggests. However, when the therapist begins to advise the helpless patient, he may be doomed to failure. The patient is quick to point out that the advice is no good. The patient is not only victim but harsh critic. The therapist's insights are treated as criticism of the patient's way of looking at things and criticized in turn. This way, he can be both parent and child simultaneously.

CLINICAL EXAMPLE OF ROLES PLAYED
BY THE THERAPIST

The complex interrelations between the feelings of the therapist and some of their consequences in therapy are described in greater detail in the following case. It illustrates many of the complicated feelings described above.

A young woman was referred with a history of having been seduced by the social worker in the settlement house in the slum neighborhood in which she grew up. Her background was fairly deprived. Noteworthy were a history of kidney disease in childhood, requiring many long hospitalizations, and memories of her two older brothers' sadistic treatment of her, such as putting out lighted matches on her arms, a practice in which she herself now engaged.

The feelings of the male therapist were a mixture that varied over the four years of treatment. Initially, there was a desire to nurture and care for the patient, and to protect her from the many sado-masochistic situations and relationships she became involved in. This was the therapist's experience of the complementary feelings aroused by her history of deprivation and the empathy resulting from it. But there were also feelings of having to exercise consider-able care lest she interpret his responses as a seduction, repeating her experience with the previous therapist. Her repeated plea was for closeness in therapy. Could she sit on his lap? Would he hold her? This would make her feel better. He felt overburdened by her requests and often felt drained and empty at the end of an hour. This was apparently how she had felt when unable to gratify her mother's numerous demanding requests. These feelings could be understood as the results of the patient identifying with her mother and placing the therapist in an emotional situation similar to the one in which she found herself.

The patient seemed to make very slow progress over several years, worrying throughout that the therapist would soon terminate with her, leaving her deserted, while continuously seeking physical closeness with him. He tried to find alternate ways of being close without being seductive. One that seemed successful for a while was reading the children's books she wrote. However, she claimed that this was a poor substitute for physical intimacy and claimed that he alone could help her achieve an orgasm. If he would only sleep with her, was an implied request. It was difficult to find a way to deal with this therapeutic deadlock, and he found himself increasingly bored. He did not feel sexually attracted to her, but rather was feeling very frustrated because of his response to the draining infantile level of her demands, which seemed fixed and too far from her awareness to work with. Discouraged at the lack of progress, and wishing to place some boundaries on the relationship, he began to think of terminating.

The interviews seemed to bog down. The patient was angry at the thought of his expecting too much of her, and he was angry at her for her failure to progress. At this point, during one interview on a bleak winter morning, when she was talking about her sad early experiences, he found his eyes filled with tears, which began running down his cheeks. He felt futility and despair that such hard work on both their parts seemed useless. It was impossible for him to hide his feelings. The patient seemed quite ill at ease, not knowing what to do, until finally she came over and put her hand on his shoulder, a gesture he had made with her on a few occasions. She said that at last she was sure he cared for her. The therapist was not sure what to think.

This was a turning point in the treatment. Many previously made interpretations seemed to take hold over the ensuing months as though the incident had validated them. The patient moved into a much more womanly stance, and over time became much happier and clearer about herself. She did not again demand to be held. The issues dealt with were increasingly over heterosexuality. What seemed central was that the tears were enough proof that he cared for her. Finally, she moved steadily toward termination, which involved both finding a man to live with and love, and a closer yet independent relationship with her parents.

This example is not meant to suggest that being moved to tears per se is an answer to multiple demands from a patient to show how one cares. Here, the therapist had worked in an orthodox and flexible way with the patient over several years, and they had built up much experience of the ups and downs in her life and the therapist's reactions to her. The moment of weeping in frustration and sadness had a large, shared past, which had implications for the outcome. Another patient, if the therapist wept on her behalf, might have become terrified that he or she was destroying the therapist with the burden of the demands and fled from therapy unable to talk about it. Yet another might have taken it as a cue for even more sexual involvement, reading the tears as proof that the therapist wanted to be with her in a mutual way. The reaction of this patient suggests that she had, throughout the previous work, slowly felt less of an inner void. She had reached a point of being able to empathize for another person while appreciating his separateness. The therapist's spontaneous, uncontrollable response really put it to the test, and the experience turned out to be useful and confirming for both patient and therapist.

THE THERAPIST'S OWN DYNAMICALLY DETERMINED RESPONSES

Certain situations, reactions, and feelings arising with patients are due to the therapist's own psychological makeup and individual ways of dealing with life. In supervision and by self-examination the therapist can begin to recognize these. Experience in therapy or analysis may help to explore and deal with them. In spite of these aids, all therapists have their blind spots.

One may recognize that certain phenomena occur over and over again with different patients in different contexts. For example, one may realize that he is nearly always too early or too late for appointments with patients whom he anticipates may be angry; or that he is generally uncomfortable when patients try to express their warm feelings; or that he has a tendency to "go after" sexual material in detail to the exclusion of other issues a patient presents; or that he becomes angry with patients who are not "grateful enough"; or that he tightens up in the presence of any strong affect. These are general tendencies that a therapist may have difficulty elucidating on his own. If one is aware of them, and possibly of their derivations, then he can be more alert to their influence, making it easier to decipher which part of the interaction is due to himself. They may still be hard to deal with, since one may become self-conscious and overcompensate for them. There is no easy answer. The first patient a therapist sees on Monday morning will probably evoke some different responses than the last one on Friday afternoon.

More specific areas may be noticed. Some therapists like to treat people with dynamics similar to their own, since they feel they understand them better. There may be pitfalls due to overidentification, but there may be advantages of easier empathy. Other therapists may have mainly positive or mainly negative feelings about hysterics or obsessionals or young women with babies or old men with recalcitrant sons. Sometimes the idiosyncratic aspects of the therapist's feelings are evident because they clearly represent an overreaction or underreaction to the patient, that is, they are out of character or unwarranted. For example, the therapist may be more worried about something than the patient is. His patient may point out to him that he is in error. For instance, one patient said to her male therapist, "You seem more concerned with my career and its success than I am." The therapist had to agree that perhaps he was fostering a neglect of her family, and to consider whether he was perhaps too proud of her professional success when she was at least as proud of her children and her ability to look after them. When the therapist has made a misjudgment, it is useful to acknowledge it, and even apologize to the patient if it has caused unnecessary pain, and rethink the position.

THE THERAPIST'S SOCIAL VALUES

The sociocultural values of the therapist are mentioned here because they do exist and may influence a therapy to a greater or lesser extent, depending on the therapist. Much as one's professional training teaches him not to let personal values interfere with the patient's treatment, goals, and expectations for his or her life, they do influence even the most experienced therapist in very subtle ways. One need not, however, make a mystique out of this recognition. There is no simple way to approach the problem, but at least it is a start to think about it for oneself and allow that it may happen. For example, in middle-class American culture, it may be hard to separate oneself from the value of education and be entirely objective about it in a particular patient's case. Individuals have private views of sexual mores, religion, politics, or how women or men should be, and at times, they can, even unknowingly, influence the treatment situation. Many professionals are currently thinking a lot about this topic and its implication for both therapist and patient.

CONSULTATION

Often a useful adjunct to the therapist's consideration of his own feelings is a consultation with a colleague. What is critical in the choice of this colleague or consultant is that the therapist know he can be open with him about his concerns and not feel constrained to report only his successes. For instance, a therapist consulted a colleague about an angry, somewhat paranoid man who was an expert marksman. The patient was phobic about shooting anything other than targets, though grouse hunting was a hobby in his family. When the patient began to discuss several patients recently reported in the newspaper to have killed their therapists, he sought a consultation. The therapist knew himself to be inclined to enjoy risk taking and described it to his consultant. He did not feel particularly anxious that this patient would hurt him, but he was concerned lest he deny certain dangers. In this connection the therapist was reassured as far as was possible by the consultant. The consultant agreed with his perspective on the patient, and the future course of therapy continued smoothly. This proved a helpful validation of his approach, in that his own style did not seem to be overtly interfering with therapy.

It is not incumbent upon any therapist to be perfect, only to try to be professional and to acknowledge his own limitations. This implies fostering an ability to work with someone else's interests at heart, but not to such an extent that he becomes overburdened.

One does not have to be for the patient a model person who has solved or has the ability to solve all life's problems, or knows all the answers. Neither does one have to be overly apologetic for one's humanness. As with other parameters, some middle ground is sufficient for therapeutic purposes, whatever one's ideals.

8

Thinking about Money

Among the many things that are difficult for patient and therapist to discuss together, money stands high on the list. Often, money is harder to talk about than sex. Jokes and folklore, which used to emphasize the psychiatrist's preoccupation with his patient's sex life, now also pay a great deal of attention to the psychiatrist's interest in money. The jokes acknowledge the importance of both matters and the difficulty that the patient and the therapist have in talking directly about them.

In many outpatient clinics, teachers, supervisors, and administrators find it hard to agree about fee scales, whether the patient's fee should be set by the therapist or by the business office, and even whether it really is important for the therapist to discuss the fee with the patient. Arguments on these issues go on year after year.

Therapists in outpatient training are often instructed early each year in the fee-setting arrangements currently in force, and in the possibility of using the discussion of fees with each patient as an introduction to important relationships and feelings in the patient's life. Although there are always some trainees who handle it quite well, some have difficulties. For example, the therapist in a clinic may repeatedly "forget" to bring up the matter with the patient, or the patient may always seem to have something more pressing to discuss. The therapist may allow a series of hours to begin with long silences until the patient begins talking, because the therapist feels the patient may have something more important on his mind than the fee. Or, the patient may actively avoid the issue when the clinician brings it up, by changing the subject or saying, "I don't want to talk about money." The therapist then has to assess in his own mind whether to press the subject even though it may anger the patient, drop the issue and wait until the patient is ready to talk about it, inquire as to why the patient does not want to talk about it, or seek some other compromise. At the same time he must decide whether or how to stall off the business office while he and the patient are trying to find ways to discuss the issue.

If the clinic administration gets tired of waiting, arbitrarily sets a fee on the basis of the information it has from the patient's registration, and sends bills to the patient retroactively for all appointments to date, the therapist may feel guilty: "It was my fault for delaying so long." He may be angry that the administration acted unilaterally. In such circumstances therapists may argue for a reduction of the hourly fee, or for the patient to be excused from payment of the retroactive balance, "because it was no one's fault," even though he still may not have discussed the matter with the patient. In such cases the clinician may feel he is supporting and helping the patient. When the matter is brought to the attention of the clinical supervisor, the chances are good that a useful discussion will ensue, which will help the clinician to deal more satisfactorily with the issue in his interviews with the patient. The supervisor may bring up the matter himself, as part of routine inquiry about major important matters, or in recognition of its absence from the discussion reported by the clinician. But he, too, may forget.

In private practice, while it is reasonably hard not to make a good living as a psychotherapist in most American cities these days, some people manage not to. They may do this by consistently charging their patients far less than the current standard of fees in their own communities, and often less than they can afford to charge. Some allow patients to accumulate larger and larger bills month after month. In private practice, the issues become more complicated than in the training clinic, because the private practitioner's income does depend on his fees. If he undercharges, the therapist's resentment may build up because of the hardships for himself and his family. The patient may feel uneasy about it — he may feel guilty, or he may wonder why his therapist is charging less than other therapists in the community.

Medical doctors sometimes turn to their psychiatric colleagues for help with financial problems that they are having with their patients. A patient may persistently avoid paying a doctor's bill that he can afford. Or he may complain that he should be charged only for materials used or specific procedures but not for the doctor's time or knowledge or judgment.

SETTING UP THE CONTRACT

The therapist should clearly inform each new patient of his usual hourly fee and his rules about payment, such as for missed appointments and when he expects to be paid. When appropriate, he may be able to offer a reduced fee to conform to the patient's ability to pay. It is usually not sufficient, however, for the therapist merely to ask the patient if that fee is acceptable to him, even if the patient consents. One may relate the discussion of fees to the discussion of how often the patient will come and how long the treatment might last, since the cost could become a major financial burden over a period of months. Whether the fee is set by the therapist or by the business office of a clinic, it is helpful to inquire how the patient will meet the cost — from current income, savings, an extra job or new job to be undertaken, contributions from parent or spouse, medical insurance — to consider any sacrifices the patient or his family might have to make in order to pay for this treatment. Whether the patient can realistically afford the fee depends not only on hard facts of dollars and cents but also on his ways of dealing with others who are close to him, for example, whether he takes into account their needs as well as his own, on his work history and his ability or inability to support himself and his family, and on the intensity of his own sense of need for treatment.

Financial considerations are usually inseparably intertwined with myriad assumptions and behavior patterns. These details of everyday existence are so familiar to the patient that he may assume automatically that they are equally obvious to the therapist without being mentioned. Another reason for hesitancy in the discussion is that the patient may be embarrassed to reveal the details of his money management because he feels it is so mundane or otherwise undesirable that he expects the therapist to repudiate him for his habits of private thought and behavior. Such patients usually have been excessively criticized in the past for every thought and deed, and have grown up feeling that all of their basic assumptions are wrong. They may tend to spend much of their energy keeping their private thoughts protected.

As with other matters that are difficult to talk about, the patient may feel that if the therapist does not talk about finances either, he must consider them unimportant or too dangerous to talk about. Either of these conclusions can be harmful to setting up the contract or to the progress of therapy.

PAYING FOR MISSED APPOINTMENTS

Many people feel that the patient should pay for all scheduled sessions, regardless of the reason for missing. Others feel that the patient should not be charged for appointments missed since no service was given face-to-face. Some therapists choose a middle position, informing the patient, for example, that in general all missed appointments are paid for unless there is something that patient and therapist agree is a very unusual circumstance. Others, particularly in once a week psychotherapy, ask the patient to pay for the missed hour only if the therapist has been unable to use it to see another patient. Still others set a minimum notice requirement, such as three or four weeks, understanding that the patient will pay for appointments missed at short notice for any reason. The dynamic issues involved are too complicated for exploration here.

A general principle is to try to keep any rule simple and direct. It will protect the freedom of the therapy atmosphere for the patient, and it will protect the therapist's income, since the patient has contracted for a block of the therapist's time. If one sets some guideline for the patient at the beginning of therapy, the issue is easier to cope with when it arises. There are times when any of these approaches makes sense, depending on the length of treatment and the frequency of visits, the patient's tendency to miss appointments for reasons that the therapist might consider avoidable, the administrative arrangement of a clinic, and the preferences of the therapist.

Many therapists starting private practice, in particular, learn from their mistakes before evolving a style which suits both them and their patients. The therapist needs to know that he can afford to spend time exercising his professional skills with the patient, without significant financial cost to himself. He may also learn to enjoy some gratification from payment for his work, especially if he is dealing with a particularly demanding patient. The patient should be able to pay current charges regularly, with whatever resources he can arrange without undue strain. He probably should not undertake an overwhelming financial burden to obtain psychotherapy or any other medical care if he can possibly avoid it. Even a successful outcome of treatment may not be worth years of debts, overwork, and family deprivation, for either therapist or patient.

BILLS

There are many ways to write bills. In practice, if one has no secretary, a bill can be written out by hand on headed notepaper. On the following page is a suggestion about how it could be composed.

Many people give or send bills to patients at the end of each month, asking them to pay by the tenth of the next month. Patients have many feelings about bills; it can be useful to explore these. Occasionally a patient will pay in cash. One paranoid woman paid her therapist immediately after each session. Some of the meanings of this behavior had to do with her irrational concerns for privacy. She had a delusional system about the postal service and had many

John Smith, M.D.
950 Main Street
Cincinnati, Ohio

February 1, 19___

Mr. Lewis Jones
245 Maple Avenue
Cincinnati, Ohio

Re: Patricia Jones

Psychotherapy: Jan. 8, 15, 22, 29	$140
Parents' consultation: Jan. 3	35
Letter for school	10
Total	$185

John Smith, M.D.

feelings about her mother's possible investigation of her treatment. She also felt unable to give any guarantee at the end of each session about whether she would be able to tolerate returning. It was thus indicated not to send this woman a bill but to accept payment on her own terms.

THIRD-PARTY PAYMENTS

Owning a medical insurance policy with psychiatric coverage is part of a patient's planned financial assets. The therapist may regard his contract as with the patient, and the patient's contract as with the insurance company. Thus, the patient may pay the therapist's bill directly and be reimbursed by the company. This may avoid the lack of clarity in transference and countertransference issues that may occur if the therapist views his contract as with the insurance company, and the patient as merely the intermediary. If the patient is seen privately, or in a public clinic with a sliding fee scale, he may be charged a full fee by the clinician. Many insurance companies will pay a percentage toward the full fee. In these cases, discussion along the lines described earlier is appropriate, with assessment of the patient's ability to make up the full fee. At times, it may be appropriate, to accept what the company will pay, without any addition directly from the patient.

Some insurance companies will only reimburse a patient in therapy with a psychiatrist. When an intake worker in a clinic is considering recommendation of private therapy, it is wise to insure that the patient has read the fine print on his policy. This may prevent the unnecessary pain of seeing a private therapist whom he likes but who does not have an M.D., only to discover later that the therapist is excluded from the limits of the policy.

In order to protect the confidentiality of patients, therapists often use vague categories of diagnosis on the claim forms. In most cases, the companies seem to be sensitive to these issues and rarely question them. Thus, terms such as "emotional adjustment of adolescence," "emotional problems," "psychoneurotic depression," or "anxiety" are sufficient. It is usually unnecessary to disclose to a third party any diagnosis with wider import.

The insurance company as "provider" for the patient may become symbolic and personalized in discussion. The patient's wishes or fears about what the therapist will disclose on the form often lead to rich discussion. Concerns about his revealing anything, lest it be misused, may be obvious. Other patients want to be formally designated as very ill, to prove to the company and their families, to whom they may use the form as objective evidence, that their disturbance is not to be taken lightly. Some may express irrational guilt about "getting something for nothing," since there is not enough sacrifice involved because it seems that the money is not coming directly from them. Others may feel bad about "robbing" the company. Many of the comments may be regarded as displacements from fantasies of what the therapist thinks and, more basically, of what their parents might think about their present situation.

It is a good idea to have open discussion with the patient about exactly what is written on the form, and show it to him. One may give him the facts without closing off his numerous concerns, which are described throughout this chapter.

Examples of setting fees could be drawn from almost any therapy. In working with adolescents, fee-setting may be particularly complicated, since often the patient cannot pay for his own therapy. Should the fee be set in accordance with the parents' ability to pay or the patient's? The issues about the payment cannot be considered in isolation from other questions. Should the parents be involved in the therapy situation, and, if so, how? In conjoint interviews or collateral interviews? During the evaluation or during the treatment? Should they pay the bill? Should the patient be responsible for a portion of the bill? The answers to all of these may depend on the maturity of the patient's judgment and on his ability to manage his own life responsibly. They also depend on the nature of his relationship with his parents. It may become apparent that the patient sees his parents as cold and unloving, for instance, and wants to burden them with a high psychotherapy fee as a way of getting even with them for the misery they have caused him. It may be a way of finding out whether they care enough to recognize how upset he is and pay for professional help. Another patient may feel that his parents are too overprotective and smothering. They may rush in to pay for anything he seems to want, and be overenthusiastic about his interest in understanding himself better through psychotherapy, as if it were another elaborate present.

It is really not enough to make decisions about the fee and about the parents' involvement in the therapy and then stop thinking about the matter. In each case the patient's feelings about his parents, his perception of their feelings about him, and his sense of the role of money in their dealings with each other may be central in his life and crucial in the therapy. His expectations of how the therapist will respond are important — will he call the parents right in or exclude them entirely? Will he side with them or with the patient? Setting a low fee or a high one may introduce the patient and the therapist to an examination of the patient's values, conflicts, self-esteem, and basic assumptions about himself, his relationships and his future that have far wider meaning for him than what his fee should be and whether his parents should be notified.

Open discussion of money matters that have been avoided or forgotten often overcome periods of stagnation in the therapy and may lead to new understanding of the patient's inner experience, sometimes with sudden relief of symptoms. This is true, of course, in relation to every issue that is important to the patient.

GENERAL MEANINGS OF MONEY

There are wide variations in the ways people incorporate money considerations into their personal value systems. Willingness to spend money on another person may be taken as a measure of caring for him. Material possessions provided may be a measure of how others feel about one, and may affect independence, control over, or dependence upon others. Ability to earn money and judgment in saving, investing, and spending it are related to how a person feels about himself.

It is common for anyone to experience a powerful inhibition against talking too openly about finances. A person may feel that he is giving away something vital if he talks too frankly about money, even someone else's money. The sense of vulnerability may be in the fear that his property will be seen, and therefore somehow taken away. There may be a feeling that his self-sufficiency is under scrutiny or attack; or there may be a troublesome sense that he is revealing something particularly personal of which others might disapprove. Some of the feelings involved may be pride, envy, joy, and disgust. A person may hope to be admired for money manners but also fear ridicule for being considered too stingy, covetous, too generous, or careless. Personal scales of values vary widely on all these parameters. The roots are within the unconscious. Perhaps the frequently seen tacit collusion between a patient and a therapist, or between a trainee and a supervisor, to avoid discussing the money arrangements of a therapy is due in part to this multifaceted sense of vulnerability that each party may recognize in himself and may sense or assume in the other person.

PERSONAL WORTH

A therapist in training is often unsure of the value of his professional skills. This uncertainty may be reactivated when he emerges from training, and a salaried position, to enter private practice. Young therapists usually have been in school for most of their lives and are in the habit of paying for professional services, rather than being hired for them. Trainees recognize that they are learning at the same time that they are performing a useful service for the patient. What they do for the patient sometimes depends on the immediate advice and guidance of clinical supervisors. It may seem like cheating to ask a patient for payment, especially if one is not directly dependent on the fee.

These doubts may be enhanced by an image of oneself as an all-giving healer who would not offend his patients by charging more than a token fee. This may be a source of inner conflict, and may lead to erroneously low conclusions about the patient's ability of willingness to pay. Dovetailed with this is the patient's feeling that he should be treated for nothing. To have to pay someone to talk to him? As one patient said angrily to a psychiatrist, "Doctors are supposed to be interested in the welfare of their patients, and not in their own personal gain." Patients and therapists may share the wish for a nondemanding Good Mother to take care of them. Doctors and others in the "helping professions," such as nursing, social work, and the clergy, may deal with this wish by becoming the "good mother," and even they, when they become patients, may experience the same desire to be taken care of with nothing asked in return. Patients and staff in a public clinic may feel that *that* is the place where selfless care may be expected and given, whether or not the clinic's financial structure is set up to provide free care.

DEPENDENCY STRUGGLES FOR PATIENTS

Most people like to be taken care of, to have someone else ease the pains of life, make difficult decisions, point out the path to happiness, and the like, but at the same time they want to be grown up, responsible, and worthy of others' respect. The resultant conflict manifests itself in peculiar ways in therapy. The following is an example of the strong feelings involved.

An intelligent 20-year-old boy whose thought disorder prevented him from getting admitted to the Ivy League colleges, or from keeping a job, was referred to an outpatient clinic by his private therapist because he could not afford the private fee. He tended to blame all his problems on his family's limited finances. After much discussion, in which the patient only reluctantly participated and then with much blocking and circumstantiality, a $2 a week fee was set.

The therapist, who was both kind and competent, sometimes felt that he was being deceived by the patient. Therapy in the clinic began in the summer and progressed slowly; in late September, the patient enrolled in a community college and did reasonably well for about six weeks. He then became increasingly withdrawn and irritable, and began to come late and miss appointments. Discussion of Christmas, final exams, and the new semester looming up did not lead to significant clarification or improvement. Inquiry about his passing reference to the therapist's departure from the clinic at the end of June led into his feelings about one more change, being abandoned and that no one cared about him.

About that time, late January, the business office notified the therapist that the patient had not paid his bill for several months. The therapist thought it would be unkind to demand payment at the time that the poor fellow was feeling so badly. With encouragement from his supervisor, however, he brought up the matter with the patient, who brushed it aside, saying that the $2 a week could not make that much difference to anyone. After further unsuccessful efforts to understand what the patient was feeling about it and why he was not paying, the therapist told the patient that he would not be able to continue seeing him if the bill were not paid in full within four more weeks, by early March. The patient became progressively more involved with the therapist, more agitated and angry, insisting that the therapist did not give a damn about him "as long as you get your stinking $2!" The patient arrived for his appointment on the fourth week with a check for only a small fraction of the outstanding bill. With considerable trepidation, the therapist told the patient that he would be unable to see him until the bill was paid in full. The patient stormed out.

Several weeks later, he called to make an appointment and came in with the money. He was angry but not withdrawn, and reported that things were going well in school. With the therapist's inquiry it became clear that the patient had taken the therapist's laxity in letting him get away without paying the bill as an indication that the therapist did not care. If the therapist would allow him to be so irresponsible, how could he help him "grow up"? The patient's anger went in both directions, angry that the therapist did not care enough about him to treat him for nothing, and angry that he did not care enough about him to insist that he meet his responsibilities. While both motives were at work, it was the latter, leading the therapist to side with the patient's more mature ego functioning, without ignoring his needs to be dependent, that led to the patient's greatest forward strides in the therapy. The related issue of the therapist's anticipated departure from the clinic a few months later then became a readily discussable issue.

Another young man, an unemployed high school graduate of 19, used the fee issue to demonstrate his dilemmas.

He entered therapy because of suicidal preoccupation related to nearly impossible communication with his parents, indecision about whether to go to college, and ambivalence about his active homosexual life. His well-off parents had agreed to pay for his treatment, at the maximum rate on the clinic scale. A small part of the first month's bill was paid after extensive discussion with the patient, which focused on his ways of negotiating with his parents for the payment they had promised. He would characteristically bring up the matter with them in a provocative, antagonizing way, such as, "The shrink thinks you're all messed up, and you're messing me up, so you'd better pay him so I won't go crazy." When they delayed any further payment until well into the fourth month of therapy, the patient seemed unwilling to change his style with them. Neither would he consider getting a job and having the fee reset in accordance with his own ability to pay. When the therapist said that the therapy could not continue until the back balance was paid in full, again offering to adjust the fee to what the patient could afford if he would go to work, the young man smashed the therapist's ashtray on the floor, stormed out, and did not return.

From many things the patient and his parents had said, the therapist surmised that the gratification of maintaining the stubborn, angry battle with his parents was greater than the anticipated gratification from self-sufficiency and more mature independence. The young man described earlier, on the other hand, was more withdrawn both from his parents and from the therapist, and made his choice for the other side of the ambivalence, toward more self-reliance.

Sometimes a patient in psychotherapy may feel that he or his therapist is prostituting himself in the relationship. The therapist may be seen as a person who shows friendly interest, and who sees the patient's most intense and intimate feelings but only for a price and without sharing his own feelings or life experiences in return. The patient may feel he is degrading himself by consorting with the prostitute therapist in order to get someone to show some interest in him. He himself may be the prostitute, in that he is revealing his most private self to someone whose personal life does not depend on the relationship with him. The following is an example:

A severely anxious young man had been in psychotherapy for several years. He had had recurrent disruptions of his ego functions following an acute psychotic episode at age 22 and was repeatedly troubled by the feeling that he was prostituting *himself* by coming to therapy; he felt he was repeating a well-established pattern of his immediate family, in which he had to confess his private thoughts, and sometimes be punished for them, because of his parents' threats that they would give him away or send him to an institution if he kept secrets from them.

He went through complex machinations around the therapist's fee. Early in therapy, while his parents were paying the bills, he wanted it to be as costly as possible for them, while he accused the therapist of maliciously trying to destroy his good relationship with them by refusing to reduce the fee. He took a vengeful pride in making his parents pay for his telling his personal thoughts to an outsider; but he felt very guilty about it and felt very much in danger of being cut off by them forever.

When he began to earn his own money, he was torn between wanting to be treated for nothing, while fearing that that would give the therapist unlimited power and control over him like his parents had had for so many years, and now and then sensing some glimmer of feeling that he would like to pay his own way like other adults. He was furious when charged for an extra hour that he requested in time of crisis, complaining that the therapist's heart was a stone and his mind was a cash register. He seemed both proud and sulky when he paid his monthly check, but he was always a bit better integrated after each crisis around money.

When he got a job that provided health insurance covering outpatient psychotherapy, he chose to pay the therapist's full fee for several months before deciding to make an insurance claim, and then for a few weeks he openly avoided the therapist's efforts to discuss what diagnosis should be entered on the insurance company's medical form. He wanted the therapist to decide that; but he was afraid of what he might say and afraid that any diagnosis might impede his chances for advancement in his field.

He wanted his employer, the insurance company, his parents, or the therapist to underwrite the costs of therapy, but he was scared to death of being considered sick. His conflicting feelings about his own sense of worth included the sense of demand that someone else pay for his therapy as proof that they cared for him and that he not be thought of as sick, damaged, or in need of treatment. He felt he wanted to pay his own way and thereby have some control over his therapist and reduce his parents' power over him, and he wanted to have someone available with whom he could discuss his terrible anxieties. He did not want to feel forced to expose his private thoughts and feelings, and so on, into more complexities, all real, all important to him, and important to take into account in working with him toward the development of a stronger, more self-respecting ego.

Among the basic underlying issues was his fear that he could never be loved, neither as a child nor as an adult. Many years of experience as a child with trying to buy his parents' love through great sacrifice of his own privacy, autonomy, and self-respect underlay his angry, insistent feeling that he must be repaid for the anguish he had suffered and be reassured that he was worthwhile before he could feel ready to assume the role of a self-respecting adult. The therapeutic work involved slow, careful, repetitive identification and clarification of these interwoven issues as they became manifest in the interviews. He gradually became able to recognize the memories of the terribly painful childhood frustrations and to separate them from realities of current everyday life. In this patient, the financial considerations in the therapeutic relationship were inseparable from all the issues of self-worth.

GETTING AND GIVING MONEY

The feelings that are generated around getting money often concern the comfort of being taken care of and loved, resentment at being dependent, and the pleasure and pain in accomplishing something through one's own efforts. Alarm that one will not get enough money may evoke an old, familiar fear that one will not be loved, or the newer fear that one's own skills will be inadequate. The child quickly learns that he is not capable of taking care of himself and that he needs adults to provide physical care, love, teaching, and limit-setting appropriate to each developmental advance. As he gets older, the gratification of getting what he needs through his own abilities increases.

Concerns about getting enough money may be especially important in the thinking of depressed and psychotic patients, for in those disturbances, regression to an oral adaptation is the pathologic mechanism. A young compulsive patient phobically avoided eating with people he did not know well because of his distressing obsessive preoccupation with the thought that they would think he was eating money.

The feelings around holding onto money, and around spending it or losing it, are related to those around getting money. They commonly evoke the childhood worries as to whether one has what he needs, whether his skills are adequate, whether he is in a friendly or a hostile environment. The worries whether one has enough money and whether it will be left alone or taken away are commonly on the same wavelength as worries about having the love of others and about having self-respect and self-sufficiency. Issues of autonomy are more important in the management of money than in the getting of it; fear of incompetence and of being overwhelmed, cheated, and robbed are more important than fear of being abandoned.

The constellations of feelings about money reflect the history of the child's psychosexual development. Knowledge of the early psychic origins of feelings about money is very important for the therapist, and is to be found in the psychoanalytical literature. It is a vast topic and beyond the scope of this book. These origins of feelings about money, such as early feelings about defecation, do not usually come into explicit discussion in psychotherapy. This is particularly true in time-limited or once a week therapy. One may hear more of the primitive material in therapy with borderline or psychotic patients.

With a well-defended patient, much of what the therapist thinks and knows about the meaning of the patient's productions at this level is best kept to himself. He will try to address the available level of the patient's awareness. The patient's defenses must be respected. The goal of the therapy should not be to have the patient confirm each of Freud's major theoretical contributions but to help the patient extend his level of self-understanding step-by-step in a way that is relevant to his own life. The theories are of more help to the therapist in doing his professional work than to the patient in therapy or in leading his daily life.

PSYCHOTHERAPY IN A NATIONAL HEALTH SERVICE

In the foreseeable future a national health service or its equivalent may be introduced in this country. If the government assumes major payment responsibility, how will this affect financial discussions with patients?

Present "Free" Therapies

No treatment is truly "free." Patients pay an inclusive medical premium for prepaid or group health care plans; veterans pay a symbolic fee of sacrifice by serving in the armed forces; low-income groups are supported by taxpayers in programs run on federal grants, and within these some patients pay on a sliding scale according to income. In a national health service, participants will have to pay some general medical fee toward its support. "Free" indicates only that no money changes hands directly between patient and therapist. The similarities between existing "free" programs and a national health service are that patients are not financially strained and the therapist is assured a fixed salary. The differences revolve around the patient's and therapist's current awareness of the special nature of their contract as opposed to psychotherapy conducted outside the aegis of a health care program.

Many reactions to an American "free" system can be observed. Some patients feel it is a privilege and a rare opportunity to have psychotherapy without financial burden. Others come most unwillingly. Compared to private practice, where patients usually come expecting to get help, a wider spectrum of value placed on psychotherapy is seen in "free" outpatient clinics. At one end of the scale are poor but very sick patients, ignorant of psychotherapy, who may view outpatient treatment as the bastion of the rich and assume it is unavailable and inapplicable to their life situation. They can be surprised by its personal benefits. At the other end are well-educated, financially comfortable people who regard themselves as being in minor trouble. They may approach treatment experimentally, saying they despise psychotherapy and would not feel it worthwhile to waste money on it. These people often turn out to be as needy as others who value therapy more highly. Adolescents often feel much freer within such a system, since they need not be dependent on parents for support. This independence may be a matter for rejoicing, but, it may also be mingled with sad feelings that parents do not care because they are less directly involved. Nevertheless, the privacy of being able to seek treatment on their own can be a valuable adjunct to the therapy.

In programs offering time-limited therapy as a way of coping with oversubscription, patients may experience more guilt than they would as private patients, feeling they are "taking up too much time" and shortchanging sicker people. Some may be angry for whatever reason but feel restrained because they feel the therapist is doing them a favor by not giving them a bill. Others may become angry with the limits and long for free, timeless therapy, or feel that they are receiving inferior treatment compared to those who can afford private care. Any of these issues may be real; but where reactions are very strong, one can assume that coming to terms with the system has a significance wider than the rules themselves indicate.

The impact of money discussions fades, the further one is removed from the fee-for-service position. However, although the actual dollars may no longer be a burning issue, the money-related concerns mentioned in the chapter are just as vital. There is a less obvious springboard for discussion. These concerns are often avoided even in the presence of a payment issue, thus it may be tempting to neglect them in the absence of the financial perspective. This need not be the case, because there are still elements of the treatment contract that bear on self-worth, estimations of what is offered and received, and all the other personal ramifications of values.

Impressions from Working in the British National Health Service

I (R. M. B.) worked as a psychiatrist in training in Britain from 1964 to 1967. Many of the comments made here apply to any hospital-based outpatient service in which trainees change at intervals. Some psychological aspects of the therapy dyad within the established British system will be mentioned.

In the United States no generation of therapists and patients has been raised to assume automatically that there will be a no-fee-for-service basis within the therapeutic contract. The reverse is the situation in Britain. There is an undoubted human advantage to the ideal that whoever needs or wishes treatment, regardless of income, may have it. For the therapist there is the security of a fixed salary scale; he will never be rich, but he will not starve. The therapist with a guaranteed income ideally ought to be free of pressures to cling to patients, to need to please them for fear of jeopardizing funds, to overselect them on the basis of ability to pay, or to offer therapy out of guilt for their poverty compared to his own well-being. The financial aspects of patient care in Britain are thus less likely to interact with feelings of the therapist's self-worth in ways described in other parts of the chapter. However, there are other pressures on therapists that provoke conflicts not unrelated.

Most mental health workers in Britain are hospital-based. There are well-defined categories of advancement in the National Health Service with corresponding pay scales. The hierarchical structure is mainly built on centralized examinations. In order to have the best chances, one may choose a training program in a big city where the major medical centers are located. People choosing lower-grade posts with tenure, often in minor medical facilities, sometimes have an internal battle in coming to terms with their position. It is possible for patient care to become interwoven with the therapist's ambition and self-value. The competition within such a structure constantly tests the therapist's faith in himself and his own worth. Assessment of his worth vis-à-vis his seniors is involved, and the value he places on himself is reflected in his work accomplishments and success in examinations. In other words, reactions to the system are reminiscent of concerns of trainees within the academic system here. The sense of competition may be heightened in Britain because of little sideways independent mobility due to lack of private practice and the relative lack of middle-grade tenured posts in the National Health Service.

Pressure, which can exist, to produce "results" with patients is much more complex than the personal aspects contributed by the therapist. Government-sponsored programs of any sort often provoke pressure for objective good, speedy results. It is understandable that the financial administration would wish institutions to function in the most effective and most economic way possible. As is well known, "results" in psychoanalytically oriented therapy are particularly difficult to reduce to measurable quantities. Apart from the few famous psychoanalytical centers in Britain, I think it is true to say that psychotherapy as described in this book is less generally developed in the United Kingdom. This is a very complicated topic with many facets which cannot be explored here. Other modes of therapy are more popular. In any individual institution or unit, however, the emotional climate can minimize any of these external pressures for the mental health workers. Very high-quality psychiatric care is available and can be geared first and foremost towards the particular patient and his needs.

Ideally in this system the patient should be free of financial burden, being satisfied that the therapist is interested primarily in him and not his money. He should be secure in the knowledge that treatment will not be stopped abruptly because of lack of funds. And yet the familiar disgruntled complaints are heard: "The treatment is no good." "You mean I can't see somebody else?" "You don't care two hoots about me as long as you can leave at 5 PM to avoid the traffic." My former chief used to say that if at termination the patient was grateful, then there must be something amiss. That, of course, is an exaggeration, but it points out that the absence of money from a contract with the patient neither eradicates the angry feelings about the therapist nor enhances the patient's warm feelings toward him. Transference and countertransference factors will exist regardless of the system. Money-related themes emerge in terms of time offered to patients or in whatever symbolic "offerings" the therapist gives the patient to receive or reject — empathy, understanding, or interpretations. Issues of autonomy, self-respect, family dealings with money, work undertaken by the patient, and talk of his possessions can be discussed. Only the avenue of approach is altered without the ready access through money being exchanged between patient and therapist.

The more impersonal the source of financial support for the treatment, the more uncertain the time element of the treatment may become. This can occur in spite of any pressure to produce "results" mentioned earlier. Uncertainty in setting termination dates has to do not only with the ubiquitous fantasy of timelessness shared by patient and therapist. It also has to do with supply and demand in the system. If the clinic is very pressured, less treatment than is needed may be offered in order to try to give all a fair deal. If the clinic is less pressured, treatment may take place with the patient being passed from one therapist to another. No fee is involved. Therapists are available, and a common fantasy is that the next therapist will do a better job than the preceding one. A decision to terminate a "perennial patient," based on clinical judgment, takes courage. The system colludes with him, since it fosters passivity on the part of both patient and therapist in the implicit notion that "someone will take care of it" (Mother Britain in this case).

In the National Health Service I think it may also be easier for the "savior fantasy" to flourish. Many therapists in the United States are uncomfortable making the transition from public clinic to private practice, having to take money from sick people, "penalizing" them for their unfortunate illness; it may violate one's altruistic principles. In a national health service the therapist does not meet this conflict head-on. If he has tendencies in this direction, it is easier to be unaware of the existence of the conflict for a longer time. A British therapist in this situation will temper his idealism, lack of self-preservation, and "omniscience" in other ways than by facing money issues in his practice. For example, as his clinical experience grows, like any therapist, he can begin to accept the difficulties and complexity of his art, be less frightened of the intricacies of his patients, and have less need to "save" them or become overcommitted due to personal guilt.

Just a few of the dimensions are represented in the above comments. However, I wish to convey the notion that conflict is inevitable for both therapist and patient regardless of the system This is really a fact of life, of human existence, and of the practice of psychotherapy.

9

Administrative Aspects of Therapy

All of the administrative aspects involved in a patient's therapy
will have transference and countertransference overtones. They can
be viewed as part of the therapeutic process, and the practical handling of these often complicated, delicate issues can turn out to be
more or less useful to a patient. They may involve value conflicts
for any therapist, which could lead to too slow or too hasty decisions,
too much openness with either the patient or colleagues, or the con-
verse, when nothing is said or written, to the detriment of the patient's welfare. The main aim should be to keep the air as clear as
possible in the therapy. This means attempting to create an atmosphere in which the patient feels as free as is internally feasible for
him to state his views and say what he wishes about his feelings toward the therapist or others. In order to do this he must have the
best privacy the therapist can provide and protect for him. Many a
patient finds it extremely difficult to have any trust in another person, and his experience in therapy may be a vehicle for building his
first reasonably trusting relationship. Therefore, external practicalities cannot be treated as only external. They will provide discussion,
observation, and testing ground for both therapist and patient in
their mutual experience of each other's respect for individuality and

ways of approaching or thinking about things. The values of psychotherapy are thus intimately interrelated with the values of individual privacy, and as a professional therapist one acts upon those values in the conduct of his work.

In any single case, the situation may be extremely complex for both patient and therapist. Suggested here are some coping devices and policies that may help protect the therapy in a general way. Full discussion of their intellectual dimensions will be found elsewhere in the literature. The views of senior teachers can be sought as a sounding board while one is creating his own style or while treating any particular patient with whom an administrative matter becomes an issue.

NOTES AND TAPES

It may be reasonable to take a few notes in an intake hour, as when a patient has had frequent changes of residence and it is important to know all the locations. One should either ask the patient if he minds or explain why he is doing it. It is distracting to take notes in a regular therapy hour. One cannot follow themes and affect, be aware of nonverbal communication, and be alert to all the levels of meaning while scribbling notes. Sometimes people are tempted to do this "secretly," if preparing the case for presentation to a group. They may be nervous that they will be questioned about missing facts. It is more important not to jeopardize the therapy. Many therapists use tape recorders or one-way mirror windows, and have different degrees of comfort in doing it. If it seems second nature to the therapist, it will not seem second nature to the patient, at least at first. One should have a meeting without tape to explore freely the patient's feelings about it before switching on the machine. The same is true of videotapes. No matter how good "teaching material" a patient is, his wishes about being seen or heard by others should be respected. A patient may not mind, on the grounds that the material will be kept confidential and only shown to other professionals who may have opinions helpful to his treatment. If he knows that he has been discussed, he may be curious about the results. The therapist may be prepared to say something about it, while also hearing a feeling of exclusion from the group discussion. The destruction of such tapes after their professional or teaching use has expired may be indicated.

RECORD KEEPING

The legal aspects of record keeping will be found elsewhere in the literature. Therapists vary greatly on their attitudes to records. Private therapists, in particular, nowadays, may keep no records, or brief records with only initials or numbers or fictitious names. Clinic records may be more problematic, since more staff are involved, and there may be solid reasons for wanting pertinent information. This applies particularly to drug information, for example, in efforts to prevent duplication of medication, if the patient is attending other medical facilities within the clinic. Drug records may also be requested if a patient is admitted with an overdose and the psychiatrist who prescribed the medication is not available. Clinics try to work out ways to meet this problem, while keeping the information as private as possible.

Records about anyone who is publicly known require particular caution. Some clinics have specially protected files to which a few authorized personnel only have access. Identification by a code number or an initial may be added protection.

Where records are kept regularly, therapists vary from one- to two-month summaries to a few notes written after every hour highlighting the main themes, particularly with very disturbed or potentially suicidal or homicidal patients. Forgetting facts in any single case can be outweighed by the records being too publicly available. Initial summaries and termination summaries, excluding the most personal detail, may be helpful if another therapist is scheduled to begin therapy and there is, for some reason, little chance for mutual discussion.

Verbal exchange may be one of the best ways to communicate about patients when necessary. Thereby one can still maintain confidentiality and be more sure of the information not being disseminated.

If a patient has been in therapy elsewhere, it may be helpful to request, with his permission, a summary of the treatment from the previous clinician. Therapists vary as to whether they read the previous opinions before seeing the patient for the first time. One has to work out what is best for himself. On the one hand it is good not to be biased. On the other, it is good to be prepared. In either case, the notes, if available, may be read eventually; they may add an important dimension that was missed.

All records should be kept as privately as is humanly possible within the situation.

LETTERS ABOUT THE PATIENT

Patients often request a letter describing why they are in treatment. This may be for a job application, entrance to school, or other purposes. Institutions have different policies about this, and one should first check the policy before acting.

Suppose it seems appropriate to write a letter. With the patient's permission, one might first find out directly from the third party (1) exactly what information they had in mind and (2) who will see the letter. A phone call or a letter can clarify this. One may explain that these are routine inquiries to protect confidentiality and have nothing specifically to do with the patient.

Before one writes a letter, it is good practice to get a signed release from the patient. To make doubly sure of keeping open communication, it is wise to at least discuss each point of information released with the patient. It may be indicated to have the patient read the letter and react to it, and then to negotiate changes to reflect both patient's view and therapist's position. One can usually phrase a letter in simple descriptive terms and give a supportive opinion upon the value of the patient's having entered psychotherapy. There is rarely a need for a psychiatric label, since most inquiries revolve around the patient's ability to function, his reliability, and his interest in the project in question. One may merely want to suggest that the third party assess the patient as it would any other applicant. This may be usefully discussed with the patient, and it helps to clarify his motivation, the assets and liabilities he would bring to a prospective job, and his readiness to undertake the project. Useful discussion can ensue about his illness, what he thinks of it, and what the therapist thinks of it. Distortions may be corrected and perspective gained in such discussions. The patient will always have an avid curiosity, "What does he think of me? Now he has to commit himself to paper." Behind this one may detect, "Does he like me?" The open, tactful, careful discussion of the letter will do more for the patient's trust than the reassurance, "Of course I like you." Both may gain more from questioning the close link between the patient's expectation of being disliked and his own discomfort with his childlike qualities, anger, sadness, selfishness, or whatever he repudiates about himself.

If a former patient requests a letter, if possible the therapist should see him and talk face-to-face with him to assess the current situation. It is not really enough to rely on old notes or a telephone conversation.

As the political climate takes various turns, letters describing evaluation for therapeutic abortion may or may not be required. Writing such a letter is best viewed in the context of at least a few interviews. One may recognize with the patient at the outset that the letter will be formed with her to address the most sensible and reasonable solution possible. One may create an atmosphere in which all her conflicting feelings are considered with her in private. One should offer further sessions, or decide with her whether it would be helpful to arrange at least short-term treatment around the time of the abortion. Her partner may also be involved in discussions if she wants this. One should see each individual separately as well as together.

FORMS FOR ADMINISTRATIVE PURPOSES

Institutions may be responsible for supplying statistics, which are used for overall planning of programs by the organization itself, the state, or the federal government. Debates are often conducted, as in the community mental health centers and within the British

National Health Service, regarding the amount of information to be disclosed. Many clinicians grant that general statistics about age, sex, diagnosis, and length and type of treatment may be of value. Patients' names, addresses, and details of problems are usually withheld. The latter approach gives rise to opposition from professionals and administrators who are interested in building up computer data banks of information. At best such a system could expedite treatment of itinerant patients and facilitate dissemination of clinical information. Many people hold more dear the value of individual privacy. It takes more work to telephone information between cities, but this should involve less risk of violating the patient's autonomy and privacy.

Whatever his opinion or practice, the therapist should discuss with a patient any such personal forms completed. Questions may arise in therapy about how the patient feels depersonalized or categorized, and how much and to whom he wishes information about himself to be entrusted. At one extreme, a paranoid patient may be enraged and struggle with intolerable feelings of invasion. At the other, a patient may say he cares nothing because he feels so helpless and empty. A typical patient may either object or agree, want to know the limit of the revealed information, and decide how much it may or may not interfere with his personal treatment. It may revolve around how much he can trust the therapist. In the United States, if a patient feels strongly violated by the rules of a system, he has the option of seeking private treatment.

MISSED APPOINTMENTS AND TELEPHONE CALLS

Missed appointments can be viewed in the context of what is happening in therapy, particularly in relation to the previous hour. Of course, external events may occur, but the therapist may wonder about their meaning.

If a cancellation occurs in advance, there is opportunity for discussion and a decision for or against an alternative appointment. Cancellations which occur immediately before, during, or immediately after a scheduled session are intriguing. The message is that that particular hour still belongs to the patient. These calls clearly raise therapeutic issues. Calling just before an appointment may indicate anxiety and ambivalence. It is as if the patient is at the threshold, but something acute stops him. He still has allotted time with the therapist in fantasy, and he knows the therapist will have time to sit and cogitate about him. Sometimes a comment about his anxiety, asking if it is connected with his absence, will clarify the situation or encourage him to come in for part of the time. At other times, agreement to see him at the next session and discuss it is all he wants.

The call during the patient's own time slot is often an angry reaction. It may not be far from the patient's awareness. This cancellation results in most inconvenience for the therapist. He waits; he may worry or get angry; he is unable to settle to another task; and by the time he is notified, the hour is wasted. Calling after a scheduled hour has passed can be a passive-aggressive phenomenon. It, too, may bespeak anxiety, anger, and ambivalence. The caller who says, "Woops — I'm sorry — I slept through the appointment," usually has some heavy issue to discuss, which part of him wishes to avoid.

Borderline psychotic and psychotic patients can be quite unpredictable about missing appointments, with or without notice. At one time or another, they may wish for more distance, and if they fall into a pattern of missing, say every other week, the therapist may want to renegotiate the contract to take the need into account. The patient may call, primarily to insure that the therapist is still alive, at a time when closer human contact seems too overwhelming.

With phone calls, sensitive secretarial help is a valuable aid in forming a picture of what is on the patient's mind. One may ask: "Did he sound upset?" "Did he call locally or long distance?" "Did he ask to be called back?" A knowledgeable, interested secretary can say: "Mrs. Smith canceled her appointment an hour ago. She sounded sort of vague. She couldn't remember your name, and there was a lot of background music. Her voice was slurred. She said, 'Tell him just not to bother with me anymore!' " With this alcoholic-depressed patient this may be the major clue that she is furious and contemplating suicide. In this case, the therapist would certainly call back. A less observant secretary might give the message, "Mrs. Smith called and canceled her appointment. She said you needn't phone her back." The therapist might query, "Did she say she'd keep her next appointment?" And the secretary might reply, "No, I didn't ask her." A secretary does not have to be intrusive and initiate a lot of questions, but a description, using every piece of evidence, may be invaluable. In interpreting phone calls, the therapist may add his assessment of the secretary and balance it with knowledge about the patient. Secretaries should be instructed about the privacy of any information.

If a patient does not leave a message to be called back, the therapist usually respects this, unless he is concerned that the patient is disorganized, suicidal, or homicidal. All sorts of intrigues may go on via telephone messages, and the only reliable rule is to bring them up for discussion, reaction, and clarification at the next appointment.

ANSWERING SERVICE

One should try to maintain a good relationship with his answering service. First of all, a service may be chosen by recommendations from others on their politeness and reliability. A personal visit to the operators at the beginning may help. If they know what the therapist looks like and how he talks, the contact may be less inhuman, and they may therefore treat patient calls with more skill.

It is very important to tell patients exactly how to get in touch with the therapist, and what to expect when they lift the phone to call him. One may talk in advance of any anticipated waits. In the event that the patient calls in the midst of an acute upset, he may remember that if the call is not returned immediately, it does not mean abandonment.

CONFIDENTIALITY

There are legal and ethical considerations surrounding confidentiality. The clinician should know the strictly legal concepts, such as "privilege," and where legal protection of patients' confidentiality becomes vague. The care of minors and outpatients who are legally defined as "not competent," and the legalities of commitment of a patient to an institution warrant careful attention. The therapist should know the implications of "informed consent." There are local laws on these aspects. Fuller discussion will be found elsewhere in the medicolegal literature.

Complications can arise when the therapist is given permission by a patient to divulge information, and the therapist does not wish to do this. One should know what may be required in a court case. The beginning therapist should never participate in anything with legal implications without discussing all details with a senior. If one anticipates that his first dealings will be with adolescents, where prescribing narcotics, treatment for drug addiction, advising about contraception, or perhaps therapeutic abortion might be indicated, it is essential to have detailed discussions about one's responsibility, both to patient and to parents, in the training orientation program.

There are simple human and professional reasons for keeping one's counsel in this work. Therapy involves the most intimate detail of a person's life. Even the most exhibitionistic patient needs a therapist who can listen and be discreet. The more tightly knit the society in which one works, the more crucial becomes the automatic rule never to talk about a patient personally or in any identifiable way to anyone socially. It is damaging and disrespectful to break this rule. Even among colleagues, when one is asking informally for constructive help, it is best not to mention the patient or family by name. False names can be used at open case conferences. If there is any possibility that the person might be identified at a public meeting, that case should not be discussed, regardless of its teaching value. The sooner one begins to practice watchful caution in talking about his patients, the better. It may be hard, especially as a beginner, to withhold information which will awe or titillate one's friends. However, if the therapist treats the patient with as much care and respect as he would wish for himself in this regard, he will not go far astray.

10

Ending Therapy

Termination of therapy is a time of intense mixed feelings for both patient and therapist. With each patient there will be different emphases on the quantity and quality of the feelings involved in the separation. Regression may be more or less evident. It may be hard to try to maintain a holistic view of the person and what he wants of the therapist while listening to the themes and often intense feelings. This may be doubly difficult if the therapist is sad at losing a "favorite child," or angry at renewed rebelliousness. The task of the therapist in some ways is similar to the task of a parent in that he attempts to help the patient prepare for life without him.

This discussion will be confined to a clinical account of what may happen, concentrating on some of the affects involved for the patient.

A young, single man called a female therapist to ask if she had time available to see him. They agreed to meet in consultation. He had just terminated three months' therapy in a local clinic. Becoming acutely depressed within a week, he had tried to reach his former therapist but had found she was on vacation. He said he could not understand why he was so depressed and panicky because therapy had gone well and had been an enriching experience for him. In referring to his therapist he referred to her as Dr., then Mrs., then Miss. The therapist did not pick up on this with him, but noted to herself the confusion of wishes and fears that the relationship with the former therapist represented in his life. A few days after termination he had attempted to have intercourse with his girlfriend for the first time and had been impotent. He told his story in a burdened way. Toward the end he smiled slowly to himself. The therapist asked about the break in the story. He reflected slowly, "I was just thinking of the difference between your technique and Mrs. X's. That's not to say either of you is a better or worse therapist. I do speak slowly, and I guess I have a limited time with you, since you said this was a consultation . . . [Sigh]!"

Therapist: It feels very different talking with me?

Patient: Yes — you ask more questions. It's a more incisive experience.

Therapist: It's hard to talk to me, when you must have liked her very much and wanted mostly to see her again.

Patient: That's true. I liked her a lot [Blush]. How could you know that? I suppose it's obvious. I really want a woman therapist. . . . I suppose you don't want to see me in therapy?

Therapist: We can discuss that, but why would you suppose that?

Patient: Well — I sort of said I liked her better and — well — I can't see how you could want to see me after that.

Therapist: It's very important to you, that you feel I am pleased with you?

Patient: Of course. I have to feel I please everybody. I suppose that's a big part of my problem. I would think you would be angry and hurt and feel like crawling away — [Silence]. Once I was talking to Miss X — it all took me by surprise — you understand I really liked her — I fell silent and then I felt like screaming. It came out that I was *angry* at her. I don't understand. I was *angry* at her. . . . I must have been rude to her, I didn't mean to be rude. Well, no, I wasn't rude, I was just angry. I felt like it was my fault that we had to stop. Maybe if I'd been nicer we could have continued. That's not right either, because she said it was clinic policy that we stop.

Therapist: Sounds like you felt you had pushed her away and that she went off on vacation in disgust.

Patient [Brightening]: Yes [Blush], I actually think I felt she needed a vacation from her dreadful patients — especially me.

The discussion continued with elaboration on other problems, and they agreed that he could benefit from longer-term therapy. His present depression seemed very much connected with his recent termination experience, though representative of pervasive problems in his life.

When a patient changes therapists, or when he has separate experiences with different therapists, the new therapist may find himself beginning work around the termination issues of the previous experience. This does not necessarily mean that the previous therapist was neglectful. In the example, from fuller discussion it became clear this was far from the case. It may have to do with the readiness of the patient. It may be easier to talk with a new person about the involved feelings concerning the person seen earlier. The passage of time may also help in working through of issues unavailable at the time of termination.

Termination will represent a distillation of the themes which have arisen in the therapy, the situation that brought the patient to treatment in the first place, and the positive and negative aspects of transference and countertransference. The young man had come to therapy complaining of difficulty in getting along with women. He had chosen a female therapist with whom to begin to work upon his problems and had, much to his surprise, become very attached to her. His antennae were acutely alert for any suggestion of rejection. Before therapy he had been relatively unacquainted with his anger in such situations. Now he was beginning to be able to experience the strong feeling. With his previous therapist he had identified the feeling but had not been able to focus it on her. There was a suggestion that it was too dangerous for him. He had turned it toward himself and had become depressed. He viewed himself as a worthless burden from whom she had to escape. Guilt about his warm and sexual feelings for her was shown by his blushing and feeling that his thoughts were transparently obvious. His attachment to the consultation therapist was too ready. The episode with his girlfriend suggested he was searching for a quick replacement, perhaps to avoid feeling anger and sadness at the loss of his therapist. Fear of the future without support had led him rapidly to seek a substitute for her. His sense that he needed more treatment than his short-term therapy offered was quite accurate.

The dialog in the example could have wider meanings, but the point here is to introduce some of the feelings seen in termination. The common thread in all terminations is the effect of separation upon the person. The patient's feelings that are not available to awareness often are centered in the therapist and involve individual concerns about leaving or being left by the therapist.

WHEN TO STOP

Therapy may stop electively. This may be a complex decision. Patient and therapist may not see eye to eye on the matter. The concept of "enough improvement" bears on all lengths of therapy for both patient and therapist but is particularly relevant to elective termination of long-term therapy. There must be as many levels of satisfaction as there are people who become either patients or therapists. A stolid, externally oriented patient may be satisfied with less than an intense, introverted person who is fascinated by the workings of his own mind. Therapists may influence the timing of termination, depending on how quickly or slowly they feel satisfied. Elective terminations are more subject to the personal vagaries of both individuals involved. However, the therapist and patient may arrive at a point of mutual agreement that enough work has been done.

First of all, symptoms may have disappeared or may have been ameliorated. During the therapy there may have been repeated situations in which the symptoms became troublesome but were experienced with increasing ease. The patient and therapist may now be more confident that the improvement is potentially solid. Enough work may have been done to help the patient live his life closer to the way he desires. His interpersonal relationships may have improved. Longer, steadier close relationships with mutual give-and-take may have been observed. Sticky, neurotic involvements may have been discarded, or their nature and expectations may have changed as a result of the patient's growing awareness and decreased need to repeat unsatisfactory aspects of emotional ties from the past. He may be less timid and more open to risk in everyday life. His need for multiple energy-sapping security operations may be lessened, and in general he may be more comfortable. Sexual relations may have improved. More satisfaction may be forthcoming from his work. These are a few of the indications of possibly solid internal change, and they may indicate a point has been reached at which patient and therapist can begin to assess the need for continued treatment.

BEGINNINGS OF TERMINATION

All "improvement" for a patient involves giving up something. It is very hard to give up familiar and repetitive ways. They may be cozy, well-known, and comforting, no matter how self-destructive, conducive to anguish, or alienating they may seem to the patient or to the therapist. When one is a child, the center of the universe is his parents, family, and house. This territory is jealously guarded. It is only in the process of becoming involved with other children and families, and their homes and later of comparing different views of the family world that one can reassess the situation and become aware of other possibilities. Growth and change may be involved in this process. Choices have to be made. Some modes of behavior are continued. The modes that are threatened or changed probably cause the greatest anxiety and conflict, even though they may ultimately be regarded by the person as "improvement."

A person coming to a therapist is usually asking implicitly or explicitly to change something. Within the prospective goal of giving up some way of being, the first harbinger of final separation from the therapist may be experienced. The threat of change may be seen in those patients who improve very quickly and want to terminate therapy "before I get too involved." "I'm frightened of getting too dependent" may suggest an internal fantasy of vast and insatiable dependency needs that the patient senses will be "too easy" to fall into and "too difficult" to work through to the point of giving up the therapist. Depending on what such a patient wants from therapy, it may be perfectly legitimate to respect such fantasies. One may decide to leave them untouched or to touch upon them only briefly and agree with a rapid termination if this is what the patient wants.

Another patient may come to treatment asking help with repetitive relationships in which he has become so dependent and demanding that the other person has fended him off because he is a burden. He may want to change this pattern. He, too, may experience an urge to leave therapy at the point where he is becoming involved. He may need to separate first, saving himself the pain and also the pleasure of involvement, lest the therapist make any demands of him, or lest the therapist see how childlike he can become as he becomes attached to him. If one has enough information, he may wish to interpret the patient's behavior to him at this point in order to help him stay in therapy or at least to encourage his reflection about his actions. This may help him introspect or draw some parallels between this and his other relationships which he found difficult. In brief, time-limited therapy the unilateral urge of the patient to separate before risking getting into deeper water may occur around the sixth or seventh session,* and in fact many patients terminate at that time. There is a clinical impression that if a patient states initially the length of time that he will spend overcoming his problem, be it four sessions or a year, that often correlates with the number of sessions or length of time spent, even if the contract is open-ended. This too may be a parameter of a person's desire to change and may be related to how he intuitively perceives he can withstand separation.

TERMINATION DATE

The date of termination may be agreed upon according to many variables. In brief therapy by choice, the termination date may be fixed almost from the beginning. At various points in the therapy it may have been reviewed to test whether it still makes sense. If still mutually agreed upon, patient and therapist will proceed with a definite date in mind.

The projected termination date may play a role in the pacing of the therapy. It may internally urge the patient forward, and increase his motivation to work in therapy by reflecting, allowing himself to become involved with the therapist, and perhaps experimenting with situations outside the therapy. He might experiment by visiting parents after a long absence to reassess the situation, or taking steps to change an unsatisfactory career goal, or breaking up a relationship that has been difficult for a long time. On the other hand, knowledge of a termination date may slow down involvement on the outside and encourage the patient to be more introspective and

*Prelinger, E. Personal communication.

tolerate some of his strong feelings, such as sadness, loneliness, and anxiety. Perhaps his usual way of coping with them would be to stir up external turmoil in order to distract him from his internal pressures. Some patients may therefore be spurred on by the goal.

Other patients may try to do too much, allowing too little time to integrate the experience. It may be part of the therapeutic task to slow down such a patient. One might make observations on his too fast pace and wonder if it has to do with his feeling rushed because he knows he has a limited time in therapy. For one patient the meaning of rushing to the finish concerned a wish to please the therapist and to "be perfect" at the point he stopped therapy. He said he felt as if he were awaiting "a grade" from the therapist at the end, and he hoped it would be a good one. In further discussion it unfolded that a good grade would mean that the therapist cared about him and that he had been an especially responsive patient.

Treatment may be terminated by circumstance. Money may be limited, the patient or therapist may move, or the patient may anticipate a life change which will necessitate stopping treatment. Usually in these cases also a termination date will be mutually agreed upon early in the therapy. Even if the time factor has been fully discussed in early interviews, the therapist should give the patient plenty of warning of the date of the last session, say four to six weeks in advance in brief therapy and several months in long-term therapy. Occasionally a therapist will assume that the patient knows. As he reminds the patient of the date in the next to last session, he may be quite disturbed to find that the patient is shocked and had "forgotten."

One highly obsessional patient was in once a week therapy for a year. He had told the therapist six months in advance that he was leaving the area on a certain date. From time to time he talked of what it would be like to stop therapy. The therapist too was aware of the date, and had mentioned it at least four times in the six weeks prior to the last session. In the last session the patient began to talk about something important that had happened the evening before. Since the therapist had such pressing issue on his agenda, he interrupted him at the beginning of the hour, saying, "That sounds important, and we can talk about it, but first I wanted to remind you that this is our last session."

The patient said, "Our *last* session? That's ridiculous. That's crazy. You never told me before that we were stopping!" He berated the therapist for not telling him sooner. The therapist said that he may recall they *had* talked of it, and he brought up some of the issues they had discussed in connection with the termination. The patient denied that these had occurred. (Sometimes one is caught off guard and is not sure if indeed one remembers correctly; in this case it is, of course, best to acknowledge the possibility of a mistake, hear the patient's feelings about it and work out the misunderstanding.) In this instance the therapist knew definitely that they had talked of the date. The defensive maneuvers involved were a reflection of the patient's problems. This was the first time for a long time that the patient had been able to be angry at the therapist. The therapist pointed this out and asked if there was some connection between the patient's anger and the "forgetting." The young man thought for a while and then told him what he had been about to relate before being interrupted.

The previous night he had felt suicidal. Nothing seemed to matter. It was exactly as it had been before he started therapy. He had written notes to various people and then, he said, there was a note to the therapist: "You are a nice person. You tried your best, and you shouldn't feel guilty. I couldn't help it." The therapist asked what that was about, and the patient slowly elaborated: "I've been such a burden, you must be glad to get rid of me [etc.]." He said the last thing in the world he wanted was that the therapist should feel guilty.

Therapist: I think that you're very angry with me for stopping seeing you.

Patient: I *am*. I really couldn't understand last night why. As I was writing those notes, I didn't *seriously* plan to kill myself, but I felt so low and confused. I *am* angry. How can you let me stop if I'm in such bad shape?

Therapist: You feel angry and helpless about stopping seeing me. Sounds like you feel nothing is worthwhile.

He agreed and compared his feelings this hour to those at the beginning of therapy. This developed into appraisal of some of the gains he had made and reflection on how he could suddenly become so angry. He felt "just awful and ashamed about being so angry when it really isn't your fault."

Therapist: It's hard for you to be angry at me when you like me. I also think you'd like to hurt me.

Patient: I never told you I liked you, but I told you in the note, didn't I?

Therapist [Agrees]: It *is* very hard to leave someone you like.

Patient [Silence]: You know, maybe I'm so angry because that, somehow, seems easier to say.

He then went on in a more direct way about how *he* usually ended involvements because he got angry and walked off.

Therapist: Like the idea of killing yourself rather than coming to the last session?

Patient: I suppose that's it. I have to put on this big show that *I* don't care and everybody's rotten to me, when actually I *do* care.

The hour finished by his connecting this experience to one with a girlfriend who left him before the therapy had begun. That was the first time he had had suicidal feelings. The therapist saw him in the street a few months later. The patient greeted him cheerfully, introduced a friend, and said that school was going well.

This example illustrates the importance of establishing and acknowledging the date of stopping treatment well in advance. Even when this is accomplished, some patients maintain a state of internal denial that the event is taking place even in the last hour. Resistances may be increased because of the power of the feelings of separation.

FEELINGS ABOUT TERMINATION

For a beginning therapist facing his first termination experiences, a simple, practical, descriptive listing of the feelings most frequently observed in a range of patients, and the way in which they may come up, might be useful. Termination is talked about with a certain awe among more experienced clinicians, and it may take away the mystery and relieve anxiety to name and think about the components involved. The authors here merely present a plea to listen for which groups of feelings seem most relevant to the patient's psychodynamics. This is easier if one has an idea of the range of possible feelings. The following feelings rarely emerge in pure form. There may be complicated derivations of them, appearing in a seemingly haphazard manner.

Loss

Separation calls forth primarily feelings of loss and grief. In terminating therapy the difference is that the patient can talk of such feelings with the therapist before the event, which gradually helps to integrate the experience for the patient and make it bearable. For more disturbed patients it will be a first experience in talking to the living, available object of the grief and in talking to a person who can bear the feelings while remaining whole and undamaged, while still caring for the patient.

The person's characteristic way of handling feelings of loss will come into focus. Thus he may gloss over them pushing aside the discomfort of the feelings of loss; he may deny the importance of the feelings while appearing elated; he may become increasingly anxious while avoiding the topic. Or he may become extremely sad and depressed. It is appropriate to be sad and wish that the experience could continue. With a patient who has had many losses in his life, through actual death or more subtle losses due to emotional unavailability or fantasied losses of any kind, one may hear much more of these experiences. This allows him to work through them further, with such feelings nearer the surface. One may hear sadness about the loss of the therapist mingled, for example, with sadness about an abortion or with sadness at the death of a parent in childhood. Some patients allow themselves to weep. Others may talk of the impossibility of shedding tears lest the therapist think they are "unmanly," "weak," or "impotent." Others do not experience the pain so deeply, since they have not allowed themselves to become so involved, or have not admitted that they care for the therapist. A loss of interest in outside events may be observed. Some of these reactions are more like those described by Freud as mourning.

Borderline psychotic patients may begin feeling the loss of the therapist very early in therapy and alternate abruptly between total loss of the therapist and being with the therapist till eternity: "I am sad and totally empty without you" may occur in the same hour as "I am not sad because we are one for ever and ever." Masochistic patients may experience some pleasure in the grief itself along the lines of "I am the helpless victim and you are the torturer." They may withhold their participation in the event and experience every interpretation made to this end as an accusation. One patient said, "Not only do you torture me by leaving me, but you turn the knife by telling me I'm sad and angry about it. I have no right to be sad. This is a 'clinical relationship.' You do your job." At the same time she was smiling and seeming less than perturbed.

In other patients grief about the birth of the next sibling is often at the fore. Termination is an analogous situation, in that the patient is expected to give up nurturance and "be more grown up." This concern may come up in the form of comments such as, "You'll have more time for other patients" or "Will someone be taking my hour?"

Loneliness

Feelings of loneliness may be described. This is appropriate at the level of having seen the same person regularly for a time and naturally preparing for withdrawal. It may touch on deeper levels of aloneness in growing up and bearing responsibility for oneself, his life, and others in his life. One female patient said, "Without you, the future looks bleak." This was connected with depressive fantasies of deprivation akin to melancholia as described by Freud. The patient needed the contact with a caring, nurturing therapist to continue the struggle of daily life. She needed someone "to feed upon." In confronting the loss of the therapist's support, the patient's emptiness and difficulty having independent thoughts of her own came into focus. When growing up, as soon as she had had the beginnings of an independent idea, her parents immediately suppressed it. This involved everything from doing her homework for her to organizing where she would go on weekends. In therapy, when her own ideas and expression of feelings were encouraged, she had begun and carried out some independent actions and had experienced a new joy in the process. Faced with the loss and loneliness of termination, her depressive symptoms were exacerbated.

Anger

Anger is an integral part of separation, and many patients have a great deal of trouble recognizing it or tolerating its existence. Patients may terminate treatment in a more or less angry way. There are those for whom this may be the only affect available. This may be seen especially in very deprived patients whose therapy is terminated by circumstance. It seems the world is against them, that they are cruelly victimized, and that the therapist in particular is taking away the only promise of fulfillment of their dependency needs, even though they may know this wish is irrational. These patients may therefore spend the last sessions in fury. At the same time they may be frightened of the power of their anger and feel as if this alone is the reason the therapist is "kicking them out." The therapist can make interpretations along this line, for example, "You are so angry with me that you feel like I'm getting rid of you because I can't stand it." The patient may agree or disagree, but it may lead him to an awareness of other feelings he may have, for example, the fear that may be behind it.

Patients who have a great deal of difficulty with tender feelings may mask some of them with an outburst of annoyance. It may be easier to seem angry and repudiating of the therapist or the therapy than to seem too attached. Or it may seem that any anger expressed will detract from the appreciative feelings (as in the example early in the chapter). In the closing hours other patients may bring themes that suggest they feel the therapist is so angry and drained that he is stopping therapy. This may be a projection of the patient's anger and may be used in interpretation. If the patient feels that the therapist is "too nice" to him, he may feel a painful amount of guilt in showing his anger and may turn it upon himself. With such a patient the therapist's main task is to help him externalize his rage.

Anger may come up directly or disguised in many forms. Patients for whom termination feelings are too difficult may miss hours. They may do it in a hostile way, for example, by phoning ten minutes into the hour to say they cannot make it, or having sudden problems in scheduling hours, or requesting to be seen impossibly early or late. Suicidal patients may find it easier to talk of veiled threats to their lives or to retreat to symptoms rather than face the pain of their anger in leaving. Anger may not be the only feeling that is avoided by missing hours.

A therapist may decide not to contact a patient about missed hours if he feels that, for example, the paranoid patient's unexplored fury is necessary for his integration and functioning. The therapist may feel that it is too painful for him to become fully aware of it, since there is not enough time left together to work it through to a manageable level. With other patients he may decide to call and inquire, if he is worried about their welfare or feels there is practical value in working further on the issue. It might be, for example, a repetition of previously discussed incidents in the therapy. The therapist may also choose to contact a patient whom he has reason to believe is missing hours to prove mainly that the therapist does not care.

Caring or not caring on the part of the therapist may be a very ambivalent issue. The patient may fantasize that there are only two options, that is, either the therapist does not care at all, or else he is too caring and overinvolved. The overcaring fantasy may be quite terrifying for a given patient. Rather than phoning, where the patient may have less ease in regulating the emotional distance he wishes, it may seem appropriate to write the patient a letter such as the following:

Dear Mr. Adams,

Since you did not keep our last appointment, I wonder if you wish to stop at this time? We do have the option to continue for two more sessions, and I think it may be worthwhile for you to come and talk more about the difficult issues that we had started to discuss. However, if you do not wish to come, you should feel free to return to the clinic at any future time. Perhaps you could let me know of your decision by October 15?

Yours sincerely,

Rosemary Balsam, M.D.

This leaves the patient an out if he needs it but also assures him of continued interest. Something should probably be said briefly and simply about what the therapist feels is the reason the patient missed the session, on the chance that it may free him to continue until the end. One hopes the interpretive comment will not be so threatening that it makes matters worse. When a patient can terminate therapy with some self-respect, it will be easier for him to seek therapy again later. This should also be borne in mind when constructing a letter to a patient.

Guilt

Another central feeling that often occurs in separation is guilt. The patient may feel "too much has been said." As Dr. Schafer says about the elaboration of feelings during psychotherapy, it involves feelings that the patient "blushed too much or wept too much to acknowledge." The patient may want to be rid of the therapist quickly, in an effort to reconstitute his defenses and feel more "whole," like his old familiar self. The patient may feel guilty about his sexual feelings toward the therapist, having harbored some hope of reciprocity, and when faced with stopping therapy, be ashamed about the unilateral attachment in this respect. Sometimes a patient in short-term therapy will save talking more openly about his sexual attachment till the last session, when he feels "safe." Listening and perhaps commenting about why he feels safe enough only in the last session may be all that is needed. If it is part of a repetitive pattern of having to break a relationship as soon as tender or sexual feelings come up openly, then one might link it with previous situations described. Patients are often capable of "working" right up till the last moment, and in such a situation one may hear the patient's reflections about the therapeutic relationship and more about why it was not "safe" before.

A patient may feel guilty about his pleasure in "being free." He may have a need to tell the therapist how badly off he is in order to disguise his joy at "release" from the therapy. This kind of patient may have had difficulty admitting to any feelings of joy throughout the therapy, for whatever reason.

There may be guilt about expressing anger or death fantasies, lest they hurt the therapist. Many patients feel guilt about being "bad and disappointing" patients. They may feel that they have wasted the therapist's time. This can be a projection of their anger at being abandoned, for which they feel guilty. It may be connected with familiar old patterns of feeling like "a bad child" who "deserves" the punishment of the parents' withdrawal.

Fear

Many patients experience fear in separation. This may emerge as fear of the future, fear of the unknown, fear of the intensity of the feelings themselves, fear for the therapist, his welfare, his finances, his future without this "special" patient, fear that the therapist will die, or fear that the patient will die if his supplies are cut off. With symbiotic patients or those in touch with primitive fantasies there may be an intense fear of emptiness, expressed as a fear that the therapist has "sucked off" all the substance of the patient. The patient may fear that he will cause the therapist's dissolution or else be annihilated himself. Paranoid patients, and others for whom trust develops by millimeters, may have an acute exacerbation of fear that the therapist will betray them and reveal "the secrets" in order to destroy them. One paranoid schizophrenic's parting words were, "My last word is that if you breathe a word to a soul about what I've told you, I'll kill you with my own hands." This was after months of work on issues of trust on different levels, often intermingled with the reality of confidentiality.

Pleasure

Separation may evoke pleasurable feelings too. There may be satisfaction that "the job is done," a feeling that something has been accomplished, and a feeling of completeness. It can be very good to a patient to savor the idea of being on his own. He may feel that it is a vote of confidence on the therapist's part that he has not insisted on more therapy. The patient may know that he can come back if he needs to, and that may help him have confidence too. He may want to tell the therapist that it was a good experience for him. Some therapists have as difficult a time listening to these positive emotions as others have hearing painful feelings.

If a patient becomes very elated in termination, the only feelings available being how wonderful it all was, the therapist may reflect on what depressive ideation is being avoided. It is a delicate matter sometimes to phrase one's investigative comments in such a way as not to put down the patient. One manic-depressive patient said in these circumstances, "I felt as if you took my toy boat and tore off the sail." By that time he was in tears. He experienced being brought down from his elated state as a cruel aggressive act on the part of the therapist, who in fact had attempted to phrase his comment as gently as possible. When the patient explored further, he concluded that the use of "toy" suggested to him that the elation had a "pretend" aspect and was therefore fragile in its own right. Having had an opportunity to hear some of the painful feelings before stopping treatment, the therapist felt a little more confident, that there was less likelihood of the patient's suffering a severe depressive reaction after termination.

WAYS OF TERMINATING

Not every possible feeling will come to the fore with every patient. The less disturbed will be mainly involved with "mourning," the more disturbed mainly with "melancholic" feelings as described by Freud, although these two conditions may overlap in any individual. Some will use the opportunity to review their life, past, present, and future. Others will emphasize the details of future planning as if to carry the reactions of the therapist into the unknown future. Still others will use the time to demonstrate how they are "stuck," to re-enact all the situations that brought them to therapy and do everything to prove that therapy should be interminable. With these patients, in particular, the therapist may have a hard time keeping his head, being aware of any progress no matter how small, and sticking to the mutual decision previously agreed upon. If a patient manages to get an extra few sessions after the termination date, he may ultimately feel quite undermined and guilty. Little is usually gained by these "few more" sessions, and they may be granted on the basis of the therapist's guilt in not having been able to help enough. However, if a seriously suicidal patient has a determined plan to harm himself, which he tells the therapist in the closing minutes, the therapist should not feel in conflict about seeing him again. This is more in the nature of a reassessment of the situation, to see if indeed the decision to terminate made sense at that particular time.

With many patients the therapist will hear a little of all the feelings with varying intensities, depending on the patient's basic problems. Some therapists feel cheated or feel it is less valuable work if they do not hear everything, first-hand and involving themselves. This is not possible for most patients, and they are able to approach the feelings only indirectly through displacements. One patient in brief treatment, who did not talk about her loss directly in relation to her separation from her therapist, used the termination hours well in expressing grief about a recent death of a teacher, who was more important to her, and a more real part of her everyday life. She felt there might be some connection with stopping seeing the therapist, but the teacher's death was a greater and more absolute loss in the course of her life. The same principles regarding not forcing the pace of therapy still operate at the termination.

Vacations taken by the therapist or patient may act as mini-terminations and may prime the patient for a richer termination experience. The same or similar feelings are operative, but since the experience is temporary, there is more of an as-if quality. One experienced therapist who was in the first year of his analysis described what may happen. His female analyst's first vacation passed, and though the topics had been introduced by the analyst, he felt they were still abstract. The second time his analyst went on vacation, he anticipated the same bland experience. He left the hour, drove off in his car, and at a nearby junction was jolted by a minor accident due to his own carelessness. Shaken by the unusual event, he entered his house, lay down on his couch, and tried to "catch his fleeting, random thoughts." He realized that at the moment of the accident, he was toying with a fantasy of his analyst being in a plane crash. Till that moment the impact of his separation was not conscious. His next association was, "Yes, Virginia, there *is* an unconscious!"

After stopping therapy for many months the patient often carries within him an image of the therapist. In dealing with the loss he may take with him a part of the therapist by various mental processes such as identification, introjection, and incorporation. He may or may not be aware of this. In brief therapy it will not be possible to explore fully the implications of all the patient's impressions about the therapist's personality and the patient's actual knowledge of or fantasies about the therapist's life-style which he imitated. Valuable aspects of the intensified internalized image of the therapist may be present. For example, the patient may still talk things over with him and anticipate reactions in his imagination. The work of the therapy and termination goes on for a long time after treatment stops. Some patients do not find any improvement in their way of being till after termination. Some report gradually feeling better months after termination, and decide that the state was connected with having been in psychotherapy. This presumably has to do with the pace of integration of the experience for each individual.

Termination is an evocative experience for both therapist and patient. Feelings that the patient dwells on are part of the therapist's experience at some level too. There can be overemphasis and underemphasis by therapists, forcing issues and avoiding them, collusion with the patient, and shared denial. Perhaps in termination, above all experiences in therapy, there are more countertransference issues involved, because of the universal meaning of the experience of separation.

11

When There Is Little Time

Brief individual psychotherapy is a term generally used to describe a course of therapy which lasts anywhere from a few sessions up to about a year. The term has different meanings to different therapists. Some therapists offer frequent sessions per week during the course of a few months. Others may offer a nonintensive, once a week therapy of variable length. The brevity may be viewed in terms of overall time spent with the therapist, not necessarily in terms of the length of the therapy. There is probably more demand for brief psychotherapy than there used to be. This is a very interesting state of affairs, but one that is beyond the scope of this discussion. Most therapists offer brief treatment, whatever their ideology, and try to adapt techniques from their basic school of thought. In this chapter some aspects of brief, once a week, nonintensive, psychoanalytically oriented treatment are described.

There are two broad categories in which brief therapy is offered. It may be a treatment of choice determined by the therapist with a patient, or it may be a treatment of circumstance because of external time limits imposed by either the patient's or the therapist's situation.

BRIEF THERAPY BY CHOICE

As a guideline for recommending or choosing the mode of brief psychotherapy, one may consider the kinds of problems for which brief therapy might be helpful. This decision cannot be made independent of what the patient wants. The therapist will weigh with him alternative available modes of therapy that might offer help. The following are situations in which it might prove useful.

A developmental crisis may present problems amenable to a time-limited approach. Adolescents who are not severely disturbed may profit from the experience, which will help them weather a stage in growing up. This may be more desirable than intensive, long-term therapy, in which the treatment relationship could become a major focus of life. Frequent meetings may emphasize regression and dependency, and diminish the impetus for peer and adult involvement. This might be less fruitful for a particular adolescent whose energies, one feels, would be better used in experimenting with ordinary life situations. A brief therapy, however, might give him enough time to reflect about his problems. It is often helpful for an adolescent to talk about his experience with an adult outside the family. Putting his puzzling and often overwhelming feelings into words may help make them more manageable. Talking with a therapist not involved in the parental conflicts offers a safe environment in which to explore painful or mixed feelings about his parents. Talking with the therapist about sexual matters and his first tentative involvements with the opposite sex may be easier for him than talking with adults whom he sees in daily life. In some cases it will help him to withstand pressures of the parents or school, realistic or unrealistic, to sort out his own aspirations, and to test them against the therapist.

Another kind of patient who may benefit from a short-term experience is a young adult, in late teens or early twenties, who already has many resources — for example, college students. He may need only a little help to make a maximal gain in his or her growth. He may have difficulty with separating from home for the first time, or with a first serious sexual relationship that is faltering, or with choosing a career. These problems could also, of course, indicate more serious pathology, and careful evaluation is recommended before settling on brief therapy as a preferred treatment.

Acute life crises in adults who are reasonably well able to stand the stresses of everyday life may be worked out in brief therapy. Much has been written about various aspects of "crisis intervention."

Patients with fairly fixed character problems, such as obsessional patients, schizoid patients, or passive-aggressive patients, who have overlying anxiety due to current difficulties, may benefit from brief therapy. The current problems may result from the deeper issues, which might indicate psychoanalysis, but they may not wish to make the time, energy, and money commitment involved. Remaining within reasonable goals for brief therapy, such a patient can sometimes reach a point of feeling better, with improved functioning.

For many of the patients who choose brief therapy, one or two periods of therapy may be sufficient to help their functioning. The therapist cannot always be sure that x months of therapy will be sufficient. He may feel that x months will be needed as a minimum to give therapy a chance, depending on what the patient wants and how ready he is to use the experience. An obsessional, constricted patient who is breaking up an important relationship but has earlier experienced much isolation and fear of people will need a longer period of therapy than an adolescent who has basically good relationships with caring parents and peers. Perhaps the adolescent is depressed because of reaction to rules at home and school. He may be a senior in high school, anticipating going off to college. For the adult in crisis, one might suggest something like six months to a year to see what unfolds in the course of therapy, whereas one might think in terms of three to six months, perhaps terminating at the time of graduation, for the adolescent. Any patient may turn out to have more serious underlying problems than one initially anticipated. One may need to reconsider and recommend more intensive or longer-term therapy.

For long-standing character problems for which the patient asks help, brief treatment will not be a treatment of choice. Borderline psychotic and psychotic patients are best viewed as needing long-term treatment, although because of circumstance they may often be seen briefly. This topic is further elaborated in Chapter 14.

A reasonably functioning adult with more serious problems than those which can be helped by brief therapy sometimes tries in a number of briefer therapies to tackle more available aspects of his problems and even may be helped. However, there may come a point when the therapist and he decide that brief treatment no longer makes sense for the kind of major change he wants. A current brief therapy may evolve into an exploration of why he should or why he does not seek intensive therapy or psychoanalysis. In this case, it might be a preparation for analysis.

BRIEF THERAPY BY CIRCUMSTANCE

Absolute time limits may be placed on therapy either by the patient or the therapist. In these cases it is really a matter of doing one's best in the time available, recognizing that a scaled-down set of expectations may be in order. A patient may anticipate a change in his life situation as the end point in therapy — a move, graduation from high school or college, or marriage. Money may not be available for more intensive therapy even though it is desirable. Therapists may be limited by administrative demands posed by the numbers of people applying for therapy at an institution. There may be a more or less defined limit to the period of therapy offered in order to try to accommodate as many as possible. Psychiatric residents or other therapists in training may have a limited time to spend in one program.

Suggested aims of brief therapy may be to help a patient explore and identify those problems which are hindering him or to communicate a way of thinking about his situation, which may be new to him. Another broad aim may be doing beginning exploratory work with him with the view that he may seek more prolonged or intensive therapy at a later time when his life is more established or when he can afford it. For some patients, having a termination date in mind from the beginning seems to speed the work of therapy. For others, there may be a sense of haste in trying to achieve too much in too short a time, not allowing sufficient time to integrate the experience. Integration of the experience will continue for months after the patient has stopped therapy. What a patient says about it during termination may not give the full picture. For example, one patient said during termination of once a week therapy for three months that characteristically it took her a long time to "percolate" any experience, and that it was impossible at that time to assess whether it would have any effect on her life.

Another patient, entering brief therapy for the second time in five years because she was experiencing anxieties about handling her children, said that her previous treatment with another therapist had made a tremendous impact on her life for the better. This had been limited to two months because she had moved away from the area. She had been able to free herself enough from domination by her parents at that time to get married. Although she still had many problems, she had made a reasonably good marriage, which had brought her happiness. Aspects of her early problems were beginning to show themselves again in raising her children, but she felt that without the earlier brief therapy she could not have progressed to this stage of development.

Thus, even if the problems of a patient seem all-pervasive, it may be well worth trying therapy in the brief time that patient and therapist have at their disposal. There will be patients who remain virtually untouched by the experience, but one hopes that the therapy was not seen as damaging or too threatening, permitting the patient to seek more intensive treatment at some future time.

HOW BRIEF THERAPY MAY HELP

The nature of the helping process of brief therapy is a complicated question. There are many opinions and few answers, in contrast to the clear theories that exist about how psychoanalysis effects its improvement. However, it is clear that brief treatment often does help. Described in this section are some of the potentially useful processes that can be observed.

From the patient's point of view, *ventilation* of the problem and the associated feelings, even on a seemingly superficial level, may be helpful. The therapist is likely to be more interested in the patient's feelings than are others in the patient's life. A patient who has been going around in circles about the intricate content of his problems may experience a freeing up of feelings in the presence of the therapist. A patient may find it easier to talk to the therapist about real or irrational worries — anger at a husband, shame engendered by parents, or anxieties about a child — than to talk to the people who are deeply involved in his situation. Living with them, he may be fearful of real abandonment or retaliation. Keeping the feelings contained may result in symptoms. Relieving the pressure of feelings through a safety valve, to a person removed from the situation, may help to deflate their intensity and resulting symptoms. With the feelings lessened in intensity, the patient may begin to examine how they came about and explore their irrational components. A nondirective climate in therapy similar to long-term therapy may help the patient to feel free enough to bring up discussion of forbidden wishes, fears, or fantasies and assess how these impinge on everyday relationships. Expressing them to a therapist who does not react in the assumed way, say with discouragement, may help a patient to understand that the thoughts are not unique or inherently "bad."

Clarification is another process which may occur in brief therapy, that is, clarification of the order of events leading up to a crisis. Many patients preface statements with, "I've never told anyone this before, and it may come out garbled." True, it may sound garbled, but the experience of having questions asked about the sequence and comments made about inconsistencies may help a patient mentally to restructure an event or an interaction. This may lessen a feeling of being out of control or being at the mercy of unseen forces. It may lower a patient's general level of anxiety. Clarification of feelings and their direction is helpful, as in any therapy. Sorting out the pros and cons of the meaning or worth of relationships while helping the patient to keep his own welfare in mind may facilitate decision making. It may mobilize his resources for making a decision or help him withstand pressures to make impulsive decisions.

The *encouragement of reflection* and the emphasis on thinking out actions is helpful and may be communicated in brief therapy. This can increase impulse control and suggest that a person's behavior, thoughts, and feelings are not based on unconnected accidents. In a general way, this can reduce anxiety and strengthen internal control. In other cases, where too much rumination is a problem, the therapist may help with examination of the patient's need for the resultant inhibition of action and indecisiveness.

Even in short-term therapy the therapist offers a *constant experience* under a set of fairly regular conditions. From hour to hour he is usually relatively consistent in whatever approach he uses. This promotes internal integration and communicates a sense of reliability which may bolster a patient's sense of internal cohesiveness. It may help his sense of trust in himself and others.

A patient can use, to a greater or lesser extent, the therapist's *interpretations* of his motivations, leading to insights that may make his behavior more understandable and tolerable to him even if there is not enough time for him to attempt and experiment with behavior change.

Support from the therapist may be helpful in many ways. Some therapists are very supportive while saying very little; others talk more. One can be supportive of a patient's autonomy by allowing him to struggle with all the pros and cons of a decision, having faith that the person will be able to reach a conclusion in his own time. If a proposed decision seems based mainly on urges of self-abnegation, then it may be supportive to point this out and help the patient think through alternative plans. Support can also mean a kind of comfort. One's agreement with a patient about his difficulties or an affective comment about his pain or anxiety, may be experienced as supportive comfort and interest in his welfare. Concrete support in the form of encouragement may be appropriate. At the same time, one should try to hear the patient's reactions to it.

One patient was hovering at the brink of acting on a career decision, having struggled with all the pros and cons and arrived at a conclusion. The therapist decided to encourage him, since he had complained bitterly that no adult had faith in him, and the therapist felt confident that he could take this step. At the same time he inquired about how the patient felt about the encouragement. The patient said that usually if anyone encouraged him, he would feel like "blowing the opportunity." They might expect too much or want something in return, or perhaps they did not understand the enormity of the step before him and its associated anxieties. The therapist asked how this applied to his comments. He said that though he had mixed feelings, he was surprised to find that he felt supported. The most supportive aspect, he said, was the therapist's interest in how he felt about the encouragement. Because he was sure of the therapist's interest, he felt less like missing the opportunity and could bask more freely in the warm feeling that the therapist must have some faith in him. The patient was able to take steps to further his career, and he began to talk more in therapy of his own lack of faith in his abilities and to reassess this in light of his recent better academic experiences.

Giving support is a complex issue, and the forms of support offered range from a concrete sharing of the therapist's opinion to more subtle forms of ego support, such as siding with a patient's adult resources or supporting his successful defenses.

Some therapists use *direct suggestion* in therapy, and others tend to avoid it. If a direct suggestion is made after one knows all the facts, and it is expressed in a discussable way, so that the patient feels free to criticize the therapist if it fails to work, then this may be helpful in brief therapy. For example, a troubled adolescent with difficult parents may need to move out of the house temporarily. If this is introduced as the therapist's suggestion, based on a belief that the parents are unable to modify their approach to him, then such a suggestion may prove helpful to a patient. If a patient is complaining of memory lapses and is taking a lot of drugs, one might suggest that he give up the practice, at least for a while, on the basis that drugs can cause physiological effects on the brain. A direct suggestion accompanied by good reasons, which are comprehensible to the patient, may be helpful. A direct suggestion given with no reasons will not be useful.

One patient reported that her therapist told her to "stop thinking" when she found herself going off into complex abstractions that troubled her. If he had explained more fully what he meant, the patient might have understood and been able to use the suggestion. But she experienced it solely as an impossible order that could not be questioned. One questions why the patient did not tell him of her bewilderment and why she did not feel that the "suggestion" was a discussable issue.

The therapist's stance in once a week therapy is often oriented toward *current life situations*. When there are frequent weekly sessions, there is more leisure to explore developments and themes on many levels. In once a week therapy, attention may have to be paid to working out ways of handling immediate events, particularly if the patient's life is in flux. The therapist may feel it necessary to interview other individuals in the patient's life, together with him. Some therapists keep the therapy in the context of exploration with the individual. If they see another member of the family, they may do so only once or twice with the emphasis on helping to clarify some issue with the patient or helping him to facilitate some process. The other persons will not be seen in ongoing, conjoined therapy, although they may be referred to another resource. For example, marital therapy with someone else may be recommended while continuing the present one-to-one treatment. Some therapists work in the broader context of a social or family structure. These modes will not be explored here.

While the therapist may find it useful to keep in close touch with the patient's daily life, and at a time of crisis may need to intervene at the patient's request, it is still possible to think from a psychoanalytic framework, along the lines suggested throughout this book. In other brief therapies, one's therapeutic stance will be little different from longer-term therapy.

Medication, if needed, can play a part in brief psychotherapy, as in longer therapy. The patient's feelings about receiving it and his feelings about his physical reactions are very important. Mild and major tranquilizers, sleep medication, and antidepressants are sometimes useful adjuncts to therapy. Some patients may use medications to maintain a connection with the therapist outside the hours, perhaps even to feel they are taking in part of the therapist. One such patient who complained about feeling empty and anxious, particularly when alone at night, found it useful to take a half tablet of a minor tranquilizer to help him sleep. The pharmacological effect was dubious, but the psychological effect was far more important. He disliked the idea of taking more medication because he was afraid of "being controlled" by the "powerful" therapist, and since his anxiety did not call for more medication, this feeling was respected by the therapist. It was therefore warranted for him to take the small amount at least till such time as he could work in therapy on his underlying longings. Some paranoid patients with serious disruptive anxiety who have a similar fantasy but who do medically need tranquilizers may agree to take them after discussion of their feelings and after hearing the therapist's explanation that they will not remove the anxiety but will take the edge off it enough for them to accomplish everyday tasks.

Antidepressants are used successfully by many therapists as an adjunct to therapy on the grounds that they may help to improve the mood of a patient and speed the process of therapy. This may be applicable to the situation in which the brief therapy is not by choice and one has reason to believe that the medication may help to relieve the emotional pain more quickly. Other therapists recommend medication only if the patient is in desperate straits. It seems to be a matter of individual judgment, according to the training and bias of the therapist and the pressure of the patient. At times it may be therapeutically advisable to choose not to prescribe medication for a patient who talks about being anxious but does not show objective signs. Even though he requests medication, he may be able to make better use of working through some feelings about pressuring the therapist to *do* something, perhaps to prove that he cares. Some patients can stand less deprivation in this area and may be sufficiently troubled in their external manifestations to justify medication.

GOALS OF BRIEF THERAPY

Most of the rest of the chapter focuses on setting of goals in brief therapy. Goal setting is in no way an absolute priority, because with many patients it seems indicated to feel one's way with a maximally flexible approach. If goal setting results in a rigid approach, then it is limited in its usefulness. It is offered here as a way of thinking about the different levels on which a patient may be talking and functioning. It is used to try to illustrate something of the process of brief psychotherapy and to address some of the inherent limitations as well as the helpful aspects of a brief therapy experience.

In an elective situation, or in an acute crisis with therapy continuing afterward, complex themes may unfold. These can be related to the situation that brought the patient into treatment, the underlying dynamics of that situation, and how these affect other areas of his life. A focus on goals therefore may include the therapist's awareness of what is going on at different levels within the individual. Primary attention may be paid to the goal the patient sets initially. The therapist also may set private goals. Either may have unrealistic expectations. Sometimes mutual discussion will help set limits on the problems to be approached. Other times the therapist's private goals may be close enough to the patient's stated goal to constitute agreement to work on the issue defined by the patient. The goals often tend to have a layered effect at least to the therapist. At the beginning of treatment the patient may ask for help touching on any layer of his difficulties.

Some patients have specific complaints, definite goals, and may have built-in expectations about how long the therapy will last. Other patients have diffuse difficulties, vague goals, and may approach therapy with no idea of how long they will wish to continue. The length projected may depend on the therapist's recommendation and mutual goal setting may or may not be useful depending on the patient. Yet others will anticipate a change in life circumstances that will carry an inherent time limit and this may naturally limit the goals. Examples of specific complaints are: "I can't do my work." "I am weak and depressed all the time." "I've had a tremendous fight with my boyfriend and I don't know what to do." "I can't do my work" may become elaborated quickly on many levels, such as in the example below.

EXAMPLE OF BRIEF THERAPY BY CHOICE

A sophomore college student had not turned in an assigned paper in organic chemistry on time, and the teacher had refused to give him an extension. The student had been doing well in literature courses but had started a short time before in a premedical program and found that he was unable to understand organic chemistry. In the first interview he asked only for help with the immediate problem of the overdue paper. He talked mainly of his anger at the teacher who would not give the extension. He was anxious, agitated, and angry. In the next session a few days later, the therapist asked if there were many students asking for a similar extension, and the patient moved to another level of discussion. It emerged that he was in the minority. It actually should have been an easy paper, and he was surprised to find that he seemed to have a study block about that particular course. The story further unfolded that the patient's father was an organic chemist and his mother a doctor of medicine. He had enjoyed literature but considered it "too sensitive and feminine" to pursue as a career. His parents wanted him to have a career in science or medicine, "the real professions." He was their oldest son. The younger son was set on a career in nuclear physics, which the patient felt pleased the parents. It was at that point of revelation that the therapist introduced the topic of the one-semester therapy that was offered at the clinic. The implicit question was, "How can we make the best use of the time available?" Or, "What goals might we have?"

The layers of the problem so far revealed were: (1) an acute problem regarding the late paper, (2) specific difficulty in organic chemistry, (3) authority issues with his teacher in the field, (4) career choice, (5) implied problems with his father, (6) probable ambivalent attempts to identify with both parents, and rivalry with his brother, (7) issues of his own autonomy and the struggle for independence. The multiplicity of these layers described for this boy in achieving independence involved other issues too. Later he mentioned his problem with girls; he felt a tendency to be passive or frightened with them. This might have opened up the vast area of sexuality for exploration. The setting of a reasonable goal with a patient will, of course, leave many stones unturned. The therapist privately aimed first at ameliorating the urgent situation. Later, he planned, if the patient moved toward further discussion, to work with whatever came up about independence issues, at least on the level of his choice of a career. The patient set his first goal, which was wanting help to get the paper done.

In the third hour the patient wanted the therapist to write a note of excuse for him. When the therapist took the more neutral line of inquiry, wanting to know how that could help, more information emerged about his fear of the teacher. The therapist chose to tell him that he did not want to write the note because he felt it would be more valuable to the patient to try to negotiate the extension himself. "Well then," the patient said, "I would have to let him know that I don't understand the material." The therapist responded, "Why would that be terrible?" The patient talked a great deal about his shame in exposing his lack of understanding in the course. When the therapist pressed further and asked about his fantasies about the worst thing the teacher could do to him, the patient laughed a little and said it sounded stupid when he said it out loud, but he thought that he was afraid that the teacher would tell his parents.

"And if that happened?" The parents would consider him a bumbling idiot and be furious, and might throw him out of the house. "They would really disown you?" asked the therapist. "They wouldn't really, but they would make life so difficult for me. They think that understanding science is the only important thing in the world." At that point the patient left the hour. The next day he talked to his teacher. Contrary to his expectations, the teacher was understanding and helped him pinpoint the area where he had ceased to understand the concepts and had become panicky. At the teacher's suggestion he arranged tutoring for himself in his organic chemistry. He completed the paper. He and the therapist then agreed on once a week therapy for the rest of the semester.

What was helpful to the patient in the section of treatment described? The therapist's initial goal was closely linked to the patient's situation of the moment. This in itself probably facilitated movement toward resolution. Ventilating and formulating his problem to the therapist, from whom he expected understanding and relief of his pain, probably helped to lower his anxiety and mobilize his resources. He felt that he would no longer be unsupported and alone. He may have seen the therapist as a benign man and therefore could separate him from the wish or fear that he would be like his more demanding father. The therapist was non-directive in letting the patient talk first of his anger toward his teacher. From this level, probably aided by the unintrusive approach, the patient himself moved to fear of the man, a more "forbidden" level for him. The less involved stance of encouraging the boy to talk to the teacher himself suggested to him that the therapist expected he could try it himself and did not need to have him collude in the regressive position of seeking protection. This was related to the larger theme of independence. Choosing subsequently to press the patient to think about what he was frightened of helped to focus the fear. This also often helps to make a fear more manageable, partly by bringing it up to a level where the person can assess it realistically. It does not explain the underlying fear. There were peripheral suggestions of powerlessness in the face of a fantasy of rejection by the parents and of castration anxiety. By concentrating on the fear alone, the therapist was facilitating the patient's ability to confront reality in a way he felt might be helpful. None of the concerns of the patient were brought to premature closure. In fact his ending remarks about the difficulties with his parents suggested his wish to explore the underlying issues.

There were many things about which the therapist had to remain ignorant. This choice has to do with the setting of goals. Other issues which could have been explored in more detail might have been his irrational perceptions that his teacher was aggressive and destroying. More work could have been done about his wish to hide behind the therapist for protection, what that meant to him in the transference relationship, leading perhaps to connected feelings about his mother. Further elaboration could have been encouraged about his fears of being abandoned, and his wish for this to come about. All of these were left implicit, due to lack of clarity about how much he wanted to explore and to the lack of time. Many many issues in brief therapy are not dealt with, nor are they heard in any semblance of exactitude.

The next phase of therapy with this young man also illustrates goal setting. He returned after the crisis abated and continued talking about his parents. He thus set up a new goal meshing with the therapist's goals. They agreed mutually that one-semester therapy was appropriate for him. Another patient might have wanted to stop at this point, fearful of approaching painful material. If this boy had wanted to stop after three or four sessions, on the grounds that he had received what he came for, this would have been all right, too. He showed that very little help was needed to steer him through a rough passage and that, despite his underlying difficulties, he had plenty of resources. The patient's implicit or explicit wish to continue is of maximal importance in the decision to go on with the work. Such a patient, had he stopped, might have been comforted to know that the therapist would be around and could be contacted if further problems arose. One can speculate that he might have had trouble with another paper or in anticipation of going home for the summer or in applying to medical schools or at a point in his life when he became more involved with girls.

In any case, a new goal was set. When the therapist contrasted for him his initial goal of just getting help with the paper with his present desire to continue, the patient said that the crisis had started him thinking more about his parents and whether it was really his own choice to be a premedical student. He wanted to talk more about his attitudes to them. This was his new goal. The middle phase of therapy was marked by efforts to retreat from topics involving his independent urges which he viewed as rebellious and feelings which he feared might anger and alienate his therapist, by periods of silence and passive-aggressive activity in which he wished the therapist would stop seeing him, confrontations in which he would accuse the therapist of controlling him and ordering his life when in fact the therapist was paying close attention to the patient's bearing his own responsibility for the discussions. Throughout this he talked of his mother and father, their control of him, his passive acquiescence and anger, their brilliance, his feeling of stupidity, his brother's "masculinity" and his own "femininity" and his fear of competition with his father, and his unsuccessful ways of handling these painful feelings. Very little was explored about his relationships with girls. However, toward the end of therapy he fell in love with a girl student and had intercourse for the first time, successfully. This involvement may have had to do with his fear of being abandoned once again and avoiding feelings of pain at the loss of his therapist. Balanced against this was more freedom in pursuing his wishes, the dawning of a new sense of autonomy, and a more experimental approach, appropriate to his stage in life. The therapy ended with the onset of summer vacation, during which he planned to discuss on a more equal basis his choice of career with his parents. He had not decided whether to pursue literature or continue in medicine. As his premedical grades improved, he began to wonder whether this indeed was his own best choice in spite of his parents' devotion to the notion of his being a doctor. He struggled in anticipation of his anger if his parents simply said, "Just as we thought," without appreciating that the decision involved much soul-searching and pain for him.

Thus this young man's goal of "talking more about his parents" was achieved. It meshed with the therapist's goal of exploring further his sense of autonomy. As a result of therapy, the patient was probably able to achieve a more solid independence. In therapy he had some live experience in transference of familiar feelings of helplessness and anger aroused by his parents. His actions and plans in the outside world showed hope of progress through this phase of his adolescence. No true "working through" of feelings was possible — it is not possible in brief psychotherapy. Glimpses of the sources of his problems were seen without full exploration, again impossible in brief psychotherapy. Many levels of development were touched upon, which presumably helped him begin to work through feelings at a level not visible in nonintensive therapy. The therapist has to be content in brief therapy with less "finished" work in the analytic sense, and this is where it becomes important to try to match one's goals closely to the patient's own sense of what he wants while taking into account the time available. In this example the brief treatment worked out well. At the end, the patient said if he had further problems at a future time in his life, he would seek therapy.

EXAMPLE OF BRIEF THERAPY BY CIRCUMSTANCE

A female graduate student came to the clinic in crisis at the breakup of her relationship with her boyfriend. A therapist had seen her several times during the acute aspects of the crisis, and she came now to a different therapist with the explicit knowledge that they could work for one semester in once a week therapy. In the crisis, which lasted for about two weeks, she wept a great deal, stayed away from people, wrote endless letters of remorse to her ex-boyfriend (which she tore up), ate very little, and slept a lot. She had talked to the first therapist about her anger and hurt, her feelings of worthlessness, and her sense of shame that her friends might despise her for not being able to keep this boyfriend. She felt he had left her for another, prettier, livelier girl, and she was scorned and enraged.

In the first session of regular therapy with a female therapist she briefly mentioned that she was going to terminate treatment at the vacation. The therapist accepted this, expected to hear more about the implications later, and kept an open mind about goals. They talked a little about her recent upset, and she said that since it was all over now, she did not want to talk any more about it. The therapist suggested that she might have feelings about changing therapists. She denied that this was important. She wanted to talk about school. She recited the details of the courses she was taking, and how hard it was for her to write papers, but that in general she found school satisfactory. She looked calm and talked in an orderly way, and though there was little feeling in anything she said, the therapist felt that might have to do with being emotionally drained after the recent upsurge. The therapist expected to hear more about her reaction to her recent rejection. The patient indicated she did not wish to be pressed, and the therapist decided not to. She always had the feeling that there must be a great deal going on within the girl and that sooner or later it would emerge.

The next hour she entered, curled herself comfortably in the chair, and said, "You know I haven't talked to anyone for years about my family and how it was at home in childhood." The following fifteen once a week meetings were all about her childhood, with scarcely an interruption from the therapist, who felt at times as if her presence were unnecessary, since the patient seemed to ignore any interpolations. The therapist wondered why she came every week, on time, and what she expected of therapy. She herself seemed perfectly contented. Once the therapist canceled an appointment, and she inquired about her reaction to this in the following hour. The inquiry was dismissed, and she continued her story.

The therapist was never bored in a single hour. The patient was a wonderful storyteller. Her session was in the afternoon. She settled back in her chair with the warm sun enveloping her, cigarette smoke blurring her edges so that she looked like an impressionist painting, and talked in a nostalgic way about the vast extended family on the West Coast and how each related to the other. She painted mental images of the beauty of the countryside, the sea, riding over horse trails, episodes with family dogs. Sometimes the stories were sad, sometimes humorous, sometimes tender. Often the overwhelming task of keeping track of the interrelationships of the extended family for several generations baffled the therapist, who was listening for themes and trying to weigh their implications for her life. She seemed to be speaking the first volume of her memoirs. She was very involved in the content and seemed to resent any intrusion. The therapist pointed this out, and she said "Well, yeah, maybe," and, unruffled, continued dreamily with some tales that seemed unconnected to anything the therapist had said, although she listened hard for displacements. The patient seemed to be talking as if the therapy relationship were timeless. Yet from the first sentence in therapy it was clear that the patient was aware of the clinic time limit. Once she mentioned that she rarely talked to anyone. This would have caused the therapist to be more active, except that she knew from the previous therapist that the patient went to school regularly and lived in the dormitory with two friends who knew her well and had brought her to the clinic in the first place.

Four sessions before the end, the therapist reminded her of the termination date, to which she replied, "Yeah, I know." Now, surely, there would be more themes of sadness, anger, loss, or the like at a displaced level from the therapist, or an upsurgence of her recent loss. None were obvious. The timeless pace continued. The last session she began talking as usual. One quarter into the hour the therapist noticed she was wearing a gleaming engagement ring. It was so obviously an engagement ring that the therapist interrupted her to ask about it. She blushed scarlet, smiled, paused for a long time and said, "Yes, I've been very, very happy — happier than I've ever been. I am deeply in love with my fiancé." They talked a little about him. He was not the original boyfriend but someone she had known several years before. Her whole life plan had changed. She was leaving school, had been accepted at another, and was leaving for the West Coast in two days. The therapist was most startled, congratulated her upon her engagement, and said, "How come you never mentioned it to me?" This was by now the closing minute of the last hour. "Yeah, . . .," she said slowly and with a bemused smile, "I guess in our big family, secrecy was the only way to maintain privacy!" She thanked the therapist, said she felt much better than when she started treatment, and left. She maintained her image of mystery.

This patient's explicitly formulated goal had to do with talking of the distant past. The therapist accepted this but expected to formulate other goals as she learned why the patient wanted to use the short-term therapy in this way. At the end, she was left with only speculation about why the patient wanted to do this. Perhaps having opened up at the time of her upset to the previous therapist, who "handed her on," proved to her that it was dangerous to get too close. Perhaps the therapy served a reintegrative function in getting over her loss of her previous boyfriend and preparing for marriage. Perhaps it was mourning for her seemingly idyllic, cloudless childhood as she approached a new phase of her life. Perhaps it was all resistance having to do with the need for secrecy, mentioned in her closing comments, lest her privacy be invaded and something of the current real-life experience be taken away. Perhaps it was all of these.

Had the therapist been more insistent about framing goals after the first few hours, as a way of keeping herself in the picture, she might have reached the area of importance of privacy earlier, and the tone of the therapy might have been different. But this might also have been less helpful for the patient, due to her presumably complex feelings about her privacy. Perhaps her need for secrecy to the point of exclusion of the other person pervaded her relationship with her fiancé. Had she been in longer-term treatment, there might have been, after the comment about privacy, more of a struggle and involvement with the therapist, revealing more about herself. She showed the therapist one aspect of the transference in the closing sentence — her inclusion somewhere in the patient's large family. Perhaps the therapist was behaving in timeless fashion too, and colluded too much in the patient's need to keep the therapist tantalizingly at the periphery of her poetic imagery. On the other hand, a great deal of movement had taken place in her life. She was not painfully "stuck" in her growth after the breakup, and she seemed very happy with her new relationship and the anticipated move back to the west. She seemed satisfied with seeing the therapist. The reasons for her improvement must remain puzzling and intriguing.

THE VAGUE PATIENT

The layering of goals and how the establishment or nonestablishment of mutual goals affects the shape of the work attempted in brief therapy have been mentioned. The patient who has a very vague idea about why he wishes to be in treatment may present a problem. Helping make his reasons more specific may be a legitimate goal of the entire therapy time. The patient may come in talking of all kinds of issues, with no overriding reason for being in therapy except that he feels it "is a good thing." One may spend the time in a stance of inquiring and exploration, following him down every avenue of his life he cares to bring into discussion, wondering whether and how these things relate to why he feels he needs help. In some instances one may decide with him after a few sessions that he does not need therapy, if one feels that his life is proceeding fairly smoothly and there is little evidence of pain. In other cases the therapist may begin to understand more clearly only when a strong enough relationship develops and the patient begins to demonstrate problems in transference. The goal of determining the complaint may then be resolved, permitting a further set of goals to be defined.

UNREALISTIC GOALS

Unrealistic goals may be conveyed by a patient overtly or covertly. A senior in his last semester of college came to therapy saying he wanted to change his homosexual orientation before graduation. Discussion of this led the therapist to feel that this was the patient's "passport" to therapy. It was a very real conflict, but it turned out, when the therapist explained that the goal was unrealistic, that the patient already knew that resolution was impossible in the fifteen or so sessions probably available. The therapist detected anxiety about other topics that were more urgent — fear of leaving college, a forthcoming unstructured trip to Europe for an indefinite time, chronic difficulty in making commitments, worries about his parents, and choice of a future career. The therapist suggested that these topics seemed important to discuss. The patient agreed that these topics were most important, and began to reflect on why he always "blamed" homosexuality for all his problems. He continued to talk of his homosexuality but as a less central current factor than his other anxieties.

A more covert way of presenting unrealistic goals, which is sometimes unwittingly supported by therapists, is giving primary importance to dream material in short-term therapy. Dreams or aspects of them can be very useful in furthering understanding, but giving them continuous priority in once a week therapy may convey an expectation to the patient that the therapist can work with them in the same way an analyst can. There is simply not enough time to hear all their associations nor is there the opportunity to know many of the complexities of the patient's life or have the kind of developed therapeutic relationship which allow the patient and the therapist to do justice to his dreams. Too often it ends up with snap interpretations that promote closure of topics. If the patient insists on talking about dreams every hour, perhaps the therapist should ask himself, for example, whether the patient feels he is boring the therapist and wants to titillate his interest. Perhaps the patient has misconceived how the therapist can be expected to help him within the time limit. It may be a form of resistance, and he may be omitting

more troublesome issues in his current life situation. He may be
trying to be "a good patient."

CONTENT COMMENTS

When the mutual goals are either established or implied, and a
therapeutic alliance has developed, some interpretive work can be
accomplished during the hours. A few aspects of this subject are
mentioned here because sometimes an attempt to set goals is connected with a sense of haste to try to achieve them. The therapist
may be surprised how much a particular patient can achieve in a
short time. At other times the goals decided upon may have to be
scaled down as therapist and patient become acquainted with the
depth and complexity of the problem.

Not all the feelings connected with interpretations can be explored
in once a week therapy, but for some patients, reworking may go on
at a preconscious or unconscious level. If the timing is right, and the
words of the interpretation happen to be on the right level of understanding for the patient at the moment, the patient may be able to
explore further, as in long-term therapy. He may experience a reduction of anxiety and a sense of internal relief. At other times one
may sense that he is almost on "the right level," but either the patient is not prepared to hear it, or one's understanding of the patient
is not sufficient to balance the feeling, content, or timing of his
remark so that the patient recognizes the connection. More work
may have to be done on the vicissitudes of resistance, more work
on either side of the conflict, or more work on transference issues
before it is at all meaningful.

Two illustrations follow. In the first example the feeling connection works well even though not all aspects have been explored.
It is akin to a trial interpretation as described in Chapter 6. The
second example demonstrates how a therapist's "psychologically
informed comment" (Chapter 6) initially did not work well, and it
emphasizes the importance of not rushing with that particular patient in the exploration, in spite of the time limit.

(1) A 25-year-old, unmarried woman was in grief, six months following her sister's fatal car accident. The most acute phase of her grief was over, and she had begun to see a therapist four months after the accident, complaining of weeping spells. The goal of therapy for both patient and therapist was to help the grief work. The most recent crying spell occurred in the therapist's office when she started to describe the activity of children in the playground on her way to her weekly session. She began to cry uncontrollably, and burying her head in her hands, she sobbed bitterly. The therapist sat quietly. After fifteen minutes he ventured to ask whether there was any way for her to try to tell him what was on her mind while she was weeping. Gradually she sobbed, "I'll never see her again. I'll just never see her again." Between tears she hesitated, saying, "I'm getting the idea that it was my fault. It *feels* very strong that it was my fault." After more intense sobbing and a further, unhurried lapse of time, the therapist, who had previously heard some episodes about their childhood together, said, "I wonder if there is a connection between that time you hit your sister in the eye with a stone in the playground and thought you had killed her?" Her sobs grew less, "I really thought I killed her when I was seven, didn't I? – This time there was no stone. I didn't – have – anything – to – do – with – her death." She stopped crying, and said slowly and with gradual relief, "I *didn't* kill my sister!" This was by no means the end of the patient's grief, but the issue of her guilt was strongly brought to the surface and was interpreted. All the details were far from elaborated at the time, such as any early fantasies of angry thoughts killing people. This episode must have been a central representation of many others, conscious and unconscious, one of which was touched upon by the interpretation, given to the patient at the right level of awareness at the right time, and within the context of the bond between the therapist and the patient. In continuing to talk of her grief till she terminated therapy, she felt that this was a most useful hour in showing her the path of connection between past and present and its potential relief. She felt much better after four months of once a week treatment.

(2) A 29-year-old woman patient came to therapy saying she wanted to find out why she was tense all the time. She wanted to talk over the pros and cons of getting a divorce from her husband. This was her goal, and the therapist agreed to explore the issues. She had described in detail the bind in which she was caught in even thinking about divorce and the recurrent childlike helplessness she felt in the face of her husband's criticisms. He often criticized her for having no opinion, but as soon as she voiced an autonomous idea he jumped on her for being too aggressive. She felt most comfortable if she pleased him, but in her predicament this was impossible; she did not even know whether she wanted to continue doing that. Her father had constantly deprecated her. While her mother outwardly appeared supportive of her, the only way to "please" mother was to be totally submissive. Giving way to mother's domination resulted in affection and being told she was a wonderful child. In that household, though her father seemed so tough and implacable, her mother had arranged a situation where he would appear strong while covertly she dominated the family. In marrying her husband the patient had mainly sought her mother's

approval by bending to her demands. Her husband, however, turned out to be unloving toward her. He was too much like her mother in seeking passivity from her, but did not give her even those rewards she had gained from her mother. He was also like her father in deprecating everything she said. Between mother, father, and husband, the only "love" came from mother, tenuous as it was. The patient talked a lot about how her mother had been "too good" to her; she had been denied nothing material in growing up.

The therapist had reason to believe that the elements of the transference observed were from the mother and that the patient was anxious to please the therapist. One session the patient finished by saying, "So my mother was too good to us. Don't you agree?" The therapist said, "Yes, she was too good." The next hour the patient came in saying she had told her husband that the therapist said her mother was "too good." "You are wrong — she was a domineering bitch!" said her husband forcefully, whereupon the patient regressed into a tearful, confused state. "Who am I to believe?" she asked the therapist.

The level that the therapist was responding to was agreement that mother was "too good" in the sense of smothering, overprotecting, and providing the patient's physical needs long past adolescence in order to keep her dependent. The patient was feeling and expressing only one side of the ambivalence, the love; her husband expressed the other side. The confusion in the patient was caused by sharply divided loyalties between therapist and husband, which caused the conflict, upsurge of helplessness, and a feeling that she herself had no opinion. The basic paradigm was probably a familiar situation of being torn between the opinions of mother and father, trying to please both. The closest emotional level to her awareness was the division of loyalties in the here-and-now between therapist and husband. This was the most hopeful area for clarification and subsequent interpretation of the connection between her present bind and the old bind between her and her parents.

An alternative and less hasty way of responding to the issue about the mother would have been to question the patient's asking, "Don't you agree?" How come the patient needed the therapist to agree? Then the therapist could have clarified what issue was being agreed upon. It suggested that much more work was needed on the topic of the patient's need for approval, starting with the therapist, and how she may be setting up the therapist and husband in conflict, before any interpretive work on the patient's relationship with her mother could be approached.

Work on the patient's feelings about criticism or approval and the perils of having her own opinion could not be separated from the goal of discussing the marriage and whether she wished to maintain it. The therapist therefore could not force the pace beyond the patient's current level of understanding. No harm was done by the comment, and it was used to further the work in the same way as one might use the transference reactions in longer-term therapy. This patient opted for long-term therapy after about three months of brief therapy in the knowledge that the problems underlying her initial complaint could best be helped in longer therapy.

TERMINATION

The goals that patient and therapist have set up come into the foreground in termination of treatment. There may be pleasure that they have been accomplished. There may be frustration because they are far from being achieved. The patient may want to continue till he reaches his goal. He may have a feeling of incompletion and may be very frustrated in coming to terms with the reality of the end point.

Some patients start a brief therapy feeling they have some simple problem that can be sorted out in a few sessions. They may be amazed during the exploration that the issues are not as simple as they seemed at the beginning. Perhaps the initial problem is solved but new conflicts come to light as a result of the therapy. Other patients may feel they have a new grasp on the present situation, which benefits them now and might help in future experiences. They may not contemplate therapy again in the near future but would return if the need arose. Some may want to be in psychoanalysis. Some patients leave feeling that the experience has been very painful, particularly those who have great difficulty in forming relationships, for whom therapy may have given promise of a closer relationship than they had thought possible. The feelings may be very intense. The brevity of the therapy does not necessarily mean there is dilution of feelings. There are all sorts of ways to conclude the experience, each demonstrating aspects of the patient's dynamics.

Thinking about the implications of goals can be an aid to understanding in brief psychotherapy for both patient and therapist. In less intensive therapy, when it is impossible for the patient to share his thoughts fully with the therapist, thinking about goals can suggest orderly ways of approaching the patient while maintaining the exploratory model of therapy.

12

Deciding about the Suicidal Outpatient

In the second supervisory hour of a therapist's psychiatric training he told his supervisor about a patient who was threatening suicide. This was an 18-year-old woman, clearly disturbed. Her closing remarks to him were, "Well, see you next week," to which she added darkly, "if I make it." The new therapist was extremely worried about this. There was no time to clarify what she meant. He was new. He was aware that the hour should be kept to fifty minutes. He had made other assessments of the patient to support his judgment that she not be hospitalized immediately, but he still felt very worried. Would she never come back? Would she commit suicide? Had he discharged his responsibility toward her? Would her death cloud his entry into his career almost before he had begun? Would he be letting down his colleagues? After examining the whole story in detail and agreeing that no immediate action should be taken, the supervisor said, "You know, we cannot assume responsibility for a patient's actions outside the therapy hours. We can try to be as thoughtful and responsible as possible about considering whether a patient needs to be in the hospital. We can try to be receptive to their feelings, and try to understand the irrationalities, but we cannot help everybody. There are people who will commit suicide despite the best efforts of the most gifted therapists."

Now it is important not to leap immediately to this position. In no way is it meant to undermine a careful judgment about whether or not to hospitalize a patient. But having exercised every faculty one has, if he decides to take a risk treatment on an outpatient basis, the therapist must face the fact that the patient is ultimately responsible for his own behavior.

Suicide is probably the most guilt-inducing form of death. It can be regarded as an unspoken massive accusation to the world of people around the patient. Friends of patients who commit suicide talk of the guilt and anger that the act mobilizes, as well as the feelings of loss. It touches the quick of the preformed guilt burden of any human being, who interprets the act according to his own psychodynamics.

No one knows the mind of the person at the moment in which he suicides. Those who have planned the act with every indication of serious intent, and who have been found and resuscitated, talk of a detached, cold moment when they are beyond reach, when no other human being matters. Psychotic patients have been inundated with voices telling them, "Kill yourself! You've nothing to lose. You're a drain on humanity." Or they may carry out blasphemous orders to wipe themselves out. The internal stimulation is so intense that the outside world ceases to exist. Absolute loss of contact with the world and reality, coupled with the self-destructive force of the patient's internal dynamics, seems necessary before a person can achieve death by suicide.

It is primarily in the former area, that is, contact with the world, that the therapist can harbor more hope at the moment in which a patient threatens suicide. If the patient has been in psychotherapy, one may use knowledge of him to try to help with interpretive comments, either about the therapeutic relationship or his life. Tranquilizer drugs, administered in a carefully controlled way, may be a helpful adjunct in the continuation of therapy.

In the following discussion, the suicidal patient is approached via a continuum of increasing contact with the therapist: (1) a patient one has never seen, (2) a patient presenting in the emergency room, (3) a patient in ongoing psychotherapy.

THE UNSEEN PATIENT

A person may telephone a clinic or a therapist out of the telephone directory, saying he is feeling suicidal. It makes most sense to persuade him to go to the nearest hospital emergency room and either meet him there or arrange for someone else to receive him. It is too difficult to assess the situation by telephone; one needs a fuller picture of the person in his distress. If he refuses, he may give his number or address. Having been contacted one may tell the patient that he will inform the police, who will come to his aid. If he gives no address and calls from a pay phone, then there is nothing to be done. One may sound as available as possible and describe the emergency services available, hoping he will use the information. One may point out that since he had the wish to telephone and contact someone, he must have a grain of hope left and that he may be able to act on it.

THE EMERGENCY-ROOM PATIENT

The medical needs of a person who has attempted suicide take priority and will often be attended to by personnel other than the psychotherapist on call. If the patient has taken an overdose of medication and is still conscious, the therapist might help the intern in charge of the medical aspects in finding out the type and quantity of medication. Peripheral evidence may be forthcoming from relatives. Where did the drugs come from? If they were prescribed by another doctor or psychiatrist, then phoning him may add important information to the confused scene. Talking with the patient's primary therapist will guide in making the diagnosis, determining the likely situation at hand, and making future plans.

If all this has been investigated, and the therapist sees a new patient who has just regained consciousness, had his stomach pumped, or has his sutures in place, the first thing is to hear what is on his mind. If this is physical discomfort, and if there are any simple human things the therapist can do, such as helping him find a more comfortable position in bed, then this is the level at which to begin the relationship. Later he may tell the therapist what happened.

In assessing the suicidal intent, the mode and timing of the attempt may suggest the degree of desperation within the patient. There may be great care taken to plan the action for a time when no one is expected to be near the scene. This may indicate a high degree of seriousness whatever the actual method employed. Some patients both plan carefully and use highly dangerous means. One business executive phoned all his clients to terminate arrangements with them, saying he was going out of business during the month before his very grave attempt. Patients who gas themselves often spend considerable time and effort insuring that no gas leaks from the room, and lay down comfortable pillows for themselves before turning on the gas.

The method used sometimes helps in assessment, and it may or may not be independent of the degree of planning. A young woman who has had a fight with her boyfriend and takes five or six aspirins or mild tranquilizers in front of him may be less in need of hospitalization than a middle-aged widower who has tried to shoot himself while alone. Decisive methods, such as shooting through the roof of the mouth or the ear, slitting the throat, or hanging, indicate deadly serious intent. Bizarre attempts at self-destruction, such as elaborate devices for electrocution, shooting off genitals, or setting the clothes on fire, may indicate overt psychosis preceding the event. Many suicide attempts will be somewhere between the extremes. They may, for example, involve a greater or lesser degree of overdose of drugs, with a greater or lesser degree of knowledge about their effects; or they may involve slashing the wrists in minor or severe degree. In these cases there may be more room to ponder whether one may risk discharging the patient to outpatient treatment or should admit him to a hospital.

When a patient is able to talk to the therapist, he may relate some direct precipitating incident: "I've just had a fight with my wife." "My girlfriend just left." "I've just discovered that I'm pregnant." If the focus is on an interpersonal issue, then the therapist may see if the other involved persons are available. After seeing the patient, he may wish to see them together to see if any resolution is taking place in the crisis between them. In other words, one's job is to try to assess what the suicidal gesture is about and then assess what effect it has had on the patient and his surroundings. If the effect on the crisis is "successful," then it may be possible to consider letting the patient return to his own environment.

Followup is of course essential, since the resolution may be subject to such unpredictable forces. Therapy should be encouraged, since the patient has shown such a maladaptive way of coping with his strong emotions — rage, hurt, fear, sadness. The attempt itself may have the short-term payoff of reuniting a couple or gaining a husband's apology, but the style of reacting says something about the patient's psychic vulnerability.

With some patients the intervention of doctors, nurses, and the therapist may be of primary importance. The middle-aged, depressed divorcée who takes an overdose of drugs may say, "I thought that nobody cared." For her, even a brief regressive experience in the emergency room, with professional people in white coats attending to her bodily needs and a therapist interested in her life situation, may be enough to buoy up her hopes in life again. If the therapist feels he has developed a rapport and alliance with her, he may feel it is "safe" for her to return to her environment, knowing that she can get in touch with him easily. She should leave with his telephone number and a definite outpatient appointment in her handbag. It may even be possible to arrange for her to stay with a neighbor for a couple of nights.

A patient may either be drunk on alcohol or high on psychedelic drugs when he makes a suicide attempt. This desperate move may make one aware of the depth of his underlying depression. If this is a first time, one may assess whether the alcohol so loosened his usual controls that he was prompted to act on impulse, whereas in a sober state he would not have carried out the deed. One may keep him in the emergency room till the effect of the alcohol has worn off, to examine his mental state. If he acknowledges his depression or difficult life circumstances at that time, and an alliance is developed with him on how to seek help, one may decide to let him become an outpatient. If, however, he denies any problem in his sober state, and views the attempt as some weird, inexplicable accident, the therapist may be very cautious and decide to hospitalize him even briefly for a period of observation. The hospitalization is really based on the patient's inability to reveal more about himself. The therapist is left wondering whether he will repeat the incident, since neither he nor the patient has gained further knowledge about the gesture.

A patient under the influence of psychedelic drugs may become very disorganized and make a very serious suicide attempt. Even when the effect of the drug has worn off it may be advisable to hospitalize such a patient, because the therapist will not know exactly how long this temporary psychosis will last. Also, the patient may have an underlying psychosis complicating the drug-induced state. This will have to be carefully weighed before returning the patient to his environment. A boy in his senior year in college, approaching final examinations, walked out of the window of his dormitory because he suddenly felt he could fly, was an angel, and wanted to be with God. After several days as an inpatient the massive fear and acute delusional manifestations disappeared, but the picture that was left was of a lonely, isolated boy, terrified about his imminent graduation and the fact that he would soon be turned loose in the outside world. He had had a "bad trip," with images of his father as a demon about to castrate him, and an Easter Island sculpture mother figure to which he wept and clung on a lonely beach. The demon (professor father) was going to make him fail, and the sculpture (mother university) was turning her back on his plight. These had prototypes in his family experience. In mentally reorganizing the recent trauma of his "trip" and talking about his years of school, he needed time for elaboration of his fantasies and his life before being readmitted to his college environment with twice a week therapy by a therapist who became acquainted with him during his brief hospitalization.

In the above instances of hospitalization the therapist could not know enough about the patient without more time for consideration. The suicidal message was reasonably clear. In addition the patient's physical state or acute drug effects on his brain were further reasons for recommending inpatient observation. The message is not always so clear.

A patient may be silent about his reasons for such a suicide act, and therefore no guarantee can be given that it will not occur again, successfully. If he protests and refuses to negotiate, he perhaps should be *committed to a psychiatric institution*. It is sometimes possible to avoid this step if one shares his bewilderment with the patient and his concern for his repeating the act. One may interpret to him that his inability to let anyone know anything about himself probably has led him to being very isolated with his problem. His action indicates that he needs help and that he needs to be hospitalized. Presented in such a way, a patient may nod in agreement and passive acceptance of someone else taking over the decision for him. When possible, it is better to avoid committing a patient. In many cases it is unavoidable and offers the best help for the person. The assaultive aspect of a commitment warrants consideration. A patient may have an ambivalent wish to be overwhelmed in such a way, but it will be accompanied by a great deal of fear. If he is paranoid, and terrified that he will be killed or brutalized in a mental hospital, some direct discussion of the matter — the setting, the wards, the staff, the other patients, etc. — may be helpful in allaying his anxieties temporarily, although after admission he may readily feel that he was deceived into agreement. The therapist who commits the patient is invariably the target for the patient's hostility. The patient may need a target on whom to focus his fury outside himself; this temporarily relieves him of the burden and his internal rage. Commitment undermines all his responsibility for himself and his actions. It may feed the fantasy that an all-powerful vengeful God is in control. The patient may seek the humiliation in commitment because it divests him of his usual social rights. This primitive "punishment" may temporarily alleviate his guilt. All of these feelings are so ambivalent that they may go in either direction. One can try taking up with the patient both the wish and the fear of being overwhelmed, for example, "You are acting as if you wish it, but I think it may be very frightening for you also." He may respond by talking of the fears and reassess whether or not he wants to go to a hospital in such a fashion.

A patient may wish to punish others by his commitment. "See what degradation and despair you have driven me to?" may be the

implied message. Again, interpretation of his anger toward significant others may help him to become more reasonable and ultimately
to see hospitalization as something of value for *himself*, as a place
where such painful issues can be talked about while he has 24-hour
protection against his self-destructive urges. Commitment and
hospitalization may be a way of a patient seeking control from the
outside, needed because he feels so chaotic inside. To talk about
this, and his fear of his internal disorganization, may lead the patient to be more cooperative and more secure knowing that someone outside him recognizes his need for controls to be put on him.
One can present hospitalization itself and drug treatment in the light
of helping controls. Another purpose in avoiding commitment unless it becomes absolutely necessary is that this lays a better basis for
the therapeutic endeavor once the patient is hospitalized. It may be
very difficult to establish rapport with a patient who has been committed.

There are some patients whom one must commit to hospital
against their will, for their own protection. Preserving the life of
the patient takes priority over any of the negative aspects of commitment. It may be a situation that the patient needs to force at a
particular time.

THE SUICIDAL THERAPY PATIENT

Threats during Evaluation

What about the patient who makes suicidal threats, direct or
veiled, in the outpatient setting during evaluation? This point in
treatment is chosen because the issue of alliance may be problematic.
The patient barely knows the therapist, and little is known about the
patient as yet. How can one decide whether it is "safe" to let the
patient wait till the next appointment, and what internal and external measures can the therapist take to ease his anxiety? Many
patients who have suicidal ideas are not patients in hospitals, and
the decision when or whether to hospitalize the person can be a difficult issue.

The patient may talk directly about suicidal ideas. One can try to assess what distance he has from them. Are they fantasies? What degree of care in planning is present? How long have the ideas been present? How has he handled such ideas in the past? Has he made previous suicidal gestures? Have individuals in his family committed suicide (this immediately puts the patient in a high-risk category)? Is he an isolated, single, middle-aged man (another recognized high-risk category)? Is the present situation a repetition of a past feeling situation? Toward whom are these feelings directed? Does he talk about the future, or is reference to the future ominously absent?

A patient who says, "Many a time I have felt like killing myself," may be very different from a patient who says, "I am going to kill myself. There is no other way." To have *felt* like killing himself occurs frequently in the despondent, depressed patient. This feeling may occur in a patient who is in remission from psychosis and is fearful about what the future may hold in terms of recurrence or in a patient with a high degree of diffuse anxiety. He may have plans, such as knowing he could get medication for the purpose if the need arose. This is less definite than if he keeps a supply of drugs in the house as a "safety blanket," or a gun or knives. If the therapist knows of the existence of such concrete aids, he should try to persuade the patient either to get rid of them or to hand them over to him for safe keeping till he feels better.

This will often revolve around an issue of trust. The mere confession of such a plan may represent a step toward trusting the therapist with an important piece of information that the patient may feel could be "abused." It may be delicate information. Is the patient asking for help in control? The therapist might present it in such a way and explicitly ally himself with the part of the patient that does not want to kill himself. If the therapist acts to take away this prop for the patient, he may consider what he is giving in return. His ready availability at a time of need when the patient feels very upset is something he can offer. If the patient can accept this, it may be a firm step in the direction of trust. The therapist should be prepared to be available and not abuse the delicate budding of trust in the patient.

The therapist may be in conflict about how much to be available, or how therapeutic mere availability is. Such times of desperate need may be regarded as analogous to a baby needing breast feeding — one can decide to wean the patient at a later time. It is safer to try to establish a pattern of getting in touch with the therapist initially. The patient will test this to see if a foundation for trust exists. If after a time in therapy, when some trust is established and more complex issues of trust are being worked through, the patient persists in phoning the therapist late at night or trying to take him from another hour with another patient, then the situation may be interpreted to him: along the lines he seems to want almost to be *in* the therapist's family or he wants the therapist's exclusive attention and is envious of other patients.

Negotiation about gradually helping the patient to tolerate some of the feelings by himself and contain them to scheduled therapy hours may be problematic. The patient's response will often be to move to his initial position, "Nobody wants me. You clearly don't care about me." If he has had some basis for knowing his therapist does care (his method of handling the referral, his attention and interest during the hours, his regular appearance, attention to what the patient feels vis-à-vis himself), then it is worthwhile to try confining the patient's phone calls to definite hours when the therapist knows he is not engaged or giving him an extra hour or half hour a week for a period. These are concrete ways of weaning the patient from frequent, unregulated contact. The therapist should not expect that the patient will show a steady progress in this direction; it may be more stepwise. A baby, too, is weaned gradually, and along the way there will be lapses due to both the baby and the mother. A patient and therapist may feel during a lapse that all is lost, that nothing has been achieved. The therapist may have some hope restored if he reviews his past experience with the patient; this may tell him of resources the patient possesses, even though they seem inaccessible to the patient in his period of lapse. This may give the therapist internal courage to continue the thorny road.

In initial interviews with a patient who talks of suicide, having established how deeply entrenched the idea is at the moment, one may hear whether such ideas existed in the past and make an effort privately to determine if there is something different about the present which makes it more or less ominous. If the patient now lives alone and is more isolated, the situation may be more anxiety provoking. One may know that he has a roommate or spouse, and may have a notion of how available he is when the patient is in trouble. This may provide grounds for feeling the patient is less of a risk to himself. His verbal description may be enough; or one may wish to invite the patient to bring in the other person for a three-way meeting to discuss ways of helping the patient when he is so upset. The other person may have an opportunity to express his fears of helplessness and may feel supported and more at ease knowing he does not bear the responsibility in a vacuum. This in turn may aid the helper's own resources and may comfort the patient. Feelings of anger and helplessness may come to the fore. There may be over-tones that the patient is "bad," the assumption being that he is con-sciously trying to provoke the other person. The symbolic act of the therapist being involved may be enough to define the patient as "needing help" as opposed to "being bad" and thus ameliorate the pressure. Better the patient be defined as such and deserving of help, initially, than be in the vicious circle of provoking such annoyance in the people surround-ing him that the very way in which he demands help be stymied by the anger in his environment.

It will be appropriate to point out to him at another time that his ways of seeking help evoke reactions in his world that mitigate against his finding it, and to explore with him other ways to ask for help that may be less ambivalently presented. Often before this dis-cussion can lead to more adaptive responses on the part of the patient, the situation has to arise with the therapist himself, producing a live effect. The demands may make the therapist feel angry and drained — a powerful indicator to the therapist of the effect that the patient is having on others in the environment — and some discussion of the patient's need to do this with the therapist may be enlightening. It may be a good experience for the patient to know that his efforts to provoke are discussable, and that the feelings do not lead to abandon-ment of him as they may have with his parents or others.

If the therapist is feeling so furious that his gut reaction is wanting to be rid of the patient, it suggests that he may collude with the pa-tient's unspoken desire to be "thrown out." Full discussion with a supervisor may help to keep the situation in perspective. In other words, the patient's provocation may become the central issue in the therapy rather than the therapist's anger. Many therapists do not discuss their strong feelings with the patient because this may place a further, unnecessary burden on the patient and detract from the central focus of the patient's conflicts, needs, wishes, and longings. In this model the therapist's feelings are utilized as indicators. Some therapists do choose to share their strong feelings, and if executed with delicate timing, this might lead to an internal feeling of confidence in the patient that in spite of heightened emotions on both sides both patient and therapist can survive and the feelings can be discussed.

If one works in a clinic setting with a very needy patient, discussion with both patient and one's colleagues on call may be helpful in handling the patient's crises. The patient may have questions about confidentiality and anger that the therapist is not always available but in general the therapist's thoughtful care wins out and is communicated to him. Dealings with others in the clinic besides the primary therapist may also help a very needy patient in the development of a "clinic transference" in addition to the individual transference. At some level it is reassuring to find that other people besides the therapist can care for him and that more than one person in the world can be trusted; for example, the yearly changeover of psychiatric residents may be of significance if the patient needs more than one year of treatment and will attend the same institution. Contact with other clinic staff may also help, if he needs to phone the clinic at night. He may be able to trust a little more someone who is covering duty for the therapist, and thus help in weaning the patient from the initial exclusive dependency position.

Threats Early in Therapy

In *the beginning hours of therapy* a patient may make covert threats about taking his life. If the therapist suspects this is really what the patient is talking about, he may try to make the implicit explicit. This step conveys the therapeutic stance of trying not to collude with the patient. It lets the patient know that if another human being is to understand him, he cannot expect the other person magically to know what is on his mind. It allows the therapist himself to exercise his judgment on how immediately concerned he ought to be and whether to consider hospitalization; it may also alleviate the therapist's inevitable anxiety. Thus a patient may comment on the windows in the therapist's office, check how many floors there are beneath him, or talk tantalizingly about his hobby of collecting guns. Coupled with other signs of distress in the patient, or with absent or bland affect, the therapist may experience a rising anxiety within himself which he may use as a signal of danger. Drawing the patient's attention to his comments about these life-threatening objects juxtaposed with his distress, or apparent lack of external disturbance, may be enough stimulus for the patient to make his thoughts more open. A direct question about thoughts of harming himself may be necessary in addition. He may say, "Yes, I've thought about it for years. I always check to see if I have a way out in any new situation. The thoughts have been more urgent in the past, but I wouldn't have the guts to do it right now." This issue may then be turned into his feeling of desperation in seeking treatment or his trapped feelings about making a commitment to see the therapist. One may wish to hear a great deal about the times when he felt tempted to suicide. Exploration of these issues would, at least for the present, decrease the therapist's anxiety as he sets about seeing the patient as an outpatient.

At the other end of the scale a patient might respond with "Yes, I am thinking of killing myself," and perhaps expand on the fact that it is the anniversary of the death of his brother who committed suicide. Then the therapist may become more anxious. He may mentally scale the future of this patient down to a day-to-day business of keeping track of his state of turmoil. He may decide that frequent contact with the patient is necessary. He might tell the patient that he realizes he is extremely depressed, and that at such an anniversary it is not surprising he should feel particularly hopeless. He might ask the patient what he feels about taking responsibility for his own safety when both of them know that it is a severe risk; or he might discuss with him the pros and cons of 24-hour care.

The *discussion of hospitalization* with the patient has many facets.

First of all, it is mutual recognition that the patient is extremely troubled and may need more care than can be provided him as an outpatient. Sometimes a patient will experience relief that this is an available option. In one case the patient said he was both shocked and comforted at the recognition that he was so desperate. His mother had thrown him out of the house cruelly, saying, "Don't come back till you are happy." In the family it was tantamount to the most terrible sin to be troubled. A great deal of joking went on if any family member was not eternally smiling and "happy," thus giving the patient the feeling that no one could take an expression of desperation seriously. He had to come to terms with the severity of his problems before he could make a commitment to therapy. Another patient felt she had been forced to keep up a front for so long that the strain of "holding together" was too much to bear, and the relief of even thinking of the hospital and contemplating an environment in which she could act as crazy as she felt inside was very tempting. Ultimately she was admitted to a hospital, but not in the initial therapy. The early discussions helped her to come to terms with the need for hospitalization, as she and the therapist talked about what she might expect in a particular hospital, and narrowed down the choice to one particular ward. Thus even at the time of hospitalization, she felt she was in some part responsible for the choice and wished for it to come about. Discussion of plans for hospitalization may help the patient maintain some self-respect. At a time when it becomes necessary, it is not experienced as an assaultive shock, completely removing his autonomy.

Having in mind an alternative to outpatient treatment may also make the therapist feel less anxious. In trying to deal with his own anxieties about the patient, the therapist may feel more secure knowing that he has at least raised hospitalization as an option for discussion. He does not *have* to take unbearable responsibility alone for this patient. The internal decrease in anxiety may help him to tolerate the patient's behavior or threats, and may help the therapy. The plan for hospitalization if the situation deteriorates further is best presented beforehand, especially to the most adamantly opposed patient, and the therapist should be prepared to act on it if necessary, even if it involves commitment, to protect the patient's life.

What if a difficult patient places the therapist in the double-bind position of saying, after veiled threats, "How can I tell you I'm thinking seriously of suicide? I know you have the power to commit me, if I tell you what's on my mind, and that is the last thing I want." This, I think, is the most difficult situation of all to be in with a suicidal outpatient. The therapist *does* have the legal power not to let the patient leave the office. The logistics of this might be something else, but could be arranged. Here is a female patient saying, "I dare you to overpower me." The therapist cannot force the patient to tell him her ideas so that he may assess her distance and decide whether it is safe to let her go. His rising anxiety may feed into a struggle with the patient, and instant hospitalization may turn into a manipulative threat, along the lines of a parent saying to a child, "If you are so naughty, then the men in the white coats will take you away and punish you." This interpretation could be made to a patient with comments about her provocation, underlining the reality that she seems to be asking for or perhaps needs more care and protection while sorting out her troublesome issues. The discussion is more about what her needs *are* at the moment in relation to what help the therapist can give her realistically. This position attends to the reality as the therapist sees it and may lead the patient away from her irrational stance.

Rising anxiety in the therapist about a patient's physical safety may be a most useful indicator about how much the patient is in jeopardy. This is, however, very subjective, since each therapist will have his own level of tolerable anxiety. One way of presenting the dilemma to the patient may be requiring him to assess his own responsibility for his safety. His taking that burden is part of the contract to remain an outpatient. In one instance, when a therapist discussed this issue with a patient, she gradually settled down to consider whether she was invested enough in seeing him to wish to continue. She was also able to elaborate more on her fear of hospitals, her fantasies of what it would be like, the attractive versus the unattractive aspects of it, and how much she felt her career would be damaged by the step. She preferred to be an outpatient.

Another suggestion may be to choose to bypass the struggle with the patient and take up one side of the ambivalence in the struggle, the fear of the hospital as "the place of punishment." Often if the struggle with the patient can be unlocked, and he demonstrates some ability to move away from this position, he is already talking more like an outpatient, albeit vastly troubled, but one who can maintain responsibility for himself in the outside world.

Issues of trust and control are at stake too. If these are prominent in the initial hours, the therapist may expect the issues to come up often during the therapy, perhaps not on the suicidal theme but in other behavioral issues. Having negotiated a rough suicidal passage does not mean that the patient will not feel suicidal again. But the amassed experience for both patient and therapist from one such incident may provide valuable clues to the message behind it, what feelings in the patient arouse the suicidal urge, and what measures or aspects of discussion might help in its prevention.

Threats Made during Well-Established Therapy

Here we concentrate more on the transference and countertransference elements, although some of these issues may be prominent in initial therapy too. The difference is that later in therapy one has more grounds for suspecting a patient feels this or that way about the therapist, and more grounds to indicate that the suicidal feelings are arising in the context of the therapeutic relationship. Threatening suicide is one of the most effective ways of tantalizing any psychotherapist — after all, he is publicly committed to help prevent traumas such as suicide. Not talking is another method patients use, since the whole process of the ideal therapy is tied to verbal communication of feelings. Failure to improve is a fairly ubiquitous way of triggering countertransference reactions. There are many other ways a patient can, with varying levels of awareness, dovetail his problems into the weak spot of any given therapist, depending on the therapist's own personal problems. A suicidal patient may manifest all three of these methods of "manipulating the therapist," as some would say. The word *manipulate* now seems to have a pejorative connotation, as if the patient consciously is *doing* something to an unwilling, passive therapist. If the therapist feels so abused, he may feel like showing his hostility to the patient by being contemptuous or fighting back with interpretations above the patient's current threshold of pain, or by sadistic banter. If the therapist does not try to understand his anger, it may obstruct rational contemplation of therapeutic action, and the end result is a futile struggle to put the patient in his place, showing who is master.

If a patient is indeed needling the therapist on a sensitive issue, which he knows is dear to the therapist's heart, then it says something about the patient's unconscious wishes and fears as well as his conscious intent. The therapist may search his mind for similar situations in which his patient has been placed or has placed himself. If the suicide threats are discussed first of all in the light of how the patient *wants* the therapist to react, setting aside the therapist's temptation to act or react on the feeling of the moment, then there may be more possibility of trying to understand the communication from the patient.

One female therapist told of treating a woman with poor impulse control, who also worked in the field of psychology and was of similar age to herself. This woman often made suicide threats and was very troubled by feeling degraded in seeking help from someone with whom she could identify so closely. Issues of confidentiality had often come up. These touched on the patient's own tendency to tell the world her life in all its titillating detail. She was convinced that the therapist chatted about her at cocktail parties, elaborating on the latest secrets unfolded to her in the office, and she was convinced that since they had mutual colleagues, all the people working in the same area would get to know how "bad" she really was. Let us assume in this example that the therapist knows the patient fairly well. A typical interaction with her was the following:

The patient comes late, stomping noisily into the office. She sits on the arm of the chair and throws her handbag across the room onto another chair in an exasperated, disgusted fashion. She remains silent and glares at the therapist. After a long pause:

Therapist: You look furious.

Patient [Smiling sarcastically]: Who me? Never. Now doctor, could I ever be nasty to a nice sweet lady like you?

Therapist: . . . Yes. . . .

Patient: Oh, come now doctor, you do me an injustice. I'm a nice sweet girl myself, and you know we shrink types never show our cards. [The patient smiles to herself, searches for her cigarettes, takes them out, and, one at a time, breaks them in the ashtray.]

Therapist: What has happened?

Patient: Nothing . . . oh . . . nothing at all. [Silent, but purple with rage.] But I've just come to tell you this one thing before I go and never come back. I'll break every bone in your body if you tell a soul what I've told you.

Therapist: You are planning on not seeing me again?

Patient: Yes, it's all over. I thought I might get help, but it's all over. There's nothing more to be said. [Silence. Lights cigarette and looks more composed.]

Therapist: Something obviously very disturbing to you has happened.

Patient [Seeming to ignore the comment]: You know I can get morphine any time I really want it, and there's not a damn thing under the sun-moon-and-stars you can do about it.

Therapist: I know that very well. You could kill yourself quite easily.

Patient: And what would you care? You'd go on just as you always do, seeing countless patients and saying "Um. Tell me more." You'd retreat into your ivory tower and you wouldn't give a shit.

Therapist: It's true I'd go on working. But it's not true that I wouldn't give a shit. [Patient looks startled at the therapist feeding back her terminology to her.]

Patient: Shit, shit — it's a nice word isn't it? And now you're using it too. [Laughs uncontrollably] That's what I'm going to do. I'm going to shit on you, disgrace you professionally, and the whole world will know what a God damn lousy therapist you are.

Therapist: I've done something to offend you and I deserve punishment?

Patient: Don't act so innocent, you prissy bitch. I'm leaving right now, and I'm going to kill myself. [Determinedly picks up handbag and goes to door.]

Therapist: If you leave the building, I'll have to stop you.

Patient: Just how can you stop me, doctor dear? By sending the strong arms and the police after me? Boy, would that be dramatic!

Therapist: Yes . . . you've told me you are going to commit suicide. You acknowledge that feelings about me are involved, and you seem to have no way of letting me know what's on your mind about it.

Patient: That's a therapeutic dilemma for you.

Therapist: You sound furious, but you also sound very scared.

Patient: I've never known fear in my life. That's another example of your flaming lousy remarks. *[Face crumples and patient begins to cry.]* And now I'm like a baby, and I hate you for making me cry. I'll never be able to look anyone straight in the face again. Oh damn! damn! damn!

Therapist: Whatever is going on with you, it's obviously very painful.

Patient: It *is.* *[Weeps]* Did you realize when you saw Jane, at Michael's party, that she was my best friend? If you knew — then it's over — I'm killing myself.

Therapist: Yes, I knew — you told me before. But we've also talked about confidentiality in the past.

Patient: My God, I'm disgraced for life.

Therapist: What did she say about it?

Patient [Slowly]: Actually she said you were distant, and she thought you must be a very cold person. She said you looked like you were having a good time and you mustn't care about your work because you didn't look very burdened or intellectual. She didn't say how much she talked to you.

Therapist: What did you think I might say to her?

Patient: Well, it got all out of control in my head. I thought maybe you'd tell her about your worries with me.

Therapist: What good would that have done either you *or* me?

Patient: Well, none, I suppose. Maybe I wanted you to tell her, since she's shunned me lately and if she knew I were sick she might be more sympathetic.

Therapist: Did it bother you that she said I was cold?

Patient: Yes — it's okay for *me* to lambast you with that, but it's different if it comes from someone else.

The patient did continue therapy. Because she was so directing her fury upon the therapist, the therapist felt that this particular situation was less likely to end in a suicidal gesture than former situations where the object of her wrath was unavailable to her. There were many issues in that session. She was using her comparable career position in the beginning as a tenuous defensive maneuver to fend off the therapist in the struggle: "I'll outwit you." She valued the closeness of the relationship but saw it suddenly jeopardized by an intrusive other who was bound to abuse her because of it and to vie for the therapist's exclusive attention. She wanted to know how close she and the therapist could be. Was the therapist so dangerously overinvested in her that she would fall to pieces if the patient abandoned her (because she herself felt so vulnerable in the fantasy of the therapist abandoning her)? On the other hand, did the therapist care anything for her, having betrayed her by talking to her friend?

The therapist tried to maintain a general attitude that she could be patient, and that they could have faith that they could sort out what was troubling her. The therapist tried to be realistic and not be swayed by the patient's volatile fantasies. Yes, she did care; particularly she cared about what the patient felt inside. Yes, she could be firm about providing her with external controls if the patient felt so out of control herself; yes, she would live in spite of the patient's fury, and yes, she did talk to the patient's friend but felt no need to discuss her case. The patient herself acknowledged both the wish and the fear of total "exposure," and in the discharge of rage at the therapist she had a true focus, which she had lacked in the past, when her anger was diffuse. This discharge could prevent her turning the anger against herself in a suicide gesture. At another time in the therapy she elaborated on her wish for closeness with her mother, and her rage and feeling of abandonment when a younger sister was born. This presumably was the paradigm for her experience of live feelings at this time, and she later talked of it in this light.

Provocation of a reaction "to prove that the therapist cares" may emerge as a suicide threat in ongoing therapy. It is important to try to ascertain what kind of reaction is wanted by the patient. The patient may wish the therapist to be her "savior," and may have fantasies of the therapist being in constant attendance, looking after her physical needs. Such a threat may be a plea for more nurturance or more "exclusive love," as when a patient wishes to be held close to preserve him from bodily harm. There may be angry elements of wishing to harm the therapist professionally. The patient may be expressing a fear of getting too close, as in a homosexual panic. The patient may want to be rid of the therapist by getting himself hospitalized. There are many, many possibilities, based on the dynamics of any particular patient. One has a rich opportunity to try to understand the derivation of feelings with a patient involved in feelings arising out of the therapeutic relationship. If one knows something of the longed-for reaction, then he has a better chance of interpreting some aspects of it or choosing to satisfy some aspects of it. For example, if the plea is for more nurturance, then it may be appropriate to see the patient more frequently during the crisis. If the plea is to escape from the therapist, one may decide with the patient to see him less frequently or for shorter sessions. If one interprets other feelings, such as the longing to be taken care of physically by the therapist, then the patient may expand more on the anticipated comforts, and he will probably talk as well of anger in the past and present deprivations. The anger of present deprivation might, for example, be traced to feelings about a forthcoming vacation of the therapist or to some incident in his life in which he wished the therapist to play a part.

With the best efforts of any therapist, a patient in ongoing therapy may become so much a danger to himself that he has to be hospitalized. Again, one's anxiety about his welfare, overflowing beyond therapy hours, may be a valid reflection of the ominous situation, indicating that it may be time for him to receive more care than the therapist can administer.

If acute suicidal feelings are due to voices telling the patient what to do, and these are accompanied by variations in his loss of contact with reality, then one may perhaps increase or start tranquilizing medication, all the time paying attention to what in the patient's environment, including the relationship with the therapist, has triggered the response. With psychotic patients it may turn out to be something which seems very minor but which is a very loaded topic for the patient.

The passive suicidal intent, in which feelings are denied, as in the patient with anorexia nervosa, may be very difficult to work with. Such a patient may maintain a bland or cheerful affect while disposing of food in the most cleverly disguised ways and becoming thinner and thinner before one's eyes. As an outpatient one has no way of controlling the food intake. The hospitalization may be indicated, depending on how emaciated the patient appears. At least with this kind of patient one has time to consider with him and talk about hospitalization.

There are other patients who talk about suicide in a cold, detached way as the only obvious solution to their life problems. They may be beyond reach of personal involvement with the therapist; or they may be superficially engaged enough to prevent suicide at the time of the therapy. With such a patient in outpatient therapy, one may quickly note every session how likely it is to come about at the present time. Having satisfied himself that it is not about to occur right now, then one continues treatment, hopes and verbalizes a wish that the patient will contact him quickly if things deteriorate. Attachment to children or to parents often seems to prevent such a patient from committing suicide, for example, "I will gas myself as soon as my youngest child is 10 years old," has been heard from a detached, despondent, cynical, pessimistic patient; or, "I would kill myself, only I know my parents would be tortured until they died." The therapist may get into a discussion, at least with himself, about the individual's moral right to do what he wants with his own life. Occasionally therapists will state their own views to such a patient in an effort to lend some of their own superego. There may or may not be value to this, depending on the patient. When working with a patient for whom children or parents provide such a tenuous bond to life, one should try to avoid hasty interpretations pointing out their ambivalent attachment, or the "worthlessness" of the chosen people. One may only delicately take this prop away if one is giving something in return, or if he is sure that the patient has ego resources enough to provide gradually his own compensations.

13

Considering the Homicide Threat

This chapter is an attempt to cover only some aspects of the
complexities of assessment and management of patients who make
homicide threats. The topic is brought up because it is something
that all therapists think about, and it is anxiety provoking. It can
be especially frightening for the beginning therapist, to whom his
patients may seem an amorphous mass of troubles. He may be very
concerned about his untried professional skill, unsure if he could
recognize intense feelings, and overconcerned about what a patient
may conceal.

If the suicide threat provokes mainly guilt in people, the homicide
threat provokes mainly fear — fear for others threatened, or fear for
one's own life. If a trainee or other therapist has reason to worry
about this contingency with a particular patient, he should talk with
a senior colleague at the first opportunity. If one is very afraid of
a patient, he may not be able to think objectively. Sharing the fear
and the burden may allow the therapist better to formulate ideas on
what may be happening in the patient's life to provoke him to want
to kill a person; or on what may be happening in therapy to arouse
the feelings of wanting to kill the therapist or someone else.

Homicidal impulses are not in themselves diagnostic of specific psychiatric entities. Murderous fantasies are part of every human being's psychological makeup. Everyone — normal people, those with impulse disorders, paranoid schizophrenics — may manifest such feelings. The problem is, how can one know if a murderous act is likely to take place as a result of such ideation? There are people who seemingly give no warning signs of homicide, even if they are in therapy. There are others who have nourished old hatreds for many years, talk about them, and may feel intermittently that they risk killing the person; and yet others for whom an acute situation, such as losing a lover, causes them to feel actively murderous for the first time in their lives. Homicide does not seem to occur in direct relationship to amounts of hatred experienced by the person, but rather the murderous feelings are provoked to a high intensity by the situation in which the person finds himself. Most homicides occur within the closest relationships, spouse, lover, parents, or siblings. It may be that these are the people with whom the most intense feelings are generated, as well as being the most likely people to share territory. Many murders seem to be done by people who, under different circumstances, might not have killed anyone.

INITIAL ASSESSMENT

Trying to assess murderous fantasies is most problematic with a patient one has never seen before. Some questions follow that one may ask himself about the patient, which may help him to understand the quality of the wrath and what the provocations of his situation might be.

What are the fantasies? How bloody or complicated are they? (Possibly indicative of psychosis.) How would he kill the person?

Is he drunk on alcohol? Is his consciousness disturbed in any other physical way?

How angry is he right now?

How fearful is he of attack or fantasied attack?

Is he paranoid and delusional? Is he out of touch with reality?

Is the object of his wrath easily available?

Does he always hold himself in and now gives evidence of losing control?

Does he possess a weapon or have easy access to one?

Has he been like this in the past? If so, what happened?

Has he attacked anyone before? (Not necessarily any indication that he is homicidal.)

Has anyone close to the patient ever killed a person? (To assess a risk of strong identification.)

If the weight of the answers is positive, then it may be that homicide will take place. However, it is really impossible to generalize about any individual's likelihood to murder. A desperate enough patient, in a tight enough corner may murder with no previous history of assault. Another may have had frequent violent fights, and the next one may cause an "accident" leading to a murder charge.

In looking at his situation, one might consider how grave was the wound to the patient's self-esteem, coupled with a consideration of how boxed-in he feels. Murder may seem the only adaptive solution available to him. He may feel he is powerless and that only revenge would make him feel whole again. Paranoid patients feel so afraid of being attacked by persecutors that they want to kill first, before perhaps being killed, raped, seduced, or exposed. In intense jealousy, the wish to annihilate the other person may be uppermost. In the interpersonal conflicts that precipitate the homicidal urge, the person may suddenly regress or feel like a trapped animal. The relationship with the likely victim should be explored too. Sometimes it seems that that person is teasing and provoking a reaction, perhaps unconsciously soliciting his doom. The last straw turning a homicidal urge into murder may be the invitation, "If you hate me so much, why don't you just go ahead and kill me?" In an evaluation, it may be important to try to interview the other person involved, as a way of seeking avenues to ventilate the anger more safely, to "loosen" the situation, and to examine the possibility of provocation.

THE EMERGENCY

A common presentation in the emergency room is a patient who is brought in by police or relatives because of his murderous threats.

This action may have intensified his rage, and he may refuse to talk to the therapist. He may be drunk or psychotic, out of control, and generally violent. There is no need to see such a patient alone if one is afraid of him. A male hospital aide, or the police, or the relatives may be present. Leaving the door of the office open may be enough to provide feelings of safety on both sides, before the interview takes place. These external controls may help the patient's internal controls, which have been shattered. Tranquilizing medication may be needed. If one explains to the patient why he is taking this step, there may be a better chance he will take the medication without a fight. One may try to talk to him about how frightened he must be by his loss of control, and about how frightening he appears. Just being in the emergency room, surrounded by people he hopes can control him, may be enough to calm him down sufficiently to talk about his situation. In extreme cases of a violent person with whom these approaches fail, it may be necessary for hospital staff to overpower him physically to give tranquilizing medication.

If the therapist has enough help available so that he can be less concerned for his own safety, he should try to resist a tremendous pressure to *do* something and act hastily without any explanation to the patient. The patient may seem unresponsive or out of touch with reality, but at some level he will hear what one is saying even if he cannot make use of it. "Explanations" may be easier to write about than to accomplish practically, if it is 4 AM and all the people involved with the patient are clamoring for action. It is appropriate to meet with the concerned friends, to hear their fears, gather information about the patient, and tell them a plan of action, if any. The patient may be informed that one is going to have such a meeting, and told at least some of what has emerged afterward. The more open the communication system around the patient, the better the chances of calming his fury and encouraging a little trust.

If the patient begins to calm down, one can go about exploring the situation in the usual way, and decide for himself, and with the patient, whether it is a risk for him to be an outpatient, or whether he would feel more comfortable in a hospital, at least temporarily.

Commitment to an institution may be indicated if he refuses hospitalization while in the therapist's opinion his own safety and the safety of others is in jeopardy. Even if one sees a furious, silent patient surrounded by police, one should tell him why he is being committed and why it is in his best interests. The therapist may tell him how he will be taken there, and something about the hospital and the treatment program. There is often a temptation to avoid talking to such a patient. This further increases his rage, confusion, or helplessness.

HOSPITALIZATION

In any outpatient setting, if a therapist feels there is a danger of the patient acting on his murderous fantasies, or that he is so assaultive that someone might be harmed, he can choose to present the option of hospitalization to a patient. The patient may have come by himself to the walk-in clinic or emergency room for evaluation or treatment. This indicates that at some level he knows he needs help and is requesting it. Therein may be a basis for agreeing on hospitalization. If the patient will not go voluntarily, the therapist, concerned about the patient's safety and that of others, is obliged to commit him to an institution (see Chapter 12).

At best, the hospital setting can serve to remove the person from the immediacy of his hostile environment. With treatment for his psychosis, or with the resultant decrease in intensity of feelings aroused in the boxed-in life situation, for example, he may be able to sort out his most acute problem and consider the impact on his own life if he were to act upon his violent fantasies.

HOMICIDE WITH FEW PREVIOUS CLUES

Occasionally when a patient is very angry in evaluation, a beginning therapist may feel that the subject of his harming someone is too delicate a topic to broach. However, if one has any thought of this happening, it is helpful to the patient to bring up the question, since this raises the idea to a high level of awareness for his own assessment. It can happen that a patient is seen in an evaluation session, gives no overt threat of homicide, but murders someone subsequent to the interview. An example follows.

A married working man in his forties came to a clinic complaining about his marital relationship. He and his wife had adolescent children, and they fought about their upbringing. The patient was tempted from time to time to leave his wife, but thought he would like psychiatric help before making a decision. He was quite reasonable and gave a coherent account of his troubles. From time to time he clenched his fists while talking about an incident. At one point he said he needed help with his anger. According to the patient, his past history was free of physical assaults. His presentation was not remarkable in ferocity or intensity in this respect. Since he seemed capable of talking of his problems, the therapist invited him to join a group that he was forming. The patient seemed to like the idea and was placed on the waiting list. Meanwhile the therapist had difficulty in getting his group together and overlooked letting the patient know. No more communications came from the man.

With tremendous shock, the therapist read in the paper a month later that the man had stabbed his wife and children to death and had been sent to jail. While trying to sort out how the situation may have been misjudged initially, the therapist talked to the patient in jail. He was not psychotic at this point, either. It turned out that asking for control over his anger was the key point, but the patient had had more distance from it at the time of the interview. He had kept from the therapist vivid accounts of previous physical fights because he felt he could talk about them later while in therapy. He was angry that the therapist had not kept his promise about therapy; feeling that he did not care, he had not let him know of his increasing desperation. This was a patient who seemed "regular" enough when first seen. There are many patients who tell the same story and never kill anyone. Perhaps the therapist should have pursued more strongly his request for help in control, and perhaps he should have given him tranquilizers to tide him over till therapy began. These were thoughts in retrospect. It was probably impossible to predict at the time that this man would kill his family.

ONGOING THERAPY

In the treatment situation, the therapist may become the object of the patient's rage. The patient may feel out of control and want to kill the therapist. Again there is a wide gradation between murderous fantasies, the urge or the act of physical assault, and the murder of the therapist or someone else. The patient may see the therapist as an intensely loved-hated persecutor who challenges the patient's favorite defenses, leaving the patient vulnerable and helpless. A schizophrenic patient whose main way of coping with dangerous feelings and impulses is to "feel nothing" or "dead inside" may, if some of the feelings become available during the therapeutic process, suddenly feel overwhelmed and want to kill the therapist. The patient may view the therapist as an attacker who has released the painful, terrifying feelings. A paranoid patient, if he begins to feel he is losing his therapist's advocacy, may feel helpless and betrayed, incorporate the therapist into his delusional system, and want revenge for the hurt caused. Borderline psychotic and psychotic patients are particularly vulnerable in the issue of secrecy, which they may feel, as one patient expressed it, "is binding unto death." It may thus be part of the symbiotic urge. One psychotic patient felt utterly robbed in having "poured himself" into the therapist, and held a delusion that the only way to recover his "life's essence" was to murder the therapist. The psychodynamics concerning why a patient may contain murderous rage coupled with poor impulse control are too complex for this discussion.

Often one may be aware of the building of such intense rage, or, because of the patient's dynamics, be forewarned that such a situation might develop. The problem is then a question of working with a very angry patient who may have a hard time controlling his impulses rather than "a homicidal outpatient." Throughout the book there are examples of working with varying degrees of anger in patients.

ASSAULT

Therapists have used all sorts of devices to try to set limits, when assault from a patient seems imminent. Rage of that intensity is as frightening for the patient in his internal sense of going out of control and "crazy" as it is for the therapist in fear of being injured. For some, asking the patient to leave the office has worked, stating that purpose of the work together is to try to understand the force of the feelings, not to assault or be assaulted. One may say that the patient can return when he feels more in control. This may give the patient the freedom of geographical distance to release a "trapped" sensation. It spells out the therapeutic contract and sets an expectation of a higher level of ego functioning, which both patient and therapist may know exists from past experience together. It may help the patient recoup his defenses.

Some therapists have emphasized the damage of an attack, both to the patient himself and to the therapist: the therapist will be injured and perhaps lost to the patient, while the patient will feel guilty or may be involved in legal proceedings if the therapist is physically hurt. This may call up the patient's better judgment and momentarily lost superego restraints. It also speaks to the side of the patient that likes the therapist very much and wishes to continue the relationship.

Other therapists have confronted the patient with a statement about their own fear of him, and pointed out the impossibility of trying to help solve anything while so afraid. This may lessen the feelings of wound and revenge, since on one level the therapist concedes and acknowledges the reality of the patient's strength and ability to assault or murder him. The threat and reality of calling for help, or calling the police, or if necessary commiting him to an institution, may help impulse control.

The therapist's behavior when his property or person is threatened may be guided by experience of previous situations with the particular patient, knowledge of the patient's life events, and his experience with other patients. After the event, the therapist may try to examine how he may have provoked the attack and explore the patient's experience of him prior to the violent feelings and during the episode. If it is an internal sense that the therapy pace is too fast, and the release of feelings of hatred is too confusing or overwhelming for the patient, together patient and therapist might choose to explore ways to slow down the process. Tranquilizing medication may be a help. Alternative ways to end an hour may be found, so that the patient does not feel raw and vulnerable, or explosive, when the therapist says, "It's time to stop for today." Sometimes even articulation of this difficulty may be enough to support such a patient. Ability to link the present powerful feelings to some old situation, when the patient truly felt powerless as a child, may help deflate the wrath and put it into context. Admission of an error by the therapist (if this was a contributing cause), may help, coupled with an exploration of why he did not feel free to complain till his rage built to such proportions. At the moment of assault what could the patient gain? How would that have made him feel better?

Many patients with violent fantasies of harming their therapists manage to discharge their affect in words, and the therapist can ask, "Do you feel in danger of killing me because of it?" The patient may be able to reassess the threat as "feeling like" killing the therapist but gives reasons himself why he would not want to go that far. This can reassure both the patient and the therapist. Often intense fury is very close to intense fear, and one may want to explore why the patient is so afraid.

One therapist described a patient in a state of paranoid fury with him. The patient lifted a heavy metal ashtray and aimed it at the therapist's head. At that moment the therapist said, "You must be very afraid." The patient began to calm himself and gained control.

AN UNUSUAL CLINICAL SITUATION

After the event, can one ever form a fixed judgment on whether or not a particular patient could have been guilty of the homicide? An example of this complexity follows.

A girl child was raped and murdered. The suspect was a single man in his fifties who was having psychiatric treatment. The police questioned every man in the city of whom they knew who fitted this description. A therapist was seeing one of these men. The patient was a chronically depressed alcoholic homosexual who was in a phase of treatment in which he was talking about his early memories of his parents and siblings. The therapist knew from another source that the patient had been questioned by the police but was unsure whether and when to broach the topic. The patient had lapses of memory from time to time, after severe drinking bouts. One of these had occurred in the week the child was killed. The patient opened the hour with comments about his loss of memory and asked the therapist if he felt that he, the patient, could do "something dreadful" at a time like that and not know about it. In answer to the therapist's question "Like what, for instance?" the patient spent the rest of the hour unfolding new material about his incestuously tinged relationship with his younger sister, of whom he was very jealous. He took every opportunity to gaze at her naked body. These opportunities were richly supplied through their childhood and adolescence with his parents since there was a great deal of nudity in the house. At 16 he remembered guiltily taking her under-pants to a field adjoining their house and trying them on while masturbating, having fantasies of assaulting her and strangling her. He said that he had always had a "lurid interest" in small girl children, and that once he had been asked to leave a cinema because he had been feeling the bottom of a little girl in the darkness. She told her mother, who sent for the manager. The patient was very distressed while telling the therapist all this. The therapist became more and more anxious during the hour, alternately doubting and convincing him-self that this person could have murdered the child. In discussing the session afterward with his supervisor, he wondered if the patient had been trying to tell him of the murder and his guilt. If so. he asked, what responsibility does the therapist have to inform the police? Is therapy bound by the same rules as the confessional? What responsibility does the therapist have to protect the com-munity? Such a patient, one supposes, could have murdered the child. He had a lot of contained rage about his feelings for his little sister, which could have be-come displaced on the other child. Under the influence of alcohol, his controls might have been severed; the horror and shock of his action, coupled with his physiological state, could have blotted the crime from his mind.

After discussion with the supervisor, the therapist decided to tell the patient in the next hour about his knowledge of the police questioning to try to get more direct information about his activities. The patient, it turned out, had accounted satisfactorily to the police for his activities. The true murderer was found subsequently. The therapist did not want to act the role of interrogator, but on the other hand he had to have extra information to decide where the reality lay. The patient had feelings about the therapist's lack of trust in him and urge to check up on him, but he was able to reassure the therapist con-vincingly that he was not the murderer. Nevertheless it left the therapist ponder-ing the issue of how one can really *tell* for sure whether a patient is capable of committing homicide. If a therapist did have good reason to believe a patient had perpetrated murder, then one possibility would be to encourage the patient himself to tell the authorities. The vast complexities of such a situation are be-yond the limits of discussion here.

This therapist was concerned that perhaps his own life would be in danger, if it had emerged that his patient had been the murderer. It would probably not have been an issue, since the murder had oc-curred in very specific circumstances. However, if the patient had felt intensely trapped by the therapist's knowing, he might have been very angry — or he might have been relieved. It is really not possible to speculate on this situation that never happened within the limits of the clinical information. It points up that one can never be absolutely sure. As with every other situation in therapy, one has to weigh each individual case with each point in the progress of events, and avoid jumping to a hasty conclusion.

14

Relating to the Borderline Psychotic Patient

The use of the term borderline psychotic diagnostically may
be regarded by some people as sitting on the fence. The very name
"borderline" suggests this. The patient may be functioning externally more like a neurotic, with no gross manifestations of disturbance. In face-to-face psychotherapy, when one hears more about
his inner life, he may at times sound psychotic. The contrast between
what one hears of his life in the world, as opposed to his internal
tumultuous state, may lead him to use this diagnostic category in an
operational way. The importance of arriving at this diagnosis lies
in its therapeutic implications.

There seems to be a lack of universal agreement about how to
classify patients who are neither clearly neurotic nor clearly psychotic. This has to do partly with therapists and partly with the
variable nature of these patients. Some therapists favor terms like
latent schizophrenia, pseudo-neurotic schizophrenia, schizo-affective
disorder, pre-psychotic state, hysterical psychosis. The use of these
labels depends on the past history, the current quality and quantity
of certain symptoms, and suggested prognostic indicators. Some
people feel that use of the term *borderline* avoids the diagnosis

of schizophrenia. Young therapists with young patients, in particular, often have negative feelings about calling a patient "schizophrenic," and seek to avoid the uncertain nomenclature, with its implications of gradual deterioration. The presence of the label and its associations may diminish a therapist's expectations, depending on how strongly he feels and on his past experience with backward patients in a state hospital. One's hopes for the therapeutic endeavor may seem dashed before it even begins, if he has not had the experience of seeing a schizophrenic who made a reasonable adjustment in life with treatment.

The fact of whether or not he receives treatment may make a great deal of difference ultimately in the course of a borderline patient's life. If the patient is an adolescent, even up to the age of 25, some therapists prefer to regard the patient as an "emotional adjustment problem of adolescence" because they feel there is no sure way of predicting the prognosis after the person's life becomes more established. If such a patient suffers many losses or abuses in his existence, he may become psychotic. If life is kind to him, he may become stabilized as an eccentric normal or a schizoid personality. He may be able to use his rich inner life in a very artistic manner. As time goes on, he may follow a manic-depressive pattern, and then one would review the diagnosis in retrospect. He may ultimately become frankly schizophrenic.

Symptom formation in the borderline patient stems from the pregenital era of his development. Thus he will have problems with faulty object relationships and narcissistic investment. Oral dependency needs may be vast. Reality testing is poor, ego boundaries are diffuse, and identity may be confused. There may be an urgent need for a symbiotic experience with another person in order for him to feel whole. Social relations will suffer. Cognitive functioning and judgment may be impaired. His ego defects may also involve his body image, and he may have strange feelings and experiences concerning his body. If these phenomena occur with consistency and are fixed in their degree of severity, with hallucinations and delusions present, the patient may be regarded as psychotic. If the propensity is present but is not flourishing or fixed, the patient may be viewed as a "borderline psychotic."

The borderline patient has a capacity to move up and down the developmental scale, short of the genital level, depending on his ability to construct defenses quickly with his partially intact ego resources. Under favorable circumstances his ego functioning may prove adaptive. It is the frequent glimpses of him in sitting-up face-to-face therapy, regressed to a low level of integration that may alert one to possibly psychotic base of his problems. Because of his fluidity and capacity to recoup his defenses even briefly, one may have difficulty in putting him firmly on the psychotic end of the diagnostic continuum.

Typical complaints of the borderline patient are "not feeling real" or "feeling hollow," in spite of external achievements. Patients complain of being numb or dead inside. They may be aware of a tumult of confused feelings that threaten to overwhelm them. The wish or fear of "going crazy" may be strong. They often have highly colored, primitive fantasy lives concerning their ambivalent views of themselves or others — either they are everything or they are nothing. One young philosophy student who was functioning in his studies described his inner experience in this way:

The other night I sat by myself. Sometimes I like that. I wrote a poem about a boy who is at one side of the street and is all alone. He sees a house burning across the road. He just looks and looks. People are screaming and running out, and being burned. He just looks on. He thinks it is just like what has gone on inside him — all this amorphous mass of fire inside me, raging and burning till I'm nothing but an empty shell. . . . I feel like Satan and God. I feel demoniacal and spiritual, so evil and so good. Everything I do and every gesture I make is God-like — I am so critical and so tortured. I hate people and they hate me, and I alienate the people I most want. I can control every situation and make it turn out badly for myself. I am also worshipped and I love the world.

Borderline patients often make superficial relationships, which may be quickly or unilaterally formed and then broken due to the intensity generated. Sexual adjustment is usually at the level of body contact for cuddling or for oral sex. Chaotic homosexual and heterosexual interests may be present. Their oblique thought processes and looseness of association may lead people to fail to understand what they are talking or writing about. They may have behavior problems as judged by their environment. Trouble in the area of social controls and impulse control may bring them into treatment. Family history will reveal very disturbed relationships, especially an early disturbed relationship with the mother, who herself may be psychiatrically ill. Often siblings have psychiatric problems.

Depending on the level of tolerance of the environment, the patient may have functioned reasonably well, especially in scholastic achievement, till points of natural turmoil and regression arise, such as age 5 to 6 at the height of the oedipal period, birth of a sibling, a family move, puberty, high school graduation, divorce or death of a parent, or prolonged physical illness.

Many of the patients who fall in this category are young. They are exciting to work with as outpatients and can often be maintained on this basis in once or twice a week psychotherapy if they can manage to keep their external lives reasonably well regulated. Major manifestations of their disturbance may occur only with some external upheaval. Such decompensation may occur around events in the therapy, too, and these can be turned to some use by the patient in his outside life.

THE THERAPEUTIC ENVIRONMENT

The reality of the therapist is important to the borderline patient. Each therapist will be "real" in his own way. Some are firm, and some are nondirective by nature. Some talk a lot, some talk little. Some tend to be humorous and some are very serious. With the borderline patient there is less evidence that it is helpful to maintain a uniform, distant stance, as one would with the neurotic. Against this background a neurotic patient may elaborate his feelings and fantasies in order to unravel his conflicts. The borderline psychotic patient requires a different quality of response because of his lower position on the developmental scale, and because of his lower tolerance for deprivation. The reality of the therapist becomes the mainstay of a live, human contact. These patients are already caught up in a turmoil of intolerable feelings, and they often feel very isolated from humans. One patient talked of living on "a brighter plane of consciousness," which was at once exciting and too intensely painful. He described it as a relief to descend from the plane in the therapy hours. The attempts to describe his inner life to another person resulted in its assuming a less "supernatural" significance, thus it seemed more manageable. He said that since he was forced by his physical body to be a "citizen of the earth," he found it useful to be in contact with a human person.

The ways that a therapist can be real are manifold. He may assume a looser approach, in which seemingly trivial things pass between patient and therapist without requiring the patient to reflect on every action. This need not stop the therapist from being aware of the significance of such actions. One patient wanted to shake the therapist's hand at the beginning and end of every hour. The therapist assented readily. It was of significance to the patient to have body contact in this controlled, "safe" way, which was within the bounds of social exchange. The patient ultimately told him that there was some "life force" that flowed into him at these moments of contact, which had to do with feelings that he was draining himself into the therapist. He said he was "too empty" to consider himself "human" at the end of the hour. Some therapists have talked of holding such a patient in their arms at times of great distress or holding their hands if requested. One therapist talked of how a patient needed to sit on his knee in a very childlike way when very distressed and talking of her pregnancy. Whether or not such responses as these in the therapist are helpful may depend on how such actions are carried out. They may prove comforting at an infantile level, but if there is any homosexual or heterosexual innuendo in the interaction, it will probably be too frightening for the patient. Such action probably should be initiated only by the patient. If the therapist is in doubt, it is very appropriate to keep the contact within the usual social realm — e.g., help a patient with her coat, provide a cup of coffee or a cigarette if requested and it is easily available, eat a candy or piece of fruit if it is offered by the patient.

Borderline patients have often offered art work to their therapists. Provided it is not something worthy of exhibition at a major art center, it is often quite reasonable to accept it graciously for display in the office. Patients will talk about their works in very personal terms, and this may be a useful adjunct to the therapy. It may be easier for the patient to talk about some internal experience using the external manifestation. One very intelligent, guarded, afraid, borderline patient complained bitterly of having no "savoir faire" in his new sophisticated environment. This was based on a real lack of learning experience due to his strange early home life, his defective ego, and intense involvement with himself. He felt that if he traveled a little, he would have a point of social contact with his peers. This was a very "real" issue in helping him with peer experience. He planned a trip, and the therapist and he discussed slides of the places he was going to visit, to prepare for the event. Meanwhile they talked of his fear of venturing on his own and his loneliness. The patient's social functioning increased outside the hours. This patient was not ready for an unstructured involvement with anyone. The visual aids were important for him in keeping a comfortable distance, while learning more about other human beings, including the therapist.

Supportive therapy is a term often applied to therapy with borderline patients. This is not to suggest a kind of condescending, there-there-everything-will-be-all-right approach. It implies a flexible, respectful, receptive, nonintrusive stance with attention to the patient's human needs. The inner experience of such a patient is so complex that no neat formulations can suffice. Try as one might, one may never be able to comprehend the enormity of the experience. Through glimpses one can try to tune in to the global affect. Even though a patient may demand control from the therapist, an uninvasive, low-key approach may be much more truly supportive of his autonomy. A readiness to let the patient take the lead, and guide one through the confusing mazes of his experience, is usually most helpful.

The therapist often has to tolerate the ambiguity of not knowing exactly where the patient "is at" every moment. Some therapists are better at this than others; some can tolerate hearing more unveiled primary process than others. These patients are highly variable. For one patient it may be a good experience to have a therapist who is internally unafraid of the patient's most raw basic thoughts and feelings, while for others, this kind of therapist may provide too great a temptation to prolonged regression. The latter may be more comfortable with a therapist who provides more psychological structure. For borderline patients, above all, there are no blueprint answers. There is a fine line between creating a permissive environment in the therapy and doing one's best to assess when he is in trouble, so that one may take action or talk with him of hospitalization. The therapist does not want to be so permissive that he conveys an attitude of being too passive, neglectful, or unduly pessimistic. Knowing the breadth and depth of the pathology with which he is confronted, a therapist can have no illusions that he might "save" the patient. He may be able to help make life more tolerable. At times he may be able to help the patient avoid a psychotic break. At other times there is just so much pathology that no matter how tuned in, thoughtful and caring he is, a patient will become psychotic or commit suicide. Thus with the borderline patient it is particularly appropriate to think of oneself as a potential helper rather than as an agent of "cure."

Hospitalization may be the alternative to trying to maintain the patient in outpatient therapy. Attempting to keep the patient within the regular world may be well worthwhile as long as it is possible. However, heroics with such a patient beyond one's human tolerance, especially if he is constantly worried about homicide or suicide, is good for neither patient nor therapist.

The borderline patient may need to come and go over time in therapy, and set the pace for himself on the basis of his tolerance of involvement with the human therapist. Many of these patients need to move from therapist to therapist and find a therapist who suits them, before they are ready to embark on a long-term relationship. A therapist may find himself as the patient's first trial, or the person with whom the patient will build up a longer-term trusting relationship, or somewhere in between.

THERAPY WITH BORDERLINE PATIENTS

Therapy with the potentially psychotic patient may be much more *reality oriented* than therapy with a neurotic. Thus the techniques involve more "closing" and encouragement of a reality view of the therapist, rather than the "opening" and potentially more regressive techniques involved in the treatment of neurotics. We might view the neurotic patient as a pyramid, where a little is seen by the therapist at the apex and all the interrelated and interdependent structures become more obvious as one uncovers layer after layer toward the base. In regressed states, the more of the wide base there will be in evidence to the therapist. In the borderline patient the pyramid can be thought of as crumbling down around him. One's task as a therapist with a borderline patient may be to construct from the base upward. With the neurotic, careful taking apart from the apex down may be in order so that the patient can reconstruct the pyramid in a different fashion. This is too rigid a view to apply to any human being, but it illustrates the technical principle.

Aspects of the therapeutic relationship with a borderline patient may be more understandable if at times the therapist suspends reality and thinks of a parent with a newborn infant. The baby cries. His body is wracked with agony. He is red-faced, accusing, spastic, and pathetically helpless. He is at the mercy of a sea of blurred visual images. He may feel hungry, or afraid, or angry, or lost in space. He may have some painful central bodily sensation from an unfamiliar appendage. He has no way of knowing whether he will be relieved and has little experience of comfort in the new world. The mother or father feels helpless too, but one of them holds the baby. It feels warm, loving, and all-encompassing, and it recreates the body contact with mother that the baby in the womb once knew. The decision is then made to feed, to diaper, or to stop stimulation to restore equilibrium. But first the baby is held. Often that stops his crying. There will be plenty of time later to help the growing child struggle with his feelings and to encourage his autonomy. The borderline patient's inner experience and needs at times have a similar flavor, and may provoke a similar protective, parental reaction in the therapist.

This idea is suggested in a metaphorical sense. Initial therapy with a borderline patient is sometimes experienced as a vast need on the patient's part for sustenance. He may feel that he is floundering. Allowing some of this dependency initially and at times of stress, and weaning him gradually in relationship, always encouraging his further differentiation, may promote a more solid trust both in himself and in his view of the world. This does not undermine the stance of listening, inquiry, and careful response that was outlined for neurotic patients. The nature of the response called for may be different at different times in the therapy.

The Maintenance of Reality by the Therapist

The *constancy of the therapist* is very important for borderline patients. In their disintegrated and discontinuous existence, the symbolic act of visiting the same therapist in the same place may provide the one continuous focus in their lives. Talking to a relatively unchanging person may generate the reconstitution of fragments of the past and present experiences into themes which begin to make sense to the patient. Such patients may be, above all, terrified of destroying the therapist by love or hate. They may search for indications of their devastation in prolonged or shortened hours, in absences, in changes of appointment, or in any change in character of the conduct of the psychotherapy. The fear of destruction may be based on the fantasied power of their rage, or their fantasied ability to suck the therapist dry in their need to feed on another's feelings. They may fear alienation from the source of their nourishment, or fear to drag the therapist to the depths of their murderous fantasies, thus contaminating him, so that he becomes a mirror image of their most hated or glorified selves. The relationship with the therapist, who is emotionally available and is neither all good nor all evil, is a primary exercise in the development of an object relationship. If one cancels an appointment or otherwise "abandons" him, these destructive fears may surface rapidly and disrupt his thinking and functioning. The demonstration that one has other patients, or is vulnerable to illness, can be used in the therapy, while being available to hear the patient's fantasies about it, and pointing out the realities. The therapist's continued appearance for the sessions will mean at a primitive level that both the therapist and patient have survived the terrifying fantasies.

A forceful, *intense ambivalence* is focused by the patient upon the therpist. These pulls between being seen as all-loving and all-giving, and being seen as cold, cruel, and withholding, may occur within the hour. It may be hard to provide middle ground between the divergent poles of the ambivalence while being buffeted about by the patient's needs. This may be one reason why these patients seem to "drain" the therapist's resources. Another reason may be the care needed to attempt to regulate and understand the primary process. One young therapist said, "I feel like I am the defensive structure and the patient is the flow from the id."

Transference comments or interpretations are worthy of meticulous attention, on the grounds that feelings about the therapist may quickly blow out of all proportion to the therapist's view of the situation. The patient may experience an urgency to act on them. The initial relationship with a borderline patient is often formed more quickly than with the cautious, defended neurotic. The therapist may have the feeling that the patient is all-consuming, very intense, and almost latching onto the therapist like a leech. Genuine warmth, friendliness, and charm may accompany this quality, but the avid intensity bespeaks symbiosis. There may be immediate feelings transferred upon the therapist from important figures in the past. Rather than the fantasy that the patient is sitting in the chair across the room surrounded by ghosts from his past, one may have the fantasy that the patient's ghosts are all around the therapist's chair, and that it is difficult for the patient to distinguish the separate forces.

A patient in his opening comments to a therapist asked, "Have you ever been in a hospital?" He meant, had the therapist ever been a psychiatric patient. This was followed by, "Are you a wealthy cold man?" which was a reference to his father. In each case the therapist was able to reflect the question back to the patient for further clarification before offering some simple details about his own training and position in the clinic. One aspect of the pressured questions was an attempt by the patient to sort out, "Are you like me?" or "Are you like my father?" Each alternative was fraught with ambivalence. If the therapist did not have identical experiences, then how could he hope to understand? On the other hand, if he had been spared this pain, perhaps he was strong enough to lean upon. If the therapist were like his father, then would he provide the cold atmosphere with which the patient was familiar? But if he were not like his father, would he be more emotional in the therapist's presence and possibly create a dangerous situation where he might feel too out of control?

As the therapy progresses, close attention should be paid to *oblique references having to do with the process* evolving between therapist and patient. A borderline patient talked about how he was frittering away his life with insignificant experience. With a neurotic patient one may wait to hear how the theme progresses over time before alluding to it directly. With this patient, the therapist asked half way through the hour, if he felt the same way about seeing him. "Of course!" the patient replied, as if this had been obvious. He was angry with the therapist about his handling of some issue in a previous hour, and was in fact thinking of dropping out of therapy in spite of feeling in a great turmoil. Thus the therapist could provide an opportunity for the patient to show his anger and focus it on him. This helped the patient continue in treatment. Had this been left in the air till the following week, the therapist might not have seen the patient again. Neither patient nor therapist would have been clear about what happened. Similar incidents and feelings may occur with neurotic patients, but the borderline patient will have tendencies to act on the feelings and fantasies.

A young female patient came irately into an hour, and railed against all her female friends who had become involved with men. Her female therapist had just become engaged to be married, so she asked the patient if she were angry with her for taking this step. "Yes, I am!" she responded furiously, and added with great intensity, gesturing with each hand in balance, "At times you are like an emerald, and at times you are like shit." When the therapist asked what that was about, she said she felt painfully excluded by her therapist's new public alliance with a man. There had been enough previous material to suggest similar feelings about her mother. The patient contained explosive anger about the intrusion of her father into her wishes to be symbiotically close to her mother. The therapist drew her attention to the parallel feelings. She had told the therapist of loving feelings toward her as well as angry feelings. The patient had not realized before the extent of her longing to be with her mother, and this was the first time she experienced recognition of something beyond pure hatred for her mother. This was one of a series of points in therapy when the chasm opened to reveal the intensity and strength of the primitive feeling for both therapist and patient to view. By the next hour the patient was somewhat more defended. The therapist with a borderline patient may be prepared to view all levels of integration within a single hour, and try to have fluidity of response, taking both past and present into consideration.

The idea of *lessening the deprivation* of the patient, which encourages a more real view of therapist, may be illustrated by the handling of a period of silence within the hour. Particularly at the beginning of treatment, long silences may not be helpful. One may assume that the patient is already full of fantasies and confusing feelings; therefore to encourage buildup of these on an outpatient basis, without verbalization or clarification, may push the patient into feelings of explosive intensity, the burden of which he may discharge on his environment. Reflective silence is in order, however, so it depends on what evidence the patient is giving the therapist whether he chooses to interrupt the silence.

A borderline patient was in the beginning phase of treatment. He entered the room humming softly and sat down slowly. A long silence ensued during which he eyed the therapist. The therapist asked him how things were going and received monosyllabic answers. He continued to make eye contact with the therapist for a prolonged period, and the therapist was unsure whether to break the silence. The patient had talked in the preceding hour of his wish to have the therapist read his mind, and the therapist did not wish to do anything that would suggest this magical power. The therapist was becoming quite uncomfortable. Finally the patient made a facial expression of exasperation, and the therapist said, "You look disgusted." "Yes, I am disgusted," the patient exploded. As if the floodgates had opened, he talked freely of his annoyance that the therapist did not recognize the sexy tune he had hummed, and followed with a long account of disgust at his sexual arousal in the presence of a girl who was friendly with him. The atmosphere gradually became less charged, and the patient thanked the therapist for listening at the end of the hour. In this case, the thanks indicated the development of some trust and increasing rapport. The therapist had the feeling the patient could have sat in silence for the whole hour. Had the therapist known the patient better or had he been seeing him more often, this might have been all right. But he had said enough in the previous hours to alert the therapist to the possibility of his decompensation. The therapist needed to know something of what was on his mind to gauge how anxious he should be about the patient's welfare. In this instance he was reassured peripherally that the patient, though emotionally uncomfortable, was in contact with friends and was maintaining a social life. The patient was full of pent up feeling, and the therapist wished to relieve it.

The silence could have been broken in several ways. The therapist could have commented on the patient's humming and asked him about the tune instead of introducing the topic of how things were. This might have led to the same material, and the patient would not have felt that his initial communication had been ignored. The therapist could have commented on his silence, and verbalized his difficulty in talking. If this bore no fruit, he could have asked if there was some connection between his silence and his humming, or he could have alluded to what he had talked of in his preceding hour about wishing for the therapist to read his mind. In commenting intuitively about the feelings shown by his face, there may have been overtones of intrusion and magic. On the other hand one may assume that such a patient feels so transparent and vulnerable anyway that internally he felt no discrepancy even though the inconsistencies were obvious to the therapist.

There are many ways to break a silence if that is indicated. One may experiment with different methods with different patients at various times. The connections between the initial withdrawal and the content of this patient's communication after the broken silence were not really clear. Perhaps he was talking in anger at the therapist and communicating how his aggressive and sexual feelings were interrelated and fused. Perhaps he was alluding to being sexually aroused by the therapist. Perhaps he was testing the therapist's mind-reading abilities. There had been hints of provocation. Any of these could be possible and the following hour might be approached with these possibilities in mind. The main thing that happened was that the therapist had helped him past the silence, and helped him communicate something, for which he seemed relieved. Future meaning of the interchange might be elaborated upon at some other time by the patient.

The Pull Away from Reality by the Patient

Patients may give all sorts of external clues about their varying levels of integration. Dress and posture may tell a great deal about where the patient "is at" at any given point. One very tall, thin girl dressed in cotton checked pastels with puffed sleeves when relating to the therapist as a coquettish little girl, in order to palliate his assumed anger. At other times she looked elegant, like a Vogue model; this would herald a distant, superior stance, when she was denigrating the therapist for some omission on his part. When feeling intensely ambivalent, she consistently wore black and white — a white headscarf with a black dress — and talked of her temptation to be promiscuous and her urge to control herself. Another patient always arrived with hair awry and with a suitcase when demonstrating ambivalence about being in therapy. The implication was that he literally felt on the move and wanted to be self-contained and self-supporting. Another asked the therapist for cigarettes and lighter when he wanted comfort, closeness, and sharing. When this wish was less intense, he carried his own lighter. When he felt giving he offered a light to the therapist.

On the same theme of variation of integration, a patient may sound "stupid" or "naive" about some matter. Ten minutes later he may display a sophisticated grasp of the issue, and then again revert to the naive position with the threat of separation at the end of an hour. Another reality theme is the patient's stance as he views himself in the outside world. He may feel that a single aspect of his visible personality may be the only one by which others perceive him. This is a distortion of reality and may show evidence of inconsistency in ego integration.

There are borderline patients who deal with their social difficulties by feeling a pressure to be continually entertaining to the group. In some instances this gains prestige, in others isolation. "I am the clown," "I can be very funny" is to these patients their passport for approval. The mask may be a tremendous strain, and this may show itself in therapy. Thus a patient might invite the therapist to share the entertainment, which is all right, as long as the therapist is aware of the patient's coexistent need to deny the seriousness of his problem. To go along with this stance without acknowledging how troubled the patient is may lead him to a feeling of being misunderstood. The patient who feels "a fake" and is confused about realities may assume that the therapist, confirming his perception of how he is seen in the outside world, has been taken in by his posture. He may be panicked or feel angry by the assumption that he is not being taken seriously. It may be a relief to a patient for the therapist to acknowledge his anguish. He may cast his need for denial as "dishonesty" and an issue for self-castigation. It is not dishonesty, since there is nothing conscious in the intent. It merely betrays his confused values, the basis of which can also be variations in ego integration. Thus he may at one time state one value with conviction, and at another the direct opposite with equal conviction. Therapists occasionally get angry, feeling that they have been purposely deceived. Realizing the possible underlying difficulty may ameliorate the therapist's reactions.

Due to internal confusion the patient may be drawn away from reality, and another theme that may emerge is *discontinuity in his daily life.* Taking a reality interest in the ordering of the patient's life is therefore helpful with a borderline patient. It helps to mobilize the patient's resources, and helps to reduce his overstimulated state, and provides the safety of a structure. The patient's daily life and relationships are sometimes in chaos, even if he is functioning within a general structure such as school or a job. It is not wasted therapy to apply oneself with the patient to a search for order or to help sort out the more self-preserving relationships. A borderline student may spend the day isolated, lying in bed, tortured or ecstatic in regressive fantasies, and try to do his schoolwork at night. It is appropriate to let him know that being in bed during the day keeps him away from people, encourages his already overstimulated inner life, and contributes to his difficulties in maintaining himself in the school program. If he were to work for certain hours and attend classes during the day, his chances of sleeping at night would be enhanced. Perhaps lack of sleep is contributing to his problems in thinking.

In establishing a regimen to circumvent the disorder, the patient may feel the therapist is too controlling. The patient's cooperation in therapy may decrease due to the therapist's assuming a stance that the patient views as too close to his previous experience with a parent. Sorting out the differences between parent and therapist then is a transference issue to be pursued. The patient's methods of jeopardizing himself to heighten the chance of failure may come to the fore (as it might with a neurotic patient). Pointing out one's evidence for his self-abnegation might be in order. If the patient responds to structuring of his situation, he may do so to please the therapist and allay his assumed anger. The application of structure is ideally worked out as a cooperative venture by patient and therapist together. If it is attempted as a unilateral suggestion by the therapist, the patient's ambivalent dependence may be too much encouraged. He may become stuck in a position of total passivity, while the therapist energetically and with increasing annoyance takes the active, aggressive role. Therefore, while helping the patient establish a pattern, the therapist may be alert to its implications for the patient.

Addressing oneself to the realities may help to *focus some of the patient's affect* and thus help him to make sense of some apparently vague and overwhelming experience that he reports. This may reduce his general level of anxiety and help him to function.

A young male student came to an hour overflowing with fury with all womankind. He talked about the "evil of Eve," his "all-encompassing and wicked" mother who played with his genitals when he was small, his violent aunt who castrated his cousin by taking him for a hernia operation, and his total abject failure as a potent man. All this was offered without interruption while the patient was becoming increasingly agitated and scattered in his thoughts. The therapist recalled that the preceding hour the patient had talked of a paper that was due for a female teacher. When there was a break in the outpouring, the therapist took the opportunity to ask him about this mundane issue. The patient collapsed in tears and told the therapist that he had thought that he had written a wonderful paper for the woman. He had had it returned the hour before his therapy with only an average grade. The therapist's comment, "You are furious with Mrs. Green" resulted in the patient at first denying it. When his attention was drawn to his angry comments about women in general at the beginning of the hour, he agreed that there was a connection. Then he said that it really felt "*as if* Mrs. Green were castrating me." With the more direct focus for his fear and fury, he began to simmer down and talk of his fear of dropping out of school and of retribution from his parents.

Trying to understand the *symbolic communication* of borderline patients while keeping closely in touch with events in their daily lives may be helpful. In this way the therapist can sometimes act as the interpreter to the patient of his primitive symbolism. One patient always talked about bedbugs in his lodgings and their nightly tortures of him after he had had some argument with his landlord and had not paid the rent. While listening to the horrors of the bedbugs, the therapist found himself discouraging the patient from calling the mayor and the vermin exterminator, and he addressed himself to the issue of the rent and the patient's financial mismanagements. With some help in revising his assets and liabilities, he paid the rent, and the bedbug theme disappeared as an active issue. It then turned into how the patient felt "as miserable as a bedbug" when he failed to pay his rent.

There is value in helping the patient *confront reality* by asking him to explain symbolism that eludes the therapist. In attempting to convey the meaning of the concepts to the therapist, the patient may be able to make more sense of them for himself. If one is puzzled and cannot follow the meaning of the communication, it is helpful to ask the patient to clarify the theme. Occasionally the therapist may feel that the patient is so intelligent and so engaged in abstractions that he will despise him for his questions or will feel that if he were more intellectual he "ought to be able to understand." Occasionally this very feeling may guide the therapist diagnostically, and he may realize that he is talking to a borderline or schizophrenic patient. Examples of this follow. A highly intelligent young poet filled the hours with talk of aesthetics as opposed to ethics, and elaborated on these two systems of thought. It gradually emerged that he was really talking of his difficulty with internal controls. He was at the mercy of swings between welling up of sexual and aggressive feelings in "aesthetics." He spent a great deal of energy turning them off as they seemed overwhelming, resulting in a barren, empty rigidity, or "ethics." Another very bright patient, an actor, talked at length about the fact that "existence" equaled "doubt" in all respects and presented both sides of the equation in metaphysical terms. This had occurred to him as a major insight. It turned out that he was telling the therapist that he was feeling suicidal, and that indeed his own existence was doubtful to him because he felt unreal. Highly colored imagery may be used to describe the feelings of what is happening to the person internally. Patients have talked of defects in their ego boundaries in terms of "cracks in the walls," "open sores," "deep wounds with my guts hanging out," "a balloon with big holes in it," or "floundering in a swimming pool where I struggle to touch the edge by coming to therapy."

The *pacing of therapy* is another theme which may be guided by reality, that is, the reality of the patient's life and how much anxiety he can stand, particularly if he is struggling to maintain his existence outside a hospital. Defense building may be attempted. A patient may, with no urging, open the gulf to vent negative feelings at a primitive level about his mother — for example, about how his mother poisoned him at her breasts. The therapist may bear in mind that somewhere the patient also felt intense love or longing for love from this person, and may attempt to balance the picture with a comment in this direction. This may lessen the risk of the patient's global hatred breaking out of control. The constant bombardment with negative feelings in response to fantasies and reactions about people may be too much pain for the patient to bear, and may result in his further disorganization. There may be a great temptation, when one is inexperienced and is perhaps hearing basic dynamics from a patient firsthand, to intensify the therapy around such an issue, hoping to hear more and more about say the patient's early and overt attempts to possess or destroy his mother. This may not be in the best interests of the patient. If one sees any patient long enough, he will certainly hear the material.

Encouraging more integration in the patient with an accent on relevant but displaced themes may help prevent a borderline patient from becoming psychotic. He may move toward an obsessive defensive position, but this is preferable to psychosis and allows patient and therapist time to unravel some of the powerful underlying feelings. Patients may be quite aware that their obsessions serve a useful function. They may more or less ask one not to assault this thin veneer. One patient said, "I know that it is ridiculous to buy a new pad of clean white paper every time I write to my parents, but I must have it, if I am to keep any communication with them." It was more valuable to this patient to be able to correspond with his parents, even if his desk was piled with virtually unused pads of paper, than for him to face every time his fantasies of soiling them with fecal matter and his guilt and shame. His urge was to "shit all over them," literally, because they had enraged him by their alternating neglect and intrusion in the past. In therapy it was possible to talk with him about "shitting" on them while talking of his other, less direct ways of accomplishing the urge. He used to invite them to arrive in their chauffeur-driven Cadillac at his house at a time when he knew it would be in squalor. He consistently failed at his job and demanded money from them. These derivations of the theme were therefore brought to light for his self-appraisal of how he wished to relate to them, and he could examine how much damage he was doing to himself by cooperating with his compelling urge. His desk remained piled with writing pads.

Serious Crises

Crises often occur in the treatment of a borderline patient. These may concern self-mutilation and suicide attempts, periods of intense vague anxiety, behavior problems such as promiscuity and unwanted pregnancy, or decompensation of a more fixed nature leading to hospitalization.

Feelings of wanting to harm their bodies are common in borderline patients. Wrist-slashing, or making cuts on the body with a razor may occur. This may not be specifically with suicidal intent, but may be on the basis of not feeling real. The physical pain feels good — at least it is a feeling and proves that the body is alive. The flow of blood may produce erotic excitement and orgasmic feelings. It is mixed up in unclear ways with the sight of menstrual blood for some female patients: it demonstrates a living femininity. The touch of the warm, cloying, running matter may be what is primarily sought after.

The need for self-mutilation has been described by some patients as having the secret, dangerous aura of an addiction. Under stress it may emerge as an attractive idea, be postponed till some point when it has reached high intensity and when the urge can be indulged in private. The act is often accompanied by a discharge of feeling, as in orgasm. Peace may follow for a time. When reality begins to dawn, the patient may recoil in horror at his or her actions. One patient described slashing at her "bad parts" with a ferocious intensity. This was the fat on the inside of her thighs, which revolted her because it was too sexual. Another patient slashed her abdomen midway in her menstrual cycle, with an idea of cutting the ovum from her body. A male patient described looking in a mirror while he used dissection forceps to pull away skin from beneath his eyes. He had fantasies of poking his eyes out and having his hands covered in bloody gelatinous matter after blinding himself. The therapist in many instances can only listen and try to develop some understanding of what these actions mean to individual patients. Sometimes they have to do with self-castration and punishment for "sins" committed; sometimes they are derivations of trying to *feel something* in desperation. Often the underlying ideas are exceedingly complex and understanding alone will not cause the self-harm to cease. The actions may alert one to the enormous stress suffered, and alternative avenues of discharge may be explored with patients. One patient decided to masturbate frequently instead, and this controlled the self-mutilation. Another patient painted furiously with red poster paint when she felt the urge. Another locked all her razors away and gave the key to her boyfriend. It is only when the patient is feeling better generally that this symptom will ebb on its own. Tranquilizing medication may be another aid in preventing disintegration to this level.

Wrist-slashing with suicidal intent may be partly related to the above body-image disturbances and absence of feeling. It may also be directed in fury at somebody or some event in the environment. One patient used to smash champagne glasses at fancy cocktail parties and slash his wrists, in order to draw "rich, bloated humanity's" attention to his plight. He felt poor, wasted, and drained. It was a form of public protest at the world that had caused him to be like this. His parents were wealthy suburbanites who attended such parties regularly and paid little attention to their troubled son. The protest was mainly directed at them. Hints of separation or loss of an ambivalently loved person may engender such wrath that the borderline patient will slash his wrists on impulse. It may take only an imagined frown from such a person to provoke the histrionic reaction. The other person may be barely aware of annoyance, while in the borderline it touches to the volcanic core of his feeling of hatred for others and self and focuses all previous rejections into one amorphous mass to be discharged.

An event in the therapy, along the lines of the patient feeling uncared for, may provoke such a response. "You don't love me enough" may be the accusation. One female patient during a long-term therapy was sitting in the emergency room with slashed wrists. Her exasperated therapist finally said, "You want too much from me. Neither I nor anyone else can give you what you didn't get from your mother when you were a baby." This proved a turning point in the therapy, and the patient stopped wrist-slashing. The patient frequently referred to it as the moment at which she began to assess in reality what care she could ask for and receive. It externalized her anger upon her mother and relieved some guilt, in that perhaps the mother had something to do with her present longings and the patient was not all bad. This "moment of truth" arrived against a background of a long relationship with the therapist, in which some trust had been carefully fertilized and tended, and had grown. The level and the timing of the interpretation perhaps were right for this reassessment to occur and a behavior change to follow. The patient's voracious wish to incorporate the therapist had been at the fore. The patient used to bite her own arm in trying to control her cannibalistic impulses toward the therapist. There had been many experiences that the therapist and patient had lived through together, such as the patient's 2 AM desperation phone calls — anything from reporting robbery of her apartment to inviting the therapist to a party. Each had been carefully talked about. The therapist had given a lot of thought to appropriate responses while hearing the patient's wishes and fantasies. It was a long uphill road to the turning point.

Suicidal fantasies of borderline patients often involve the sea. Walking into a warm sea may be a symbol of return to the womb.

One patient described a scene on a moonlit beach when she slowly and deliberately walked up to the neck in the lapping water, feeling enclosed, comforted, warmed, and seeking oblivion. Another talked of walking through the sea to be consumed by the fire of the sun on the horizon. Another patient used to sit on the dock, gazing into the water and fantasize about slowly slithering through the soft water to lie forever on the sandy, pulsating bottom of the ocean. One underlying urge seems to be a cosmic desire for merging in unity with mother nature. Overdoses of medication may involve this encompassing desired oblivion in a related way. One patient slowly took a single pill at a time to cushion the sleepy descent to death and nothingness. Borderline patients may achieve suicide in their decompensated states, while totally out of touch with human beings and reality. The major area for hope in working with these patients lies in whatever attachment they have to the human world. Since the therapist may bear the burden of being the only person who matters, this is an extra reason to be careful at all times to give close attention to how the patient is feeling in the relationship and his reaction to responses offered.

Intense, vague anxiety may be experienced by borderline patients for a prolonged period and may disrupt the pattern of their lives. This may be preceded by some external event, such as a loss, real or imagined, or frustrated demands for intensification of a relationship. The anxiety may be at panic level and grossly out of proportion to the situation. The anxiety seems to exceed that of the neurotic patient. With the latter group, one may be able to trace the source of the reaction. With the borderline patient it may be difficult to understand except in terms of breaking defenses and terror of the experience of internal disintegration. A patient may become suicidal because of the lack of relief to his internal suffering. Sometimes before a patient becomes obviously schizophrenic (particularly a young patient), this intense massive anxiety may be the only feature he is able to describe. Some people feel that this harbinger of complete disintegration may be the cause of otherwise inexplicable successful suicides in late adolescence. These patients may be quite inarticulate about the internal change in themselves, except to recognize that something devastating is going on in their minds. They talk of feelings of impending doom, and suicide may seem a simpler way out than waiting for "some horrendously awful process" to change them. Tranquilizing medication is the best hope for such patients along with psychotherapy. One 18-year-old boy described tranquilizers as "strengthening the walls" enough so that he could begin to try to reassess in therapy what was happening to him. Both of this patient's siblings were in the back wards of state mental hospitals. His grandfather who was schizophrenic had committed suicide. Hospitalization may be necessary to provide the patient with enough protection for himself. Brief hospitalization is often all that is necessary while establishing the patient on medication, and then outpatient treatment can be continued.

Especially with the adolescent borderline, behavior problems may cause the therapist a great deal of worry. The "empty" young woman lacking any definition of herself and feeling "nothing" may become very promiscuous in her efforts to feel anything. She may crave orgasm or may wish for countless orgasms in an effort for feelings of unity or oblivion. Having a penis inside her body may be for her literally to possess one. She may view her vagina primarily as an oral organ, ravenous for fulfillment. Frequent sexual acts may therefore become essential to her, with a total disregard of the man involved or how he may treat her. Pregnancy may be the more desired end. A baby, she feels, might solve her identity diffusion. The fantasies of who actually *is* the baby in the dyad may be problematic. She may feel that she can return to the womb in this way. The baby in fantasy may provide the nebulous "something lacking." It may answer her symbiotic and fusion desires. The main urge may be to fill the "gaping void." Pregnancy in a normal woman provides elements of some of the above feelings and fantasies but with less intensity. Some borderline patients are very well during a pregnancy, because in a sense it legitimizes some of their feelings. However, a realistic plan may be noticeably lacking in her urge to be pregnant. She may not be able to think in advance about coping with the needs of a real child. Practical discussion of contraceptive measures and referral to a family planning clinic are of primary importance with such a patient. In spite of the most careful advice on this matter and regular psychotherapy, the patient may, because of her transient periods of loss of touch with reality and ambivalence, become pregnant more than once. Therapeutic abortions may be advisable but may cause the patient great psychological pain, so it is much better if one can persuade the patient to take adult responsibility for her sexual activities by using contraception. Keeping the baby after delivery may cause her even more difficulty and may promote a psychotic break at that time. This does not always happen, and some patients can use the therapy support given while raising the child successfully. If the patient is married to a supportive husband and wishes for a child, the situation may be very different because she lives in a stable environment with some hope of stability in the future.

There are no easy answers to the management of promiscuity of adolescent borderline patients, especially on an outpatient basis. Some therapists assume a very directive stance about forbidding sexual involvements till such time as the patient shows evidence of settling down in the work and social spheres. The sexual activity may then become an ambivalent issue of control in the therapy. For this to work at a discussable level requires a strong therapeutic alliance. Other therapists take a less rigid stance, and may have a cooperative arrangement with the gynecologist, who may make frequent regular appointments with the patient. Still others are content to keep in close contact with the reality of the patient's involvements and constantly lend some of their ego strength to the patient by asking her to reflect and assess her involvements rather than be impulsive about her needs for sexual contact.

Finally, one may have to consider with the borderline patient, the possibility of disintegration to the psychotic level. This will require medication and may require prolonged hospitalization. The section on hospitalization, voluntarily or by commitment, in Chapter 12, will also apply to the borderline patient. With the best therapeutic efforts available, some patients may inevitably become psychotic, or may be too agitated without a protective environment. The task is to recognize the deterioration for what it is and to try to plan and discuss the need for hospitalization in advance. A facility for intensive long-term inpatient psychotherapy may be the hospital of choice. Such an institution may offer the best hope of reconstituting the person from deeper levels, and it will be equipped with personnel to help in the periods of profound regression that will occur. If the patient cannot afford such care, then one may settle for an alternative — perhaps a ward with therapy geared more toward increasing social controls. If a patient has one area of expertise which has not suffered, such as an intellectually oriented profession or study program, he may put pressure on the therapist to keep him out of the hospital in order to "save" his career. Sometimes this internal force is a factor in helping a patient to pull together the remnants of his ego resources to cooperate, take regular medication, and come several times a week for psychotherapy. Sometimes the present, unremitting strain is too great a price to pay, when weighed against the future discomforts of having a "psychiatric record." The power of the ambivalence, the regressive pull toward the hospital and the wish to remain functioning outside, is often so great a conflict that it results in unreliability on the patient's part. Then the therapist may have to insist on 24-hour care when he himself cannot realistically cope with the numerous demands and pressure any longer to hold the patient on an outpatient basis. This will be particularly true of a suicidal or homicidal patient. Each case must be judged on its own merits, and the therapist can only make the most thoughtful decision he can.

Long-term psychotherapy with the same therapist is most ideal for borderline patients. Many patients can maintain themselves and progress in their development over a period of years. They may achieve a more satisfactory work experience and better relationships with people, and organize their lives in a more comfortable way. If one works in a clinic with ever-changing personnel, the best goal with such a patient may be to try to give him a good initial experience in therapy and to help him establish himself in work so that he can pay for long-term private therapy.

Termination will be a very difficult time for a borderline patient and probably for his therapist. He should be informed of a set date, if possible, some months in advance. All the work that has gone before may look fruitless, and there may be replays of the same situation that brought the patient to therapy in the first place. Separation is profoundly traumatic for such patients as they slowly disengage themselves from the sticky symbiotic bonds and have periods of regression. The patient may need to become very distant and miss sessions as termination approaches. This can be anxiety provoking for the therapist, if his patient is acting in self-damaging ways in the environment at the same time. He may be furious, and his primitive rage may come to the fore. He may be devastated and empty. Intense desires to incorporate the therapist will be present. One patient said, "I will eat you up, and then you will always be with me." A young woman said that she had "poured my whole self" into the therapist, who was then leaving her, having incorporated her. Absence of all feeling may again come into the picture, and the therapist may point out some of the powerful underlying feelings previously experienced in the therapy to try to help to break through the thick cloud of numbness. The patient may feel excluded and excommunicated. He may be terrified that his angry fantasies will result in the dissolution of the therapist. Many of these patients believe with delusional intensity that when the therapist moves away he is dead.

All these powerful feelings may be seen at the same time that the better-integrated parts of the patient are preparing to say good-bye in a less primitive way. Often patients offer gifts at the end of therapy, and if they are appropriate — books, flowers, or a photograph and not a valuable heirloom — then to receive them is appropriate, while acknowledging and hearing the feelings that go into them. It is appropriate because the receiving of a gift respects the higher level of integration in the person who chose it. Occasionally a borderline patient will ask the therapist for permission to write to him. This is usually appropriate as well. One might explain to him the expectation that when he becomes involved in his next therapy he will feel the need less. Also it is reasonable to tell the patient that one cannot conduct psychotherapy by letter but to assure him of at least a brief reply. In other words, to treat it as an expression of his present uncertainty seems appropriate. If possible, one can connect it with the fact that one indeed expects to be alive after termination.

If the patient does not expect to see another therapist after termination, and one plans to work in the same place, then the patient can be assured of the possibility of talking again should the need arise. The therapist wants to avoid the "school—phobic mother" syndrome, showing the patient out while saying, "Are you sure you'll be all right?" At the same time it is helpful for the patient to know of one's availability; these patients often come and go in therapy at times of crises in their lives.

This chapter is not offered as a treatise on the borderline patient. Rather it attempts to give some suggestions on the management of psychotherapy with those patients who show the conglomerate of symptoms and manifestations outlined above, regardless of what diagnostic label the therapist favors.

15

The Therapist's Love Attachments

With certain patients the therapist's love attachments, lack of them, or marital status can become an issue in the therapy. Patients sometimes choose in advance particular therapists because of knowledge about their lives in this regard. They thus come to therapy with built-in expectations. They may choose a single therapist, or a married, divorced, or widowed therapist. It may be important to them whether or not the therapist has children. There may be a variety of expectations in all of these states, from "wanting to know how you do it," to "wanting to know how you can stand it." At a manifest level, there may be a wish to learn, and a hope that the therapist can be a wise teacher. While one may pursue the expectations in the usual way to learn more about the patient, one may or may not choose to use personal anecdotes to illustrate some point during the therapy. Enough has already been said about the pros and cons of deciding on this path.

For the therapist, the same general principles apply in trying to sort out one's feelings about his own situation, and separating them off from the patient's concerns so they can more easily be allowed to develop.

Points of transition in the therapist's life are times when he or she is more likely to be caught up in concerns about himself which may put him off balance in his vision of the patient and his therapy. For illustrative purposes here, some aspects of mutual involvement, engagement, marriage, and divorce will be used. There are two separate but interacting topics involved for the therapy. The first is the internal feeling of the therapist, which may affect the hours. The second is the patient's reaction to new information or to an external manifestation such as the appearance or disappearance of the ring on the ring finger or to a change in surname.

IMPENDING COMMITMENT

Often when there is an intense relationship between partners at a point before a defined commitment to each other, the persons involved may find themselves more than usually preoccupied, subject to affect changes, having a sense of vulnerability, or perhaps varying in their usual manner of approaching events or people. They may be sensitive to the possible new way that others will see them, and go through internal shifts in their view of themselves. There may be excitement and joy in anticipation of uninterrupted sharing; maximal pleasure gained in the company of the partner, feeling work or external events as an intrusion; pleasure in feeling more mature with a firmer future plan in mind; or whatever. Admixed with this happiness may be fear about having made the right decision, fear of the demands of continual closeness, sadness, loss over youth having seemingly passed, or perhaps loss over the closing of opportunities for other sexual relationships. It may be much more complicated. Engagement can be viewed as an example of this time, and for many it may imply a trial period rather than a defined commitment. Formal engagement means different conditions for different people. The trial period is only one way of looking at it, but it was the background for the following therapist's emotional state while engaged to be married. The example shows how it influenced a passage in therapy.

The patient did not know about his female therapist's new status. He was an attractive looking, vital young man, a poet. He was in therapy because of uncontrollable rages he experienced toward his wife. During one hour just after the therapist became engaged, he was particularly seductive and direct about his attraction to his therapist. He felt that if she would have an amorous relationship with him, it would solve all his problems. At more quiescent times in the therapist's life, while observing the man's attractive verbal ability and physical appeal, she could keep a therapeutic stance, allow herself her own fantasies without having a need to participate in the patient's seductive behavior. The therapist had to present this particular hour in therapy to her supervisor. She remembered that she had forgotten her ring the day of the patient's appointment, and she "forgot" to bring her notes along to the supervisor. She said that "nothing much happened." Discussion developed with the supervisor about the possibilities behind her unusual forgetting. Gradually it became clear, as she related the content of the hour during which some verbal titillation had gone on, that the therapist felt quite guilty about her fantasies concerning the patient. She was particularly guilty about allowing herself fantasies about anyone else besides her fiancé, though as yet she did not feel wholly committed. Due to the talk with the supervisor, who helped her awareness of her heightened vulnerability in this area, the issues arising from the therapist remained under control. The following hour, the patient talked further about his wish to ask her to dinner, to "tempt her" and see if she could withstand his "powerful charm" to women. The therapist having passed the "test," the patient then began to elaborate on his difficulties in drawing a line between fantasy and action with women. He liked his wife and wanted to remain married, but his philandering had led to bitter fights, after which he felt very depressed. This was new material in the unfolding of his concern. Had the therapist, reacting with guilt and anxiety, closed off exploration of the implications of his flirtation, he might have been unable to tell her about his affairs and the pain they caused to both him and his wife.

THE RING

If a woman wears a traditional engagement ring on her left hand, this objective evidence of attachment to a man appears at a time of the couple's relationship which may be more unstable than after the marriage is established. Others at similar stages of involvement who do not wear rings may be in a less revealed position in therapy hours because the public evidence is not in the presence of the patient. The patient may react one way or another to the new ring or to new knowledge from an outside source. One may expect anything from no response or a mild socially appropriate reaction, to a major response or undercurrent. One waits to see how or if the issue develops to gauge its relative importance to the patient.

A therapist with a new engagement or wedding ring may wonder,

"Should I introduce the topic with the patient, or should I wait to see if it becomes an issue?" It is probably better to wait and see how it may come up in the hour. It is understandable that the therapist, equipped with a shiny ring, may feel it is so obvious that it will bedazzle the most taciturn patient into some response. The therapist may be much more concerned about it than his patient. One male therapist referred to it as a "burr in my paw," and, being uncomfortable, he felt that every patient would detect his ambivalence, shyness, and sense of exposure. There may be a temptation to draw attention to one's brand new situation, but this urge may bespeak a high level of anxiety which is not compatible with being able to listen. Thus, it is usually preferable to try to set it aside and not unilaterally intrude the information. If the therapist is able to wait, sooner or later, if it is significant to the patient, the content of the hour will direct the therapist in his response. The themes will be very different with each patient.

What if a patient does not bring up "the ring" at all? One might assume, if there is no material in the hours relating to it at any level, that it is truly not important to the patient. Another possibility is that the patient is so bound up with himself that he notices nothing of what goes on with other people. Another possible explanation is that it is somehow important for the patient to know nothing of the therapist. In these cases, one would broach news of the event slowly, if at all. However, even after a long time lapse, in some cases it may be appropriate to try to talk about the appearance of the ring. Bringing the patient's attention to it as an omission from the therapy, coupled with one's observations of how it seems to have affected his behavior, may be indicated. An example follows.

For two years of her treatment, a middle-aged widow saw a therapist who was a bachelor. He then married, and treatment continued without mention of his new status. His ring was the only evidence for the patient. The patient, who had been eager in her regularity and often early for appointments, began to come late. There were always credible excuses for the lateness. There was such discontinuity in the therapy that the therapist felt he must mention his marriage and wonder if her feelings about that were interrupting her attendance, drawing to her attention that the irregularity began to occur at the time of the appearance of his ring. Her response was one of total amazement. She had genuinely not noticed. She was angry that he had thought "so little of her," and she stopped treatment. One can only suppose in retrospect, that to have an unattached therapist and deny that other women could exist for him was a very important part in the maintenance of her treatment. She was both unable and unwilling to discuss her feelings on the matter. Before his marriage she had been involved in talking about her loneliness and her disgust with her masturbating activities; one may conjecture that perhaps the therapist was the object of her fantasies. The fantasy was perhaps now spoiled since he had openly declared his love for someone else, and the patient had nothing more to do with him. In retrospect, the therapist decided he had made an error and waited too long to introduce the issue. But the patient might have fled from treatment anyway.

CHANGE OF SURNAME

For some female therapists vis-à-vis a patient, this may be the first external manifestation to be introduced into therapy. A secretary, for example, may say to a patient who asks for one by her maiden name, "Oh — you mean *Mrs.* So and So — she's married now you know." Or one may simply personally inform the patient of her married name and say that she plans to use it professionally. Other female therapists will be married, with or without a ring, and decide to keep their original surname. However one handles the issue, it may be of interest to a particular patient.

One borderline patient who was in treatment before her female therapist's marriage, always addressed her by her maiden name although she was aware that she used her married name professionally. For the patient, there was a fear that if identified by her married name, the therapist would be metamorphosed into a different woman, with a changed style and stringent views about the patient's sex life. This was closer to the image of her mother. It was important to this patient that she continue to use the maiden name to keep the images separate in her mind, although she was aware of some of its meaning to her.

With other patients, "forgetting" or refusal to use one's married name can be a sign of hostility, fear of abandonment, personal rivalry, or clinging to one's identity in the maiden state. For others, using the maiden name while knowing that one generally uses the married name can be "a gift" to the therapist on an assumption that the therapist might not want to lose anything of her professional individuality. Use of the maiden name may be based on a hope that the therapist might not wish for children who might interfere with career aspirations.

A therapist who the patient knows is married, and who continues to use her maiden name, may be viewed positively by a patient as being serious and interested in her work (and thus maintaining her interest in the patient). Or she may be seen positively or negatively as a freer individual. A patient may register dismay and assume that the therapist neglects her husband. The change of name or maintenance of the original name may therefore have many innuendos, apart from the therapist's view of herself.

TRANSFERENCE IMPLICATIONS

Reactions to the therapist's attachment may occur within the therapy connected to a patient's concerns about "sharing" the therapist. This sharing may represent, at various levels, old rivalry with a sibling, old rivalry with a parent, or perhaps rivalry with the real-life mate, in which the patient is feeling like a displaced spouse.

An example about sibling rivalry follows. This theme could begin, say, with comments about other patients in the waiting room and the patient's experiencing jealousy. It might further unfold to the patient talking spontaneously of noticing the therapist's ring; or he might ask a question about whom the therapist lives with. This may become elaborated in fantasies of the therapist, and of his or her mate being together lovingly, and having no time for the patient. In one instance, the patient's thoughts led him to notice the ring and comment on his therapist's marriage. He began to talk of feeling very excluded after his brother became married. They had always had a special, close relationship, and the patient was outraged that the brother now spent very limited time with him. The brother's wife had been the target of unprovoked verbal attacks by the patient, and as a result of the discussion with the therapist, he began to see the problem as his own internal struggle, rather than that his sister-in-law was evil.

Not wanting to share the therapist may be a superficial representation of the oedipal triangle. The therapist may hear many overtones of anger, fear, or jealousy in the fantasies about his or her mate. If the anger is being experienced, and is showing itself in oblique ways, it may be appropriate to say something like, "Such-and-such leads me to think that you have some feelings that I have become married." The patient may rebuff this entirely, dismissing it as too petty and ridiculous. But the potential clarification has been made, and one can watch later events to see the result. The same patient may become silent and sullen, accuse one of intruding one's life upon him, or he may seem to change the topic. Such a change of topic, if one is on the right line, may be a displacement from the issue at hand.

One patient in this position told the female therapist an angry story in this regard. His roommate and he jointly owned a cat. He wanted the cat to himself. The other boy had no right to have it lying on his bed. The therapist pointed out the irritations in issues of ownership for the patient, and said that it might have a relevance to what was going on between patient and her in the room. She reintroduced the issue of her marriage. The patient acknowledged that there was probably something to it and began to reflect on how he had noticed a change in the therapist, had seen the ring, and had an immediate tightening in his stomach. He began to see that what he was experiencing was anger, but felt that it was silly to show that he cared so much. The atmosphere between patient and therapist cleared, and he went on further to talk about how he used to feel "all tightened up" when his father kissed his mother. The resistance on the patient's part to further work was eased by the clarification of the here-and-now feelings about the therapist. The patient experienced live, in the hour, the "tightening up" sensation, which, incidentally, he had come to therapy complaining about, and the therapist had a precious chance to observe it, and discover with the patient that it was at least partly concerned with anger. The present anger had been allotted to its appropriate place (between patient and therapist). The patient later on was able to enter on a collaborative venture with the therapist to recall earlier instances connected with its more irrational components.

"You wouldn't do that to me!" may be the tone of the outrage from the patient who feels his "love" has been betrayed. The male patient may act like a jealous husband with his female therapist, or a female patient like a jealous wife, suddenly suspicious of every minor action of her male therapist.

The following transference fantasies are connected at deeper levels with the original "sharing" situation and internal feelings about mother or father. There is a common thread in the manifest level of a wish to be closer to the therapist or fear about assumed alienation, and a fear or wish that the therapist will act differently.

Heightened fantasies about the therapist's sexuality may come to the fore. One female patient said with embarrassment to her male therapist, "Well — uh — I always thought of you as sort of intellectual. I didn't think that you'd — uh — have those sorts of interests in anybody." The therapist asked, "What sorts?" and the patient blocked, struggled, and murmured, "Sexual interests." After that she markedly dressed up in the hours, was not flirtatious, but spoke of "realizing that the therapist was interested in all aspects of life." Later in therapy she talked of her bookish father whom she could not imagine making love to anyone, and of having admiration for the therapist since his marriage. This was all very complicated, but one aspect was feeling closer to the therapist and allowing herself sexual fantasies about him, feeling he was "safe" now. Other patients may manifest anxiety with the openly declared "sexual" therapist, for whatever reasons.

A patient may be jealous of the therapist because he assumes that he is more potent and must have a beautiful wife. Yet another may offer pity for the terrible mistake, and feel superior and deprecating. One man who was in a bad marriage adopted a "warning father" role, seeing the therapist as a naive boy caught in the clutches of a woman. His hostility about women came into focus in his efforts to protect and cling to his male therapist.

A paranoid patient became quite fearful of talking to his female therapist about sexual material because he had fantasies that the therapist would begin to share stories and tidbits from his treatment with her spouse in order to ridicule and persecute him.

Along the lines of a fear or wish that the therapist will change is the following: A male therapist who was formerly valued by an adolescent male patient as "hip" and "swinging" was berated for being so square and conventional. The therapist tried to find out why it was so important to cast him in this role. This led to elucidation of some fantasies on the patient's part that the therapist would collude with him in his rebellion against his parents and encourage in particular his abuse of drugs.

Identification with the therapist, or the patient producing his "own supplies," may prompt the patient to imitate the therapist and also get married. This may not necessarily be damaging to the patient, though one may advisedly view the step with caution. If the mate is chosen in a hurry, and the needs are clearly in parallel with the fantasied "loss" of the therapist, questions might be raised with the patient about the appropriateness of such action. However, if they have been discussed over a long time, with the identification issues to the fore, it may simply mean that the time is ripe for the patient, too, to become betrothed.

DIVORCE

If the therapist is in the midst of emotional trials of any sort, he may be too ready to share aspects of his experience because of his vulnerability. In divorce, it may be tempting to let a divorcing patient know that one is going through or has gone through a similar experience. It may also be tempting to use the information to explain to a patient one's preoccupation, new distance, or whatever. Living in a small community where one is seeing patients who may know his or her friends socially, the patient may have heard about the situation, perhaps with embellishments. Some external evidence may be there for the patient to react to — disappearance of the wedding ring from the finger, or change of name of a female therapist.

Again, for some patients it may not be a particularly loaded issue. For others it will create a lot of feelings which can be heard and, if appropriate, used in the therapy.

For the therapist there may be some problems in separating off his own reactions from the patient's problem. If one is very relieved, he may find oneself subtly encouraging a patient to leave his or her spouse. According to how regretful one feels for his own loss, one may have a tendency to encourage a patient to persevere in a limping marriage, when the patient is being indecisive and prevailing upon one to provide direction for him.

A patient reacting to news of one's divorce may directly show his feelings. These may be envy, sadness, or perhaps disgust. The patient may now view the therapist as an ally, assuming that he too has difficulties with the opposite sex; or another patient may interpret the situation as the therapist being truly, ideally, emotionally free. One single female patient, knowing of her female therapist's divorce, used the information to further compare herself to the therapist and draw strength from her fantasies of the therapist's experience. She had been involved in an unsatisfactory relationship but had been unable to terminate it. Her new thought about this was, "Perhaps if you can divorce, lead your own life, and seem to survive quite well, then maybe I can do it too?" Yet another patient may scold the therapist for being imperfect, along the lines, "How can *you* treat me for psychiatric problems when you must suffer yourself?" A patient may feel betrayed or let down by the fact that his own notion of the therapist as having an ideal marriage is called into question. Another ambivalent thought may be, "Now she/he is gone, who will you discuss me with?"

Identification with the therapist's children may be seen in various ways and will relate to the patient's own experience with his parents.

Some patients become worried because the therapist's "caretaking" abilities become doubtful for them. "If you alienated your husband/wife, you didn't take care of him/her very well. What about your children? Perhaps you are too self-involved to be able to take good care of me?" This relates, but has a different slant from the next example discussed.

One young female patient whose own parents had divorced when she was 6 years old now began to set up situations of potential conflict between her spouse and her newly divorced female therapist. She "carried tales" from one to the other and seemed to be doing her best to provoke a confrontation. Meanwhile, it was clear that she wanted to maintain her "special" relationship with both of them. This seemed to be a prototype of her earlier experience, when she still wanted each parent, in the midst of their divorce, but wanted to stir up turmoil between them. In this way she could have the "ideal" situation of childhood — the parents together but fighting. While this situation existed, she maintained an uneasy relief from her anxiety. She was ultimately able to assess whether this was the most successful way of having each care for her.

The patient of the divorced therapist may wonder if he or she contributed in some way to the disagreements leading to the dissolution. A female patient, for example, may blame herself for being angry with the therapist and taking too much out on him, so that the divorce was exhausted and could not work in his marriage. She may fear or hope that her sexual fantasies of the therapist were reciprocated, and may now appear very anxious in hours with the "free therapist." Until this material is explored fully, she may not be able to relax again in the hour. Another patient may want to "fill the gap" for the therapist and take the place of the missing marital partner. Some homosexual patients have fled in fear from a divorced therapist of the same sex, and some have become more established in therapy, for many reasons, one of which could be some fantasied reciprocity of emotional involvement.

The patient's observations and fantasies about the therapist's work environment are always important. They may have heightened significance if one is recently divorced. The therapist's behavior may be under particular scrutiny if a patient sees him while waiting for therapy, but at any time these observations play a part in the patient's reality assessments of the therapist. These will include behavior with other patients, secretaries, or other therapists. If one works in a clinic and is readily observed as he talks to other staff members on the way to meet the patient, the fantasies about a divorced therapist having affairs with other clinic members may preoccupy a waiting patient. Expressions about these will again be representative in some way of the patient and his concerns about the treatment.

Patients will therefore absorb the reality of the therapist's attachments and marital status on different levels. In many of these examples, the knowledge of the therapist's life illustrated concerns about the therapist imposed by the patient for his own needs, to show an upsurge of his conflict. These can sometimes be used in his therapy. Reactions of other patients may be less intense and may never become an issue. These include mild mixtures of pleasure or sadness on the therapist's behalf, tentative concerns about possible preoccupation (often reality-based), or mild guilt about any extra requests other than their regular therapy coming at such a moment in the therapist's life.

16

Some Aspects of the Therapist's Age

Iza S. Erlich
Rosemary M. Balsam

The age of the therapist is but one angle of the prism through which the patient's presentation is refracted. We will be dealing here with some common feelings and dilemmas having to do with this issue, with particular emphasis on the older therapist.

Young therapists are often very anxious about their youthfulness. With young patients they will often have some discomfort with interplay of sexual feelings or erotic flattery. Particularly as beginners they may become quite threatened in the presence of a peer who has severe psychopathology. Disabling symptoms in a patient may call up doubts about their own sanity or the extent of their own neuroses. Approaching an older patient they may feel acutely aware of their lack of life experience. One therapist after his marriage and early fatherhood reflected, "I think I used to get very angry when a patient implied 'You are only a little kid. How would you know what it is like to live day-to-day with a woman, or be the bread-earner for five kids?' " Single therapists, men or women, may feel uncomfortable on hearing patients' feelings about birth and delivery. Or they may feel they know nothing when a question arises about the handling of a problem child. There is really no answer to this dilemma, but its acknowledgment can be a start in defining areas where one might be especially alert in asking a supervisor's opinion, or in discussing one's anxieties with him. More extended comments on these issues are offered throughout the book. Lack of similar experiences to a given patient could be an advantage and could lead to a fresh open-minded approach when one is truly willing to learn about the patient's emotional experience.

Less has been said about the implications of being a *mature or middle-aged therapist.* There follow some clinical descriptions of a few of the issues involved. In mirror image some of these are also applicable to the young therapist. Problems may show themselves differently vis-à-vis patients of various age groups.

A young patient struggling with his relationship to his parents may put the middle-aged therapist in an uncomfortable position, particularly one who is concerned about his own adolescent children. A student may tell the therapist: "My parents . . . they are old fogies; they don't understand me or my life-style. . . . All they say is 'study, study, study. . . .' They want me to stay in school but stay away from politics, grass, and girls. . . ." The list may go on indefinitely. While a young therapist may overidentify with such a position, being still close to the conflicts over independence, the older therapist faces other temptations. One of the pitfalls may be overeagerness to give well-meaning advice, spontaneously assuming the familiar parental role. The immediate response to the question "Should I leave school?" may be "Sure! Why don't you take a year off?" or conversely "You will be much better off finishing the semester." Either of these responses may impede further exploration of the conflict for the patient since it assumes that he or she cannot struggle independently with the pros and cons.

Another temptation may be to indicate to a patient that one is *not* like his parents, or better yet that one is a superior parent, alike in no respect to the "old fogies."

A young woman told her older female therapist that she was living with her boyfriend, then added: "I know what you are thinking of me now! You think I am a slut!" The therapist asked her the grounds for this assumption, and the girl answered: "That's what my mother thinks. After all you are the same age, so you must think the same way." The session continued with the patient talking angrily about her puritanical mother, so ready to condemn her daughter. After missing two sessions the patient returned "to conclude therapy": "It is no help at all! In fact it makes me feel worse!" Reconstructing the preceding session in her own mind, the therapist recalled her private thoughts of her own upbringing and her amusement at the girl's mistaken accusation. She had smiled at the idea during the session. Thus nonverbally she conveyed to this very astute patient that she did not share her mother's viewpoint.

In the present hour the therapist brought up the missed appointments and commented that the patient seemed annoyed with her. The patient then volunteered that it was the smile that provoked her reaction. She felt confused by "the understanding smile," had gone home feeling guilty, angry, and disloyal to her mother. She was able to spell out her mixed feelings about both her mother and the therapist further, and allowed herself to stay in therapy. This smile, so natural with one's friends, might have abbreviated this therapy if patient and therapist had been unable to become aware of some of its meanings. The "knowing smile" attitude may stem from many roots. It may be a sort of self-forgiveness for one's youthful "follies." To think of oneself as a "with it" parent may bolster the therapist's self-worth: her children will have no reason to be angry with her, the way this patient was angry at her mother. It may assuage feelings of envy toward the younger woman, saying in effect: "I am still young and still a sexual being." This in turn might disrupt temporarily one's ability to listen to the patient's implication: "You have to be against my sexuality, because you, like my mother, are finished." All this need not be interpreted to a patient. Rather, it may be used to keep one alert for the vicissitudes of a seductive presentation of oneself.

Wanting to be perceived by the patient as a "now" person may be inviting. The patient's tendency toward emotional or intellectual flattery, dovetailing with the countertransference problem, may prevent the therapist from assessing reasonably the transference implications of his presentation. A gifted and appealing young man often made positive comments to his middle-aged therapist about her warm, supportive attitude to him. Nevertheless, he was consistently late for his hour, each time offering another excuse. Finally he offered the following explanation. The therapist looked very much like his mother, whom he described as a controlling and intrusive person. The resemblance preyed on his mind and, he said, interfered with his being more open. He said that he would appreciate being transferred to a male therapist in the same clinic. The therapist readily agreed. Partly disappointed, partly angry, partly afraid of being seen increasingly like his difficult mother, she found it easier to accede to the request and its rationale than to inquire more closely into the issues involved in this particular manifestation. The patient's lateness turned out to be a chronic problem central to his difficulties.

The transfer to another therapist may or may not have been ultimately indicated. However the ready closure of discussion about the underlying feelings might not have occurred had the therapist been less invested in the patient's flattery.

One way of thinking about adolescent problems is to say, "After all, isn't that what the younger generation does nowadays?" Sometimes such a stance results from a patient's identification with the therapist's own children. Taking a mild view of the young person's life-style may serve to reassure oneself. Drug use, for example, may occur as a part of normal experimentation of adolescence. On the other hand, it may be part of a schizophrenic picture.

Somewhere along the line, one ought to expect an overt *comment about one's age*. The patient may be simply pleased that one looks mature. That may have to do with "the wise old woman" or "the wise old man" image and an expectation of being well cared for. Young girls baffled by their sexuality may feel more comfortable with an older woman; young men may find it less threatening and competitive to talk to an older person of either sex. However, the same patients, hurt, bewildered, and angry, will often verbally attack their therapists in time of stress. If the therapist is young, negative comments may focus on the presumed lack of experience. With an older therapist the comments may imply inability to understand young people. The therapist who is unmarried may hear: "What can you know about real life?" One middle-aged, single, female therapist said that if her patients did not make some negative comments about her spinsterhood during the course of therapy, she wondered what went amiss! A clinical example follows with reference to a patient's perception of the therapist's advanced age:

Shortly before vacation a young woman denied hotly having any negative feelings about the interruption. As a matter of fact, she said, there was no reason for any feelings nor even curiosity, since she could envisage the scene very well: "You will have a very quiet time. . . relaxed . . . not do much . . . perhaps a bit of gardening . . . a few watercolors. . . ." After a pause she remarked: "My grandmother is very old, but she still gardens. . . ." She added that her grandmother, of whom she was very fond as a child, by now was getting quite senile. Thus the idyllic peaceful image conveyed a further message: "You are not good for much — why should I miss you?" After expanding the fantasy, she was free to talk about her warm feelings, her disappointments and unrealistically inflated expectations of the therapy and its anticipated comforts. This also illustrates a positive aspect of age, in that an older therapist may elicit in a young patient important recollections about grandparents who may have been the main source of affection and support in a crumbling family.

An older patient often expresses preference for an older therapist. There is an understandable reluctance to perceive someone younger than oneself in a position of authority. Such a patient may react with relief when confronted by an older therapist, saying that cooperation will be easier. Faced with so much eagerness and pleasure, the middle-aged therapist may overlook the formation of a rather superficial alliance, which, if maintained, may turn out not to be in the best interests of the patient. The therapy may be viewed by the patient as a social occasion between friends who will together commiserate and swap interesting stories. Such exaggeration of the "mutual friendship" aspects of the therapeutic relationship may show itself by a greater than usual curiosity about therapist's life or by multiple occasions for role reversal, as by the patient opening every hour with "How are you today?" or asking often "What would you do in my position?"

Sometimes this wish for mutuality, bypassing more direct work on the problems, may stem from a patient's brittleness or his inability or unreadiness to consider changes. An older widow whose husband died recently sought treatment primarily because of concerns about her youngest daughter. She was pleased to find an older therapist and often made comments to that effect. An accidental meeting at a local restaurant gave her further cause to stress the neighborly ties. She wanted to talk about housekeeping, shopping, and generalities about families. She was unable to talk about her husband's death, though the therapist gave her many leads. She did not even say much about her stated problem. In this case her stance seemed to be a necessary defense against her feelings, which she could not tolerate at the moment. A friendly contact was what this patient needed most at this time in her life. It is important to respect such a patient's defenses, and to accept the deep-seated anxiety rather than disturb adaptive coping devices that have been used more or less successfully for many years — particulary if the patient does not wish change.

While the older patient may have a need to deny some aspects of the therapeutic character of the relationship, the older therapist, in contrast, may have an exaggerated need to stress it. Here one's identification with a patient may be a threat to him and he may wish to distance himself unnecessarily from the patient. The therapist may be tempted to communicate: "Never forget that you are the one who is asking for help." He may thus be too authoratative, or always need to be the expert with the right answers. A balanced attitude on the part of the therapist will allow him neither to go along unwittingly with a patient's usual defenses nor to create necessarily an insuperable barrier between therapist and patient.

Age is therefore only one of the many tangible features that a therapist brings to the situation. Like all other aspects of oneself, it may occasionally hinder and occasionally help the therapeutic process.

17

The Pregnant Therapist

There is a concrete visual aspect to the pregnant therapist that is inescapable, and that of necessity evokes some kind of reaction at different levels in patients. Its existence may influence the content of the hours by highlighting facets of what a patient chooses to present to the therapist.

The internal feelings of the pregnant therapist warrant attention because pregnancy has such a biological and psychological momentum of its own. The pregnant therapist may find that her inner life varies more in intensity than before. At times her inner life may be so full and active that it is hard for her to attend to the patient. At other times it will be a rich background against which to react to a patient while monitoring her own associations and careful responses. At other times it will be quiescent and the therapist may feel calmly receptive. It is a question of balancing one's own needs and feelings vis-à-vis the patient, as in the general conduct of psychotherapy, but pregnancy may exaggerate aspects of this interaction between patient and therapist.

TO WORK OR NOT TO WORK

Many women therapists continue work almost up to the day the baby is born. Others choose to stop work a month or more before

265

the due date or not work at all. An argument can be made in favor of stopping work in very late pregnancy, due to the dramatic, increasing preoccupation with one's own feelings about the new person, the delivery, bodily changes, and the imminent change due to occur in the emotional climate of the marriage. It may be difficult to set these preoccupations aside. They may inundate the therapist and dull her response to patients.

In the scheme of things the welfare of the unborn baby and the mother is of vital importance to herself and perhaps warrant first priority. However, there are people who in the midst of turmoil find themselves capable of good, focused work.

There may be conflicts within the therapist about the quantity as well as the duration of work. Each person has to decide on an amount of work which is comfortable for herself psychologically and financially.

It may be hard to make a fixed decision in advance because the pregnant woman's vision of herself may fluctuate. The quantity of work undertaken may vary with her views about its relative importance or about the quality she feels she is able to achieve at a particular time. Any therapist who was previously singleminded in her devotion to her patients will now make efforts to balance a satisfactory work experience with a satisfactory experience as an expectant mother. This can be an uneven ongoing process. The following factors also may influence the therapist's decision on the quantity of work she will do.

The atmosphere in which she works may influence the decision. In this age of admirable effort to establish competent women in jobs of equal status with competent men, one's job may have depended on some kind of fight, on selling oneself as "strong" and not liable to the "weak" feminine position of being pregnant. Can one then have the gall to be sick in early pregnancy, or to complain about it? It may be hard for the therapist to withstand such pressures in her social field and maintain the ability to decide for herself. A more permissive atmosphere of work may also exist, in which one may work as much as one reasonably can. The therapist's physical state may be taken into account, too, in the decision. She may be nauseous in early pregnancy. Since this often occurs predictably at a definite time of the day, those hours of work may be better canceled and made up later. If she is suffering from fatigue in late pregnancy, it may be possible to lie down for portions of the day between patient interviews, to engage in less demanding activity, such as participating in case discussion conferences, to see fewer individual therapy patients. Any professional woman having her first baby is liable to be entering a crisis of identity, so she may go to one extreme or another. A therapist even in early pregnancy, may want to relinquish too much of her work in the interests of proving herself a better mother, or she may take on too much work to prove herself a reliable professional woman, thus draining off time needed to care for herself and her family. While deciding about the comfortable quantity of work, parallel countertransference factors may operate. At one moment there may be an awareness of being too encouraging of another young woman toward more professional work to compensate for a lack in oneself, and at another moment encouraging a patient toward less academic and more domestic pursuits for one's own gratification.

There are probably limitations regarding the kind of patients with whom a pregnant therapist may best work. Patients who for any reason are too draining may deplete the resources of the therapist, who is already using a great deal of energy because of biological and also psychological demands. This would apply more to late pregnancy. Practical issues, such as frequent night emergency duty, may have to be postponed till the therapist is nonpregnant. It may be particularly difficult for a pregnant therapist to remain neutral and helpful in therapeutic abortion consultations. It may also require too much of a patient seeking abortion to be asked to talk to a pregnant woman about her concerns. Excessive hostility and guilt might be expected to cloud the issues for both participants.

Doing initial evaluations may be different from doing ongoing work with patients, particularly in late pregnancy. After all, the regular therapy patient has had up to nine months to get used to the idea, as has the therapist. In a brief initial consultation there is such limited time to hear the patient's reactions that it may be unfair to overwhelm the patient when there is little chance of followup.

The therapist's pregnancy is discussed here under the headings early, middle, and late pregnancy. However, all of the examples could occur at any time in pregnancy. A temporal sequence is chosen for purposes of emphasis, selecting those aspects which may lend themselves more to one particular phase or another. The patient, too, shares the temporal element of the therapist's pregnancy. A beginning, a progression, and an end point exist. The timing of his concerns may parallel the stage of the pregnancy that is obvious to him in the office.

EARLY PREGNANCY

In early pregnancy there is nothing external to perceive. Internally there may be a variety of feelings that affect the way the therapist will listen to a patient. There may be excitement, elation, anxiety, numbness, sadness, a sense of pride — a wide spectrum of emotions, possibly not too stable. If she is flooded with one of these, the therapist may be more likely to read a similar feeling in the patient. For example, a patient may appear at the clinic smiling while relating some disturbing events. The excited or elated therapist may be too ready to accept the smile and feel that the patient must see some humor in the content, as one might find with a neurotic patient. This particular cold marionette smile may denote the detachment of all feeling, characteristic of schizophrenia. The therapist may feel all-bountiful in her fertility and react by being "too helpful" to the patient in her desire to raise all the suffering world to the same plane as herself.

On the other hand increased sense of personal worth and fulfillment may help her to withstand the many ungratifying passages in therapy, and she may allow the patient more leeway to express his or her painful emotions without requiring evidence of improvement to give the seal of approval to her work. It may be a first experience for her in allowing more primitive emotions to come nearer to surface. This may enhance her sensitivity and tolerance to the more global, massive feelings at varying degrees below the surface with certain patients.

If the therapist is suffering from physical sickness, this can be a drain on emotional availability, and in general it should prompt the therapist to wonder if she can rearrange her schedule. In one instance the therapist found the experience useful with a patient. A 21-year-old female patient was describing how she told her mother when menstruation occurred for the first time. The content of the hour triggered some reveries in the therapist about her own first period. Her next association was a sense of guilt about the gap between her sexual innocence then and her present pregnant state. She realized that the patient's monotonous voice was becoming more distant, and she felt faint and sick. Following the rule of thumb to keep quiet when one is in extreme doubt about how to respond, she wondered desperately if she were going to run out of the room and vomit in the nearby toilet, probably in view and earshot of the patient. After a few deep breaths she made a heroic effort to listen to the patient's words and push away thoughts of being sick. She felt that her fantasied actions would have made her too vulnerable in the presence of the patient and that she would have been ashamed. As the patient's voice became louder again, she heard the words, "And every time I told her about my period, mother would rush to the toilet and vomit. Now why do you think that was?" Well, why indeed! It raises all kinds of questions about how the patient told her mother, why the mother was so hypersensitive to the description. In this instance the therapist heaved a sigh of relief that she had been able to control her own vegetative functions. (One should not, however, feel constrained to control oneself against powerful odds.) The therapist's vomiting would have dramatically reinforced the patient's negative experience but would not have been disastrous because they could have discussed the issue later. The therapist sat back and tried to use her first associations to promote further inquiry into the powerful catalytic effect of the patient's telling her mother about her periods. She felt that her own feelings may have given her a clue to understanding the mother's situation and the emetic effect of the daughter's sexuality — such as fear of competition or retaliation from another mature woman. Mother and daughter may have felt themselves rivals as sexual women, perhaps evoking guilt in the daughter and fear in the mother.

The highly sensitive schizoid, borderline, or psychotic patient may sometimes perceive very minor changes in the therapist — a brighter eye, a livelier step, or changes in intonation in early pregnancy. When one feels well concealed, it may be a shock if a patient begins talking directly about pregnancy without some connecting links from previous hours. If the therapist is feeling exposed, she may leap prematurely to force the patient into talking about her pregnancy. At some moments in therapy, the therapist's physiological state may be secondary, and not a primary focus. In the following example a schizophrenic patient talked of pregnancy in both early and later phases. The earlier episode could be viewed as a harbinger of how he viewed himself in relation to the therapist at a later time. It was preferable to work more directly with his concerns at the later time because of the burgeoning visible reality.

An 18-year-old schizophrenic came into the office for the third hour of therapy when the therapist was two months pregnant. He looked distressed and tense and had difficulty starting to talk. He told about how he collected his milk in bottles every morning outside the front door. Then he suddenly said, "How disgusting pregnant women are!" The next comment was about the small size of his penis. The therapist, viewing his anxiety and scattering of thoughts, wondered if she should focus the topic by saying, "I wonder if you have somehow noticed that I am pregnant?" She decided that *that* comment had more to do with her own anxiety. Instead she said, "How come you jumped to pregnancy? Could you tell me what the connection is?" This "jump" in his discontinuity of thought turned out to be triggered by the next-door neighbor's pregnancy. This woman, in her maternity dress, collected her milk bottles at the same time as the patient. He was tortured with fantasies of having impregnated her in a magical way via his hand on her milk bottle. Filling in the connection for the therapist made his communication more comprehensible to himself and to her. The patient's anxiety decreased and his thoughts flowed in more continuity. Later in the pregnancy of the therapist, the patient had similar fantasies of having impregnated her, but the timing of the discussion about her own pregnancy was less confusing and magical than had she introduced it at the earlier time, when she did not have an enlarged abdomen.

One therapist, in very early pregnancy but clad in obvious maternity clothes, reported on an initial therapy hour with a patient. This example highlights the patient's instant private inference about the pregnancy, and how her feelings and her therapist's feelings influenced the timing of the fuller discussion of the matter.

A young married woman patient came complaining of vague nervousness. She asked the therapist about birth control methods, and the therapist embarked on a discussion of the topic in a practical way without thinking too much of the nature of her question. They continued to other avenues of her life. When the therapist was in middle pregnancy, had achieved more internal peace about her state, and had seen the patient regularly for a few months, she was able to listen as the patient described the innuendo of her opening remarks. The patient *had* noticed her loose dress and had immediately assumed that she was talking to a pregnant woman. In asking about birth control she was telling the therapist that she was ambivalent about becoming pregnant as her husband wished. She was reacting in fear that the therapist was "out of control" and that this might influence her too to become "out of control" if she embarked on therapy. With the experience of being cared for in an orderly, professional way by the therapist, the patient felt safe enough to begin to talk of her fears of pregnancy. It would probably have been too early for the therapist to introduce the topic directly in the first hour. The patient might have reacted by disappearing from treatment. On the other hand it might have been useful to tune in to the possible nature of the patient's speculation earlier, since other material may have been lost from the therapy in the interim. However the topic was usefully discussed in time, and it was important to the understanding of the patient's "vague nervousness."

In early pregnancy, while there is no heartbeat to hear and no little spastic movements in the abdomen bespeaking life, one of the primitive upsurges may be thoughts of the fetus as a tumor — something draining the body like a parasite, with a power of its own but with no relation to a human being. With this hyper-awareness of being drained, the pregnant therapist might be more finely tuned to symbiotic desires in a patient than if she were nonpregnant. Diagnostically, it may suggest that a patient is borderline or in a regressed state because he seems taken up with a desire to "suck one dry" in a desperate search for sustenance.

The same thoughts of the fetus as a tumor may be expanded into fantasies of giving birth to a monster. These are ubiquitous, and come and go during pregnancy. One pregnant therapist reported her difficult experience in working with a 20-year-old male who suffered from a congenital deforming condition. His repugnance to her painfully stimulated her own fears for the unborn baby and flowed over past her working hours. She felt that there was some basis in this for a psychological explanation of the old wives' tale advising pregnant women to avoid the physically hideous, namely that the woman's own highly colored fantasies are even more dramatic after such encounters, and it is hard to maintain distance from them and control over the fear. The fleeting notion of the patient's "evil" effect on her baby had occurred to her.

At the same time, having had this experience, the therapist was more sensitive to the patient's commentaries on his painful experiences engendered by others' reactions to him. Later in the pregnancy she had a fantasy of her own baby being a deformed child who would forever be taken care of, be eternally dependent, and who would never grow up. This helped her to understand other aspects of the patient's complaints. In spite of his high degree of intelligence and sensitivity, his parents and he seemed to be colluding in an effort to thwart his autonomy and independence. Finally she was able to help him separate from them, and from her, in a less ambivalent way.

MIDDLE PREGNANCY

There may be a long time in middle pregnancy that is internally peaceful and serene. The baby is well established. It is inevitable that a child will be born. It grows. It is nurtured and given nurturance at a vegetative level of awareness. The external world is informed of the situation too, and yet the delivery is not yet at hand. The up-surge of feelings prior to delivery are biding their time till nature more urgently begins to prepare the baby, the new mother, and their world for the event.

In middle pregnancy the reality effect of the visibility of the enlarging abdomen and the appearance of tent dresses is a powerful factor in the fifty-minute hour.

The question of telling the patient about the pregnancy, or introducing or discussing the subject in the hour, is a delicate and sensitive issue. This may be particularly problematic if the therapist is still unsure and uncomfortable about the pregnancy. It is preferable to assume that the pregnancy is noticed, and that the patient will refer to it, if not directly, then indirectly, in themes of dress, physical appearance, birth control, abortions, or stories of pregnant friends or gardening. More abstract themes that have been expanded upon are reincarnation and rejuvenation. The pregnant therapist should try to prepare herself for comments and discussion about it.

The timing of relating the patient's displaced feelings to her own situation depends on the patient, the tone of the concern, and whether or not the avoidance seems to be a resistance. Once the topic is openly acknowledged, one may discover the ramifications of its meaning to the patient. These may or may not have to do with central concerns in his life. It may affect him at any level.

What if the patient offers congratulations? There is a fine line between overfamiliarity with the patient and being so stiff that the therapist appears inhuman. A patient may notice for the first time in middle pregnancy and say, "Congratulations!" An extremely cautious silence following this would be inappropriate. One may accept the sentiment wholeheartedly at the outset. To treat the congratulations as a highly loaded comment, for on-the-spot examination, at least initially would be undesirable. Other developments will occur in the therapy within the context of the patient's experience. For example, a 24-year-old schizophrenic patient congratulated a pregnant therapist quite spontaneously. She was delighted and thanked him. It was an appropriate remark that took note of her as a separate person and conveyed warmth. Much later in the therapy a theme developed about his wish to have the therapist as an automaton. He worked with computers, and it was a strange and good experience for him to see his "therapeutic computer" manifest such a human condition. One may answer a patient directly or show the affect one feels spontaneously without ruining the therapy. These precious moments may enrich the therapy. It is possible to react verbally while thinking about the implications and whether they might be minimal or loaded for a particular patient.

The following are some ways the pregnant therapist may be viewed. She may be the here-and-now role model for the young professional woman contemplating motherhood. She may be viewed as an experimental ideal in the imagined future of the young woman. For the male patient she may be an experimental ideal, too, if the male patient's spouse or girlfriend is pregnant, or will be or wants to be pregnant, or has fertility problems. At less available levels the patient may identify with the baby and be involved in the childlike oedipal position between the mother and father (the therapist and her spouse). The pregnancy may stimulate patients to talk more of their early childhood, their views of their parents, their pregnant mother, or early situations with the birth of a sibling. The pregnant therapist, by virtue of the child within her, may be viewed as more nurturant or more sexual than in her nonpregnant state. These factors might be seen as advantages or disadvantages for any individual patient. There is really no way to tell in advance how the pregnancy will affect a patient. One can only listen carefully on all levels to a patient for guidance in one's responses.

Some patients have a strong need not to notice, even if the therapist is ebulliently fertile in her maternity dress. The omission may be cause for diagnostic speculation, as with a schizophrenic, hysterical, or severely obsessional patient. The timing of bringing it to such a patient's conscious awareness may be a matter of resistance on the part of the patient balanced against his oblique references, or demonstration of his anxieties by lateness or absence from hours. A psychotic patient who fails to notice might be involved in ambivalence about recognition of the therapist as a living, breathing human being rather than in the specific issue of the pregnancy.

"Sibling rivalry" with the therapist's fetus can be introduced in direct or more subtle ways. It may become more acute as the abdomen swells, when the termination of the pregnancy and perhaps of the therapy is becoming more and more concrete. One patient who had previously felt comfortable in a small office now began making references to her "style being cramped" at her daily work. This was a displacement from a feeling that the therapist's pregnancy was pushing her out of the room and that the unborn baby was worthy of and receiving more attention than she was. It was interesting that with a coincidental move to a larger office, this theme temporarily disappeared, but it emerged again in later pregnancy. She had the fantasy that the mother therapist would roll over on top of her, squashing her life and favoring the unborn child. She had been very angry at the birth of her next sibling when she was 2 years old, whom she felt had deprived her of a great deal from her parents.

Missed appointments "not to bother you" may come up as subtle rivalry when the hostility is marked. Requests for extra appointments usually occur over trivial matters to test the therapist to see if she "really cares" and has time to attend to the patient's needs.

One patient, a young man of 21 whose mother was a nurse, became sick for a few weeks with bronchitis while his therapist was pregnant. Each visit he struggled out of bed to come in and sat close. The therapist had the fantasy of taking him on her knee and blowing his nose for him. In his regression his eyes would flow with "tears" from his cold. He was pitifully sorry for himself and would longingly finger child therapy play blocks in her office. His younger brother had been born when he was five. He remembered that he had been sick while his mother was pregnant. The only time his nurse mother stopped work was then, and the only times of major closeness to her was when he was sick. "She'd say, 'What would you *really* like to eat, John?' I'd think and think and then I'd want soup. Real milky soup. Oh, I can even *smell* the Campbell's cream of tomato soup right now!" He was experiencing the dependent longings and mixed joys of being ill at this time. This was startling to him, since he regarded himself as totally self-sufficient. However his major complaint was of being unable to get close to people. The therapy covered some issues about his usual mechanisms of fending people off in his efforts to avoid becoming dependent. The feelings of dependency turned out to be closely associated with the pain that he would inevitably be displaced by another child, his therapist's child in the current situation, or his own young brother in earlier times.

One pregnant therapist described her experience with a symbiotic patient by saying that she constantly felt with him that "he wanted to be right inside" her. At nonverbal levels it showed itself by his sitting at her feet in group therapy, by touching things on her desk on the way out after a meeting, always leaving some object behind to be retrieved, "accidentally" taking her pen, or calling her at night on the phone. In the meetings he talked a great deal of his experiences with his psychotic mother and his emotional hunger in the context of her emotional unavailability to him. He talked of feeling empty and a feeling of urgency to fill the void. The sensitivity to symbiosis in pregnancy is complicated. Especially in middle pregnancy the pregnant woman may wonder at times whether she is mother or baby. The medical and physical care from others and her husband that she experiences is more like the "baby state." Yet it is in contrast to her feelings about her work or her marriage, or to the feelings of maturity and responsibility for the baby which are also present.

One patient said after his therapist's delivery that it had always seemed "like there was another person in the room." There were certain things he withheld from her in her pregnant state, such as accounts of homosexual anal intercourse. At a conscious level he felt that this was to protect the therapist because she was so pure. There were thoughts too of "protecting the child" based on a feeling that it could hear and understand, and that it would break the bond of confidentiality later. His paranoia showed itself in other ways in therapy, but there was no doubt that for many reasons he felt much more comfortable talking to the therapist when she was nonpregnant. It was a double-edged sword for him. On the one hand while pregnant she was a "safe" female since she was clearly someone else's "sexual property" and would there-fore never make such demands on him. This partly helped to get him engaged in therapy. On the other hand the graphic demonstration of her femininity was repulsive to him because he viewed her as a mother earth figure. In part he felt disgust with himself in the confession of his homosexuality to someone who was showing her "straightness and heterosexuality." The following was the other side to her "purity." He realted a daydream in which the therapist was a huge prostitute with vast breasts, each emblazoned with the stars and stripes. She was standing naked reading from a bible in a nightclub. His affect in the daydream was one of wonderment and joy. He had a desire to touch her to see if it were all flesh and blood, and at the same time it was disgusting and grotesquely humorous.

Some of the concerns of pregnancy are the ambivalent feelings surrounding the fantasy that the whole world knows the pregnant woman is having intercourse.

A 19-year-old married patient came to treatment complaining of a lack of sexual responsiveness. As the story unfolded, it came out that the lack of responsiveness was only present at times when she and her husband slept in her parents' house. She then noticed that her therapist was pregnant and began to ask what it was like to be pregnant. Encouragement to reflect on her own concerns elucidated some of her anxieties, not the least being that her father in particular would then know for sure that she was having intercourse. She had long maintained the fantasy that he wished her to be virginal forever. Sleeping with her mate in the parents' house, where every creak of the bed was heard, was directly related to this. She said that the therapist's pregnancy made her story much easier to tell. She commented on the pregnant therapist's poise in the interviews. The fact that she was working while pregnant was comforting to the patient. "Maybe it *can* be all right to show people you have intercourse if you're truly grown up?" she finally said. This could fall in the category of a "transference cure." The patient took only a few interviews to reach this point, saying she was much more at ease, and decided to stop treatment. She had also tried sleeping with her husband in a bedroom away from her parents. The therapist pondered on her unresolved oedipal issues after her departure from therapy, but the patient was last heard of coincidentally, and was reported to have a year-old child, a happy marriage, and work of her choice.

Patients may have a problem in being angry with the pregnant therapist for many reasons. Motherhood may be exalted by the patient in the presence of a human being carrying precious life. At the same time he may ambivalently long to damage the source of the life. The patient of an earlier example who struggled in the therapy hours with his fever and cold, and wished to be "taken care of," later commented that he had *almost* wished the baby had died at that time. He had fantasies that the therapist would contract pneumonia from him. On the one hand he did not want to lose his therapist. However if the baby were to die to make more room for him in her attentions, then she would have to die too. He was angry with the therapist for being pregnant, but he was only able to tell her after the sessions in which she turned up alive in spite of his fantasies while his cold raged. It was hard for him to let the therapist know more directly about his anger and guilt because the mothering, comforting aspect of her in her pregnant state was precious to him especially in middle pregnancy. In late pregnancy she was indeed going to terminate therapy. There was nothing he could do to keep her, and the baby was going to take his place imminently. The reality of the termination made it easier for him to be angry.

LATE PREGNANCY

In late pregnancy, from the patient's point of view, the graphic visibility of the therapist's position may be considered first.

A junior medical student described his thoughts on seeing an enormously pregnant therapist in an evaluation interview. He said that he had "screwed up" his courage to appear at the clinic with long-standing concerns. He was met by the therapist, "a woman with a huge belly, dressed in neon colors." He was so scared that he found it difficult to talk to her in spite of her admirable efforts to inquire about what he thought of seeing a pregnant woman. Being deeply embroiled with his fear and incapacity in dealing with medical emergencies, he had a recurrent fantasy of having to deliver this therapist within his fifty-minute allotted time. He had not yet done any obstetrics and was trying urgently to recall what he had learned while in the Boy Scouts. It was with profound relief that he realized he could see another therapist for his treatment.

Another aspect of the visibility of the pregnancy is in revealing a tender, caring side of a patient who perhaps has kept it concealed. A patient may see that the therapist takes the most comfortable chair, or may show himself or herself as solicitous for the therapist's health. There may be some hostility in these themes, but the greater component may be tenderness. For a highly obsessional patient constricted in all expressions of affect, this may be an important forward step.

Pregnancy may arouse envy in either a male or a female patient. For the woman patient, the therapist may represent the super-ideal, the too virtuous. One young promiscuous patient said with pain that she felt like a slut in comparison. On a preconscious level it was in comparison to her mother's values. On another, the therapist had "everything I want" — profession, husband, pregnancy, nice home, etc. On the one hand it was something for which to strive, and the therapist lent reality to the idea that it might happen. On the other hand she could not bear that another woman had something she wanted so badly, and in anger began denigrating "the therapy" as representative of her feelings about the therapist.

Envy on the part of a man was demonstrated by a 38-year-old married man.

The patient was hysterical, and his ready tendencies to imitate ailments of others in the environment had been observed by the therapist in other instances. He developed medically inexplicable crampy abdominal pains in the seventh month of his therapist's pregnancy. He felt there was "something *in* there" and the hours were all flavored with his preoccupations of labor. The terminology he used was symbolic. His work became "hard labor"; he was concerned with his "productions"; and he had "intermittent pain" in talking to the therapist. He was taking philosophy courses in night school and was producing his "own baby," a paper that was due at the end of the semester. The introduction to it was "too showy," and many a time it was "bloody difficult" to write. (He was an Englishman, but rarely was given to swearing.) The "incubation period" of the paper was three months. It took a further three months to write, and three months before its full effect was seen. The final paragraph of the paper he said "culminated in a huge explosive effort," and the job was done. He was exhausted and proud afterward, as he "delivered" it to his professor. There was a sadness at its ending, and he temporarily lapsed into a depressive phase.

A psychotic patient may become highly anxious and preoccupied with the thought that he has impregnated the therapist as shown in a previous example. He may be concerned with ideas of potency versus impotence. This theme might be introduced by questions about the therapist's husband, to reassure himself that such a person exists and that he, the patient, will not be held responsible for his wishes or fears of action. Such a patient may be internally very confused as to whether his relationship to the therapist is husband, lover or brother, father or mother, or "just another patient." Thus he readily displays the gamut between seeing himself as very close and as very distant to the therapist. Such ideas may become more explicit and therefore closer to reality testing ability if the therapist first answers simply a few questions about her husband. After that he may feel safe enough to allow some of his more confused ideas to become understandable.

Similar thoughts may exist at some level with the neurotic, and may come to light, but in nonintensive psychotherapy one will see them much more frequently with the psychotic.

Another primitive thought may have to do with sucking the pregnant therapist's enlarged breasts. Feeding on her "good" or "bad" nourishment is the issue. At times it may be a comforting, infantile fantasy, and at other moments a hideous, poisonous influence to be avoided at all costs. At high levels of integration in neurotic patients, derivations of this situation may occur. One young patient started to bring her lunch to the office in the last months of her therapist's pregnancy and sat sipping a coca-cola through a straw throughout the hour. She was involved in a phase of "feeding herself," fending off comments, suggestions, or interpretations from the therapist. She was dealing with the larger issue of autonomy from an intrusive mother in the therapy hours.

Patients may become concerned about the therapist's well-being during delivery. Some may worry about the death of the therapist, and since this is a sensitive topic with the woman close to delivery, she may either fail to hear the patient's anxious concerns or else overreact in reassurance.

A pregnant therapist may be called upon to be a teacher of sexual matters. A 13-year-old girl patient saw a pregnant therapist for six months of her pregnancy. The patient's main complaint was crying spells. She had been talking about her embarrassment at boys' glances at her budding breasts in her sweatshirt and her ambivalent feelings about her ability to attract the boys' interest. Some of her notions about intercourse were very childlike, for example, that it was accomplished by "just sleeping together." She had questions about how the baby could be born through the therapist's umbilicus. She really wanted information. One may wonder how a girl in this culture can reach the age of 13 and allegedly never before have read or discussed sexual matters. However, since her mother was a severely hysterical woman, who seemed to wish to avoid noticing that her daughter had reached puberty, the therapist decided to treat the girl's pleas for counseling at face value. She told her simply and clearly about the facts of life. The patient would think about the discussions during the week and cross-check the information with other students at school. The therapist wondered if her pregnancy was the reason why this mother had chosen her to be her daughter's therapist. At some level the mother may have acknowledged her own discomfort with the subject, while realizing that someone ought to be available for such discussion with her daughter.

Termination issues will be mentioned only briefly, since this topic is discussed in Chapter 10. One aspect of this termination that is different is that there is a reality to some of the ubiquitous concerns: "Are you abandoning me for another?" "You are more interested in the baby than in me." "I feel thrown out and angry because you will be taking care of someone else." Unlike the terminations due to illness, some of the reality involves a vision of the therapist as a happy mother, so the angry fantasies may not be so intensely guilt provoking.

"Can I see you and the baby in the hospital?" may be a question. This may be an issue of reassuring the patient that one has not actually evaporated after termination. It may be an effort to come to terms with the reality that a baby does exist after all in the therapist's abdomen, and that the mother did not die during delivery or as a result of the patient's malevolent thoughts. It may be a lively curiosity to see a new mother and baby, and to participate vicariously in the exciting experience. A wish to be caring and close, and have a more reciprocal relationship may underlie the request. There may be a hostile element, too, such as hoping to see the therapist in a weakened condition and "off guard." The request may be treated first as something to be understood. The therapist may consider how she anticipates she will feel physically and emotionally at that time. If such a visit occurs, it might be useful. On the other hand, no argument can be made that it is essential to the welfare of any patient. If the patient is healthy enough to withstand the break in therapy, then it is an elective matter. And if the patient is very sick — disorganized or suicidal — then arrangements may be made for another therapist to see the patient during the primary therapist's absence.

Some of what has been said about the effect of the pregnant therapist may be relevant to male therapists whose wives are expecting babies. Expectant fathers too are subject to affect changes, worries about the future, identity concerns, preoccupations with the new person, and concern for the welfare of their pregnant wives. The main themes presented here in doing therapy while pregnant concern the body change taking place before the patient's eyes, meshing with the psychological ramifications for both patient and therapist that are involved in the dawning of life within another human being.

RETURNING TO WORK AFTER THE NEW BABY

Timing of the Decision

Women return to work at varying intervals after the birth. It will be assumed here that the baby is normal and that the home setting is reasonably untroubled. In the discussion it will then be easier to characterize feelings of more general application. A very different set of circumstances will be operative if the new mother is plunged into acute grief after the loss of a fetus or the death of her baby, or if she is inundated with uncertainties about the health of the infant. But even in those sad circumstances, the same principle of trying to think through the physical and emotional demands upon one will apply, while trying to balance them against one's capacity for emotional availability. This may be much easier said than done.

In pregnancy one may anticipate a totally different set of feelings than come to pass after the delivery. One therapist was positive that she did not want to be absent from work for more than a few weeks. She thought that she would "go mad in the house" and would vegetate, and that her brain might never work again if she went "out to pasture" in such a fashion. She was a highly organized woman and anticipated no problems in arranging baby care and housekeeping help. Another therapist thought she might take a year's leave of absence, expressing the idea, "We who look after, and see the end results of, deprivation in other people's children know the vital importance of the first year of life in raising a child." Both therapists debated the arguments favoring quality of care over quantity. Advisedly, neither came to a firm decision about her leave of absence till after the birth.

There will be turmoil in greater or lesser degree for any new mother. It may center around the ambivalence about returning to work. The joy of watching the new infant may be boundless. Suddenly the most mundane matters of feeding and clothing the new person become of vast importance. It is as if the whole world revolves around the little wriggling mass of humanity in the crib. In addition there will be new issues in the emotional climate with one's mate, balancing responsibilities in this baby's care with that of the other children, home planning, and the personal issues of one's new identity. It may be asking too much of oneself to start work immediately and expect the same quality of work as was formerly achieved. A therapist who was a new father expressed the situation succinctly: "How can I be expected to go to work when all the action is at home?" However, some people need to return quickly to work, and describe it as "a comforting return to reality." Others simply need their salary. With a husband able and willing to share daily care, a reliable babysitter, or a good day care center, many a woman has made the transition very quickly. It is important to be comfortable about home and baby arrangements to maximize the potential for good therapy. The physical aspects of childbirth swiftly return to quiescence, but psychologically the woman can never be quite the same person again, especially after the first child. There are gains, and losses, and it takes a long time to absorb the experience. For each person there is probably a "right time" to return to work, based on one's external and internal peace and a feeling of readiness to rediscover one's professional identity and the outside world.

Planning Work

The greatest pull that a new mother may experience may be the symbiotic tie to the infant. This may be more or less intense till such a time as the child shows more differentiation in the external world. One therapist said of painful feelings of leaving her new baby, that the quality of their relationship was "like chewing gum." The presence of the patient may be felt as an assaultive intrusion trying to pull apart the relationship prematurely. If this occurs in such intensity, then the new mother ought to feel free to reassess the wisdom of her return to work. She may perhaps decide to work much less, or to stop for a couple of months.

A new mother may become depressed following the loss of the baby from her body. There may be a tendency to "fill the gap" with patients as a symbolic substitute. With the loss of the baby from the absolutely dependent position, she may find herself opposing the fostering of independence in patients where it would be appropriate. The opposite may be true, and inappropriate aggressive feelings may spill over into therapy, pushing patients away prematurely. With low emotional resources, the therapist may feel angry with patients who, for whatever reason, "take up too much time."

Being elated about giving a baby to one's mate and a new life to the world, and having a sense of power and athletic achievement, a new mother may feel that she can handle anything. Combinations of symbiotic, anxious and depressive, or elated feelings may result in a sense of brittleness. Until one is in a position to be more stable, careful work planning is essential, to prevent becoming overcommitted.

Acutely suicidal or very disorganized patients who may telephone the therapist at all times of day or night just are not practicable to treat at this time. Emotional availability is a priority for such patients. The nursing mother who is still getting up to the baby at night will often be limited in her resources to care for such a demanding patient. It may be wise to limit oneself to treating patients with less tendency to act-out. The therapist's very real conflict will come across vividly to such patients and may make management even more of a problem. Many women find that part-time work allows them to find pleasure in their roles as wife, mother, and therapist. Sometimes this option is not available, and sometimes a person may wish to be full-time in either role.

Starting Work

When one meets patients for the first time, some private thoughts might be: "Will the baby be okay?" "How do I look?" "Can I still do therapy?" "Is it obvious that I've had a massive new experience?" "Can I settle down and listen?" "How can anyone be so worried when the world looks so rosy?" "How can anyone be caught up in such trivia, when they've no *real* responsibilities like me?" It is neither possible nor necessary to conceal one's strong feelings, such as the excitement of a new baby in addition to being at work again. It is possible, however, to make an effort to set them aside or modify them enough to focus one's attention on the patient.

Patients will have all kinds of reactions to their knowledge of the new situation. If they are relevant to the central problems, one may be able to use these in treatment. Some of the situations may overlap with reactions to pregnancy, for example, "sibling rivalry," and others may be less specific to the event. One obsessional patient who had seen his therapist in the street with her husband and baby told her with distress that it was not right for anyone to look so happy. Since discontentment was a familiar facet of his presentation, the therapist inquired further about it. After he expanded on his ambivalent feelings about her family and her obvious pleasure, he gave detailed accounts of his father, who told him often that "something bad" would happen sooner or later if he allowed himself to be too happy. Ultimately they used this material to delve further into his magical notion that dire punishment would follow pleasure. Much later, in termination when the same conflict came to the fore, he began to wonder in the reassessment of his life whether he perhaps subtly influenced the events to prove the powerful pronouncement of tragedy. After all the therapist and her family had survived in spite of seeming happy. He said at the end that his major gain in the therapy was to feel less a hapless victim of circumstance. Some portion of this therapeutic work was therefore triggered by the patient's reaction to this therapist's recent new baby.

In making first appointments after the birth, the new parent of either sex may be alert to the possibilities of spill-over from the powerful recent experience. Thus divided loyalties between therapist and parent roles may emerge and overlap with conflicts and blurred boundaries about whom one is parenting (baby or patient), who is offering and about whom is being offered more gratification at the moment.

An example of the pull between "the therapist" and "the new parent" was described by a young male therapist whose wife had recently delivered. A patient whom he had seen regularly for three years had an appointment canceled at short notice because of the baby's arrival. At the next meeting the patient was fantasizing about the reasons for this unusual occurrence. He said, "Maybe your wife just had a baby?" The therapist, aglow with excitement about the new arrival, acknowledged that a new baby had come. The patient, who was a rigid, distant fellow, offered warm congratulations. The therapist described a moment of "real contact" between them which was rare. Reflecting on the incident later, the patient said that he viewed both himself and the therapist as "tight assed," and that it was a relief to him that both could relax without being overcome with embarrassment. The patient missed the next hour without notice, presumably either feeling defensive about the show of emotion, or feeling hurt by "sibling rivalry." At a normal time the therapist would have let the absence pass without intervention and awaited the next scheduled session. This time he found himself telephoning the patient to invite him to come in. He rearranged many other patient's appointments to accommodate him, although there was no evidence of gross upset on the part of the patient. Thus he was overzealous at a time when the patient wanted more distance. Much of the discussion of the countertransference feelings with his supervisor revolved around guilt at fears of shortchanging this faithful patient due to his new, important responsibility. A larger issue developed. The patient had been talking, appropriately, of terminating therapy. The therapist was now "hanging on to him" in various ways. He was not allowing the patient "to be weaned" and was worrying about too much attention being paid to his personal life at the expense of his practice. He needed this patient to prove he was still a good therapist and wanted to allay any anger the patient might experience about his new baby. After some reflection on this aspect the therapist terminated more easily with the patient.

Divided loyalties toward "baby" and "patient" may result in the patient being treated almost as an extension of the baby. To illustrate this in an exaggerated way one might consider the model of leaving a new first baby for the first time with a babysitter. The brand new mother may be filled with fantasies of what may happen in her absence:

1. The child may suffer terrible loneliness and cry all the time for the comfort of mother. This may be partially true, and certainly the baby will miss familiar arms, but part of it may be a projection of her own sense of loss. To compensate for this, or for feelings of guilt about shortchanging the baby, the patient may become the object of filling the therapist's need. Overnurturant behavior may be present, such as prolonging interviews "to make sure the patient is all right, is not upset, and gets enough." If the patient does not respond with gratitude, the therapist may be thrown off balance.

2. Something of a dangerous medical nature may happen to the baby. And as a parallel the therapist may be too interested or not interested enough in the physical welfare of the patient.

3. The baby may grow to love another, and even prefer the sitter. One therapist gave an example of how this influenced therapy. She was seeing a long-standing patient after her absence during which another therapist had cared for the patient without incident. In such situations rivalry and jealousy feelings between therapists often

occur. In this situation they may be increased. When she found herself saying, "Were you ever as angry at Dr. X as you are at me?" she decided it was time to scrutinize her feelings; "Don't you love *me* more than Dr. X?" might have come next. The most recent activated acute situation of this sort was rivalry between her and the babysitter regarding the baby's love. After her reflections the burden of proof was not placed on the patient.

4. The baby may be angry at mother for going off and having a good time. One may find herself guiltily enjoying work, and the first time the baby is forgotten can be a startling experience. One therapist was with an interesting patient who was telling her in a lively way the events during her absence. An opportunity had arisen for him to go to China as a translator for a few months, and he was relating a crucial discussion on whether or not it would be possible in light of his psychiatric history. The therapist had been with him all the way, so engaging was his description. A few moments later she realized that she had missed the vital ending. Momentarily, she had tuned out in shock, realizing that for the first time she had forgotten the infant at home. However, since she needed to know the details because they concerned a letter from her, she asked him to explain it again. He was annoyed, said that she was not as "with it" as usual, but that he would reserve judgment since she had just delivered a baby!

5. "Will the baby *really* be there when I return? Have I *really* just had a baby?" The preceding example is relevant to this point too. Some women have described brief transient periods of minor disorientation or periods of unreality after return to work. Initially there may be a feeling of altered time sense. Having experienced the drifting timelessness (in spite of the feeding schedule) of the first period with a new baby, the stark return to the fifty-minute hour and the world of office or clinic may seem somewhat unreal. There may be connected issues of the balancing of identity between "mother" and "therapist."

In one of the first hours a therapist spent with a patient in this situation she forgot to bring her watch. The patient had no watch either, so there was no opportunity to read it upside down. In her absence another therapist had borrowed her clock. Just as she was considering interrupting the session to look at a clock in the corridor, she experienced a strong feeling that the time was up. She thus ended the hour and walked out after the patient to check. It was fifty minutes on the dot! She said that she was pleased because she had not lost the "internal clock" constructed over the years in work.

A feeling related to the "culture shock" of coming back to work, may be annoyance that a patient is involved in the same old issues as before one's absence. If such a momentous event has occurred in one's own life, how can the rest of the world remain so unmoved? There may also be a telescoping effect of the experience. At one time it may seem immediate, especially if talking to a currently pregnant patient, and at other times it may seem remote.

The new mother's upsurge of unconscious conflicts with her own mother may involve "the symbolic triumph" over the old mother. Feelings from this source may flow over negatively toward an older female patient. On the other hand it may result in the therapist having more poise and "allowing" the older patient her problems.

While describing very simply some of the usual issues for the new parent-therapist, and more specifically for the new mother, there has been no discussion of more troublesome problems that can exist for her. Pregnancy and delivery may be a time of great trial. Old, irrational, intense feelings may forcefully surface, make motherhood and marriage very difficult, and interfere with efforts to do high-quality therapy. Some therapists have decided that this was a good time to seek psychotherapy or psychoanalysis for themselves with resultant benefit.

In first starting back to work one may feel like an uncertain juggler keeping so many balls in the air. With patience, wise planning, and support from one's husband, colleagues, and supervisors, even a recently delivered mother can go back to work if that is what she wants. As the months go by many problems will dwindle in intensity, and some issues that seemed almost insurmountable at the time may fade into the background as experience is gained in the new situation.

18

The Therapist's Illness

Anyone may feel ill from time to time during working hours.
This varies from minor complaints to major illness. There are all
kinds of variables that might lead one to decide to take time off,
or to continue as best one can through one hour or many hours of
therapy. This chapter is addressed to some aspects of these issues.
These are difficult conditions to work under. The emphasis here
is on some suggested coping devices, trying to make the best of one's
situation while attempting not to jeopardize the therapy. Clinical
material is presented on the theme of being as available as possible
to hear related developments in the hours.

MILD ILLNESS

Suppose a mild discomfort develops in a normally healthy therapist during work — a headache, toothache, or minor menstrual
cramps. One may have taken some analgesics and may anticipate
feeling better within a few hours. If one is having difficulty following the content and flow of an hour, it is often better to keep quiet
and follow as much as he can. Such hours, concentrated on listening with minimal verbal interaction with the patient, have sometimes

been described as the better hours conducted with a particular patient (especially if one's style tends toward the verbose!).

Some patients will notice and comment on how the therapist looks. If a patient asks or comments directly, it is preferable to affirm simply that one has a headache or a cold. It is really not necessary to reassure the patient that one can still listen. Time will tell, and the patient will have his own feelings about the therapist's response or lack of it. If the therapist is evasive, the painful expression on his face may be misinterpreted by the patient as a reaction to his story. For a borderline patient especially, it may be a useful ego-exercise in confirming his correct observation of the external world. Otherwise he may build fantasies of having harmed the therapist by his presence. A patient's concern about the therapist's appearance may add a new dimension in the realization that a patient who had seemed uninvolved or very distant really does notice one's presence, and that the relationship holds some importance for him. Mixed feelings of care and hostility may be present. There may be a fear that the therapist will be sick, or a wish that he would go away and leave him alone.

If one judges that the illness will last longer than a few hours, it may be better to cancel the appointment than to suffer through, totally unable to listen. Too many added distortions on the therapist's part may occur. One may be tempted to elicit sympathy from the patient or to communicate a double-bind position that the patient is too weak to withstand a brief absence. It can be hostile to sit coughing with a patient, believing that one is indispensable, when the reality is that one has, perhaps, influenza, cannot function properly, and is infectious. There are few patients who cannot stand having an hour or two canceled due to a therapist's illness. One may always make up time if necessary when he is feeling better again.

HOSPITALIZATION

A therapist may require a specified time off work due to hospitalization, such as for appendectomy, tonsillectomy, or disc lesions. In an emergency one usually has a secretary who can inform patients simply of the fact that one has been admitted to a hospital and ask them to check back in a few days for further information about one's return to work. In the meantime the position may become clearer regarding decisions about how much to tell the patient if he asks, and so on. In the event that the operation is an elective procedure, a therapist may be able to plan fairly accurately his expected time off work. The surgeon or physician may have practical advice in this regard.

The question that immediately arises is what to tell the patient in ongoing treatment. Often a simple direct explanation can be formulated, sparing the details or the differential diagnosis. Breaking such news to a patient is best done at the beginning of an hour, so that one has time to see any acute reactions that the patient may have and to hear the details. This applies even if the patient is bursting with information to tell the therapist. While the therapist has such an urgent issue on his agenda he is not likely to be able to attend carefully to the patient. An interruption in the beginning minutes of the hour may be advisable: "Before you begin to tell me about that, I would like to let you know about something which has come up with me and will require time off from seeing you. I need to have an operation, and I shall have to cancel our meetings from X date." The patient may then say, "How long will you be away?" and one might say, "The doctors think about X weeks. After that I expect to be recovered." Or the patient might say, "I hope it isn't serious," and the therapist might, if he wished, simply confirm that statement. If he wants to elaborate, he might say for example, "I have been having trouble with my back, and the operation is planned to correct that." Giving more details depends on the patient, how one feels the knowledge will affect him, and how well one knows him. Thus one therapist felt it appropriate to tell several inquiring patients that he was going to have a hemorrhoidectomy. He felt that certain other patients did not need to know the facts. One's affect as one elaborates on any details will often say more to the patient than the content. If one is feeling embarrassed or frightened, he may decide not to communicate the news in advance, because it might be an unnecessary burden to the patient's fantasies while he is away.

Patients will have all kinds of reactions. It may remind them of family incidents due to surgery or hospitalization. Some may want to hear nothing except that one will be away and intends to come back. Others may adopt a protective attitude. The expected separation will often be tinged with fear that the therapist might die. Since this is highly unlikely, but possible, with any operation, one might want to acknowledge the touch of reality and not read all of the patient's reactions as fantasies. There will thus be concerns for the therapist and concerns for the patient himself. Making arrangements to see another therapist may be appropriate for sicker patients or patients in crisis. A therapist on emergency call will be necessary for all patients.

An issue that may emerge with some patients is visiting one in the hospital. If the therapist has previously visited his patient in the hospital, the patient may wish for permission to reciprocate. It really depends on the patient and on one's illness. If one anticipates being in a lot of pain and on drugs for a time, it is obviously not appropriate or beneficial for a patient to visit. On the other hand if the therapist is feeling mentally alert but must stay in the hospital for a long time, then he might consider seeing selected patients. One cannot prevent a patient telephoning the hospital for a daily medical report. Some need to do this to prove that the therapist is still in existence. Other patients will phone the therapist directly in his room for the same reason. If this is anticipated, as with a deeply involved and symbiotic patient, it might be possible to discuss the need in advance and put a definite limit on when it would be possible to do this, for example, no telephone calls for, say, a week. In this way the need is acknowledged and accepted, and it saves both patient and therapist unnecessary pain, should the therapist answer the telephone in a sleepy, drugged state.

Patients will often send cards, flowers, or gifts. It can be very intriguing to speculate from a card what aspects of the transference are at the fore, for example, envy or fear of the dependent invaded state, in those humourous cards depicting patients with buxom, beautiful nurses equipped with hypodermics or enema bags. However, it is not a good idea to use these often caring, spontaneous expressions from a patient to make heavy interpretations subsequently. If they represent problematic issues, they will emerge in other ways from a patient, where the timing of the interpretation may be more elegant and more respectful of the patient's coexistent feelings of warmth and concern.

There are probably as great a variety of ways to handle one's illness vis-à-vis a patient as there are temperaments of therapists. One therapist fractured his pelvis in a skiing accident and had to be recumbent for a long time. He decided to see a few patients experimentally from his hospital bed. All the patients asked were delighted to come. They expressed a whole gamut of emotions from mainly pleasure to mainly fear. One woman obsessionally inquired about every medical trapping attached to the sick therapist except his urinary catheter. Hesitancy in talking about sexual matters was quite characteristic of this patient, but this was not the time or the place to force the issue for either therapist or patient.

Another therapist had a disc lesion for which the treatment was prolonged time in the prone position. He and his family needed money to support the medical bills, and this prompted him to see selected, nonpsychotic patients. They sat up while he lay on the couch. This dramatic reversal of positions could be painfully confusing to a psychotic patient, but a more sturdy patient may be able to say what it feels like to him and thus achieve enough comfort to continue the therapeutic work. Many issues became focused, such as dependency, and rivalry regarding who was taking care of whom; redefinition of the human therapist as opposed to the idealized therapist; disappointment at seeing the therapist in the passive position and longing for him to be "aggressive" and upright again; and also fear at the passive position, in case of the stimulation of a patient's homosexual desires.

SEEING PATIENTS AT HOME

In a prolonged recuperation period the idea of temporarily seeing some patients at home might arise. The issues involved are manifold. Some therapists can do it comfortably while others decide to wait till they are in the office in full health again. A few considerations are:

1. the layout of one's house. If there is a suite or private room with soundproofing, and a waiting area or separate entrance, this may be simple. The patient's comfort and privacy are given highest priority, in any decision involving use of a part of one's house for this purpose.

2. the effect on one's own family. Small children may find it too difficult to know that father or mother is behind that door talking to a stranger, so close, and yet unavailable to them. It may be too much to ask them to control their wish for involvement, curiosity, noise, and games. Even one's spouse may have to control the desire to consult him on domestic issues.

3. the effect on the patient. All patients are curious as to how the therapist lives, and who are the members of his family. "Everything is so perfect for you and so lousy for me" may be a theme. One might decide that since this theme often comes up anyway, it does no harm for the patient to know some of the realities. One has to judge with each patient whether such issues could be intolerable, and symbolically come into the category of "cruel and unusual punishment" for them. Some patients may feel ambivalently superior, since the therapist is clearly not the wealthy, powerful figure for whom he wishes or whom he fears. One female patient told her therapist that seeing him once at home was at last proof that she was acceptable to him, and that she felt more equal, having been received by him in his house.

4. the effect on the therapist. It is a very cozy image to be able to be with one's family in breaks between patients. This may help one person's concentration or spoil another's. The only person who can decide whether or not it is "right" for him is the therapist himself.

CHRONIC ILLNESS

The question of long-standing chronic illness of the therapist is rather different. This may be a state in which the therapist knows he has a disease that is activated in a low-grade way but that at any point might become life-threatening. He may have no way of knowing how long this state of events might last. He may need to make his living as long as he can. Going to work while he feels reasonably well may be important in maintaining his self-respect and act against a premature lapse into an invalid state.

The chronically ill therapist has usually had some time to adjust privately to his illness, discomforts, and the blow to his mortality. Trying to be aware of his limitations, and planning work accordingly is important. In elective very-short-term therapy or in consultation work, he may not need to explore the meaning of his illness with the patients. An example follows of what may be accomplished under these extraordinarily difficult circumstances.

The therapist, who had cancer, decided to do consultation work even though he was aware of a serious exacerbation of his condition. Physically he looked thin and drawn, but he was quite mentally alert, and there was nothing bizarre about his appearance. He rested for an hour before each interview to muster his maximal resources. On one occasion he saw a family in crisis. This turned out to be the last time he saw anyone professionally; he was admitted to the hospital the next day in his terminal illness.

After his death a letter came from the family, who had no knowledge of his death or illness, saying how helpful he had been. They felt it valuable to talk things over with him, and their son, who had been troubled and resistant to therapy, had elected to start psychotherapy with a therapist suggested by the sick therapist. Being able to remain objective, hear the problems, and help the decisions of this family must have taken a great deal of emotional strength and capacity for availability in the therapist, and a way of privately being able to cope with and keep separate his feelings about his illness.

In ongoing long-term therapy, how and when should one tell the patient of his illness? This is a very complex issue. It seems to depend on how one feels it may interfere with the therapy, and of course it depends on the patient. There may, for example, be irregular interruptions and last-minute cancellations due to the therapist's medical outpatient treatment clinic visits. A major issue is to help the patient's free choice concerning what he wishes to do about therapy under these unavoidable conditions. It may be relevant in this context to lay the facts before him quite simply, and discuss over a number of hours whether he wishes to stop treatment, change therapists, or continue. A number of patients may wish for alternative arrangements at this point. A number may wish to continue. One woman's ultimate response was that since nothing in life is guaranteed, she wished to continue, knowing it was a calculated risk. She felt that she had had a lot of previous experience with the therapist when he was healthy, they had done a lot of work together, and she said it had been important that there was an atmosphere in which her feelings were respected and heard. Another patient felt guilty about considering stopping, but did so, after some discussion, with relative relief of his guilt.

Whether the patients decide to stop or continue, they will have all kinds of reactions. On first hearing the news, a patient may be horrified that the therapist, whom he had hoped or feared was impenetrable, can be so vulnerable. In one instance, anger, disgust, and disappointment followed. The patient was guilty about his anger, since realistically, he said, the therapist's illness was not planned to make things harder for him. He initially regarded the therapist as too fragile to display his real feelings. This had parallels in his early life, when his father had often been ill and had seemed defenseless when the patient was angry, pleading his weakened physical state as a reason to avoid his son's feelings.

One patient, who came to therapy with anxiety in the presence of older men, felt triumphant in his physical superiority to the older, sick, male therapist. He talked of relief because now he felt comfortable talking to a second-class person. He assumed that the therapist felt like a failure. Much material followed about his envy of his older brother and his suffering due to his brother's success. Physical prowess was his big brother's forte. For a time, the devaluation of the therapist produced a feeling of control and power in him. The therapist queried the patient's new relief from anxiety, connecting it to his across-the-board devaluation of him. The patient said that his position did not feel very steady, but in his life he had never been able to feel better off than another man. He was no longer anxious but felt mainly a mixture of anger, love, and pity for his therapist. He then talked about his anticipation of his father's death, and of how his father had always made him feel a failure. He felt angry and put down by his father, but at the same time he longed to have some closeness.

Ultimately he saw the therapist as physically weak but emotionally strong, and began to talk of himself in similar terms. He wept in great sadness that he was now feeling much better, and had been promoted in his job but that the therapist would probably not be alive to see the fruits of their work together. The grief for the therapist was intermingled with further anticipated grief for his father, with whom he began to re-establish some relationship.

Most of this work took place in about six months, and therapy ended by mutual agreement at that time. Thus, in the knowledge of the therapist's illness, and with a set termination date, this patient worked extremely hard to use the time in trying to come to some peace with his feelings of inferiority in his old relationships to his brother and father. In general there was a coming to terms with the lack of omnipotence of all the important men in his life and a resultant increase in his own self-respect.

A patient may experience feelings of closeness in hearing the therapist's news, since he has revealed a precious personal fact about himself. Some patients may enjoy the role of "taking care" of the therapist, and there may be a full knowledge and examination of how this is accomplished, including feelings of hostility at not being "taken care of" sufficiently. One patient came knowingly to an ill therapist for treatment after having the devastating experience of her previous therapist committing suicide. The most excruciating aspect of this former situation for her was that she had no way of knowing that her therapist was so distressed, and felt very guilty. Perhaps she had upset him? Perhaps she could have helped him had she known? During her second therapist's illness she was devoted and worked very hard in therapy when he was available. When he was absent, she sent flowers or appropriate notes of sympathy and of missing him. The second ill therapist helped her work through her grief reaction for the first therapist. Simultaneously she had the live experience of grieving for him in his presence in advance of his death. The woman's depression cleared, and she was able to enter therapy a third time to work on painful early experiences with loss to which she had been subjected.

Some patients may not want to talk about the illness, even if the therapist is emotionally available to listen. They may try to invite the therapist to collude with them in their denial of fear of death. This may be a narrow bridge to negotiate, since the seriously ill therapist is himself acutely caught up with trying to come to terms with his own death, and he has to be careful not to force the issue with a patient who is not ready to do this work.

Worrying about the therapist's health and asking constant questions about it may be a way used by the patient to shift the focus off worry about himself or his family. This may need to be pointed out if it is persistent. Looking after another person may give such a patient a new purpose in life, and detract from the discomfort of dwelling on his or her problems.

One of the most valuable things that a seriously ill therapist can do for his long-term patient may be to help him grieve for his potential loss. He may help the patient, while continuing work in other areas, to bear his feelings of loss, sadness, and abandonment, his anger, his sense of rejection, or his guilty feelings of being angry or being free. The patient may now wish to be like him and be liked in return, may now repudiate him and his treatment and be rebellious. It will call up every other grief experience that the patient has experienced for further working through. Terminations with patients when one is in full health and can treat the fantasies as such is hard enough, but coping with the ubiquitous termination issues when one is seriously ill is an extremely difficult task, due to one's own feelings, uncertainty, and the impending reality. The accomplishment of a therapeutic stance in such circumstances must require the utmost awareness of one's own feelings, control over them, deep caring for the patient, and human courage.

If the therapist has no way of knowing when the illness will become so serious that he will be unable to work, to be of most help to his patients he may make the most careful arrangements possible for them to be looked-after adequately. For some this will mean making sure that another therapist is available for that particular patient. For some it will mean termination of therapy. For others, it will mean insuring that they can get help easily if necessary. These options can be planned in advance.

A further situation may exist in which a therapist who is physically ill is unknowingly doing poor work as a result. Other therapists may come to know of it from his patients. It may be very painful for a patient to realize that his therapist is incapable of responding to him appropriately because of a suspected illness. He may be torn between loyalty and guilt toward the therapist and concerns for his own welfare. If the therapy has gone on for a long time, the patient may be in a vulnerable state about where the reality lies. The therapist's position is a very powerful one to misuse unintentionally. If this situation becomes known by way of a patient seeking consultation to test his reality perceptions about his therapist's strange reactions, then it may be most helpful for the consultant or colleagues to help the ill therapist either seek treatment for himself if he has not done so, or to discontinue his work at least temporarly.

19

A Death in the Therapist's Family

The intensity of the therapist's grief process will depend of multiple issues. The closeness of the relationship will be a factor. If a distant relative dies, the grief may be mild, to a point of having an almost negligible effect on one's ability to work. Or the dead person and the therapist may once have had a close relationship, but the length or nature of the illness may have been such that most of the grief work is over by the time the person dies. A brief upsurge of feelings may be all that is experienced at the time. It may be possible to work well in spite of it, or to take off a few days from work and return feeling ready to see patients again.

Very intense current relationships, such as with a spouse or one's child, or perhaps a parent, sibling, or a close friend, or in some cases abortion or miscarriage, may cause deeper and longer-lasting turmoil in the therapist. Anniversary reactions to the event will also be noticed and can be taken into account as possibly influencing the countertransference for a time.

Acute major grief in the therapist's life will require time off from work. The socially defined period of mourning is society's acceptance of the fact that the bereaved person needs time to be alone or with relatives and close friends, to weep, to feel the intensity of the loss, to be cared for and comforted by others, and to allow a period

301

in which it is recognized that the person's resources for attending to others will be at its lowest ebb. When the suffering therapist has built up at least some of his internal strength, he may feel like going back to work again and emerging into the outside world. This period may be different for each person.

At the beginning, after the acute intensity has abated, one may still feel fragile and know that he is not capable of his best work. However, returning to work may be a way of affirming one's live self again and the regaining of one's ability to work may be a positive sign that it is possible for life to continue without the loved one. The old adage, "Work is the best therapy," is true, but only if it is not contributing to a great strain in setting aside one's feelings, or to a continuous denial of the state of mourning.

While the therapist is involved with his grief, it may be hard to avoid reading loss and depression into every patient he sees. The time of graduation from college is fraught with coexisting loss, sadness, and uncertainty about the future, but also with pride or joy in achievement. One therapist involved in college mental health work said that in grief he had an easy time listening for themes of sadness and loss of "mother university" but a difficult time attending to simultaneous joyful feelings of being free and independent. It may be hard to keep an even stance and attempt to maintain one's attitude of inquiry and empathy within the large range of feelings present in one's patients.

Some patients will not know or need to know the facts; one's absence may be more important than the reasons for it. Depending on the circumstances this may be true of sturdy patients who have no way of knowing about the event, as well as sicker patients to whom the facts may not be important.

After John F. Kennedy's assassination, therapists reported feeling quite shocked by inpatients under their care who seemed to remain untouched by the death. Very depressed, borderline, or psychotic patients are often already too stimulated by their internal turmoil to be able to focus on the outside world, even in such an earth-shaking event. The bereaved therapist, treating a psychotic patient on an outpatient basis, also may recognize this, and it might therefore be inapplicable to jolt such a patient into realization of the therapist's concerns. The feelings about the absence of the therapist per se, will take priority.

While embroiled in the grief process some therapists have found it helpful to take a walk for fifty minutes with a patient whom they feel needs to be seen. This is a much less intense situation than sitting face-to-face. One can still be enough in touch with what is going on with the patient. It is often less than ideal, but it can be a way of coping with the limitations of the moment. Both therapist and patient may recognize that the work together is less direct in this situation. It may have value — a new aspect of a patient may come to the fore. One patient demonstrated an interest in architecture and a respectable knowledge of birds on such a walk. He had constantly presented himself in the therapy as having no outside interests. Later, work could be done on his need to present himself in this way in the office, in conjunction with further feelings about accompanying the therapist on a walk.

Some patients will be informed about the death in the therapist's family. The therapist may have told them himself. A secretary may have told them on the telephone, as an explanation for the absence, or they may have seen the obituary in the newspaper. Any patient may appropriately express sympathy for one's loss and continue with his own concerns, which may or may not be related to a further response to the therapist's grief. Sometimes there are further implications. A patient who was usually depressed but had a previous history of manic episodes came back after the therapist's absence He began to talk rapidly of other issues. Since there was an elated quality to the outpourings, peppered with smiles and laughs, rare in this patient, the therapist took the first opportunity to start slowly to ask, knowing that the patient might have heard about the death, if he had any reaction to the missed appointments. A stunned silence followed. The patient's face crumpled, and he said with tears in his eyes, "I was trying to cheer you up." There followed hesitantly an account of his misery on the therapist's behalf, since he had read the obituary. This was an example of how this patient wished to avoid talking about, and needed help in elaborating on the painful feelings. This situation was consciously determined and available. On a larger scale his manic periods represented denial of his depression, and this instance was a mini-example of an available aspect of the mechanism of his defense.

"Being a good boy" and not troubling "mother" or "father" with his upset is another reaction to which a patient's attention may be drawn. These feelings were operating too in the previous example. Later, the therapist heard a great deal about the patient's chronically depressed mother and how she continually required him to be "good," that is, cheerful, and show no reactions which were disturbing to her. Another patient who previously had been trying to talk about his grief at his mother's death, entered the hour with, "Now you know what I've been talking about!" He had an assumption that it was unnecessary to explain further because the therapist "must know." When one is newly overwhelmed with an experience similar to that of the patient there may be a temptation to bypass the exploration as a way of saving oneself from hearing the narrative and activating one's own feelings.

A new appreciative attitude, or strength, not observed before, may be displayed by a patient. A young male patient had been struggling with his dependency needs and had experienced a great deal of anger at his female therapist due to discomfort in seeing himself in need of psychiatric help. After talking about his therapist's loss, he was able to form a more comfortable therapeutic alliance. He felt that the therapist had accepted his loving feelings and sympathy. During the hour after the therapist's return to work he had been supportive of her. Later he talked about feeling more balanced in the relationship — he could show warmth to her as well as anger. He said he felt less guilty about always being in a position of "taking" emotional sustenance. His basic assumptions were that people were either totally "giving" or totally "taking." The therapist offered some ego support, in that it was possible for him to do both with the same person at different times.

During therapy after the absence, a patient may bring up evidence of angry fantasies about the dead relative and wonder if his magical thoughts really killed the individual. He may need simple reality assurance that this could not be so before he allows encouragement of his elaboration on this or other instances in which his magical powers were "proven." One such discussion led to further unfolding about what it felt like for a female patient during her parents' divorce. She felt that "something bad" she had thought or done at that time caused the loss of her father, who subsequently became ill. Fantasies of caring more for the therapist, protecting him or her, and taking the place of the dead person in his life may result from bereavement, especially of a spouse. This can be discussed, with an attempt to understand the basis for the longing. Material will often follow about wanting more of a special relationship with either parent.

A recently bereaved therapist may not wish to begin therapy with a patient who has complaints relating to a death. It may be too difficult a task to sort out one's own feelings from the feelings of the patient, and too much cross-identification may go on, making the therapist's position unclear. It may be too hard to maintain a therapeutic stance. Temporarily one may also wish to avoid taking on patients who seem "too demanding" or too draining of one's already depleted resources.

These are but a few of the possible and important reactions patients may have. They are vignettes of some starting points for further exploration, which will vary according to each patient's dynamics.

It seems appropriate to end the book on this note. As a psychotherapist, every event that occurs in one's life, be it full of joy or pain, pleasure or grief, will have its far-reaching implications in terms of one's own emotional shifts. These can and often do influence the conduct of therapy or the facet of himself that the patient chooses to present at that point in time.

If something has been communicated about respect for the complexity of patients, about the multiplicity of feelings involved, about the intricacies and beauty of trying to follow feelings and themes; if something has been communicated about the finely attuned discipline that one seeks while bringing humanity to the therapy situation, then the purpose of this book has been accomplished. One may become a psychotherapist in terms of professional requirements. As far as being thoughtful and alert to the innuendos of each daily hour, and working out optimal ways to help each patient, one is always becoming a psychotherapist.

Suggested Reading List

Bardwick, Judith M. *Psychology of Women: A Study of Biocultural Conflicts.* New York: Harper & Row, 1971.

Blos, Peter. *On Adolescence: A Psychoanalytic Interpretation.* New York: Free Press, 1962.

Bowlby, John. *Attachment.* Attachment and Loss Series, vol. I. New York: Basic, 1969.

Bowlby, John. *Separation: Anxiety and Anger.* Attachment and Loss Series, vol. II. New York: Basic, 1973.

Brenner, Charles. *An Elementary Textbook of Psychoanalysis.* New York: International Universities Press, 1973.

Colby, Kenneth M. *A Primer for Psychotherapists.* New York: Ronald Press, 1951.

Deutsch, Helene. *The Psychology of Women,* vol. I. New York: Grune & Stratton, 1944.

Deutsch, Helene. *The Psychology of Women,* vol. II. New York: Grune & Stratton, 1945. Pp. 126-258.

Erikson, Erik H. *Childhood and Society* (rev. ed.). New York: Norton, 1964.

Fraiberg, Selma. *The Magic Years.* New York: Scribner, 1968.

Freud, Anna. *The Ego and the Mechanisms of Defense* (rev. ed.). *(The Writings of Anna Freud,* vol. II.) New York: International Universities Press, 1967.

Freud, Sigmund. *An Outline of Psychoanalysis* (rev. standard ed.). James Strachey, ed. and trans. New York: Norton, 1970.

Fromm-Reichmann, Frieda. *Principles of Intensive Psychotherapy.* Chicago: University of Chicago Press, 1950.

Green, Hannah. *I Never Promised You a Rose Garden.* New York: Harcourt, Brace, World, 1964.

Greenson, Ralph R. *The Technique and Practice of Psychoanalysis,* vol. I. New York: International Universities Press, 1967.

Havens, Leston L. *Approaches to the Mind: Movement of the Psychiatric Schools from Sects toward Science.* Boston: Little, Brown, 1973.

307

Holmes, Donald J. *The Adolescent in Psychotherapy.* Boston: Little, Brown, 1964.

Laing, Ronald D. *The Divided Self.* New York: Pantheon, 1969.

Lidz, Theodore. *The Person: His Development Throughout the Life Cycle.* New York: Basic, 1968.

Malan, David H. *A Study of Brief Psychotherapy.* Philadelphia: Lippincott, 1963.

Nemiah, John C. *Foundations of Psychopathology* (rev. ed.). New York: J. Aronson, 1973.

Parker, Belulah. *A Mingled Yarn: Chronicle of a Troubled Family.* New Haven, Conn.: Yale University Press, 1972.

Paul, I. H. *Letters to Simon on the Conduct of Psychotherapy.* New York: International Universities Press, 1973.

Schafer, Roy. Talking to Patients. Unpublished paper, 1974.

Schafer, Roy. The termination of brief psychoanalytic psychotherapy. *Int. J. Psychoanal. Psychother.* 2:135-148, 1973.

Searles, Harold F. *Collected Papers on Schizophrenia and Related Subjects.* New York: International Universities Press, 1966.

Tarachow, Sidney. *Introduction to Psychotherapy.* New York: International Universities Press, 1970.

Index